ECCLESIAE MILITANTIS

A COURSE IN SPIRITUAL WARFARE AND EXORCISM

REV. JACK ASHCRAFT

First Printing December 2013
Ecclesia Militantis/ compiled and written by Jack Ashcraft
1. Spiritual Warfare and Exorcism-Theology
2. Theology-Christian
3. Fathers of the Church- Quotations
4. Theology-Christian Exorcism

TABLE OF CONTENTS

INTRODUCTION

There is a no question that a spiritual war is being waged in the world today. It is not a conflict between nations, tribes,or governmental powers and politics. It is a spiritual rebellion stretching back into ancient times. It is a spiritual war taking place every day throughout the world in the spiritual realm. The Sacred Scriptures states that we are destroyed because of lack of knowledge (Hosea 4:6). One of the main areas in which Christians are being defeated due to lack of knowledge is in orthodox Catholic Biblical theology and spiritual warfare. The early Church understood their spiritual experience in terms of warfare. Military terminology is used throughout the New Testament in reference to this great spiritual war. Protection we are told is found only in the armor of God. The Word of God is compared to a sword. Satan's onslaughts are referred to as fiery darts. Faith is the "good fight" and faithful Christians are told to "war a good warfare." The ancient Church knew they were engaged in an intense spiritual struggle. The same spiritual battle continues today but instead of fighting the Adversary, Christians are all too often building elaborate church buildings, producing concerts, chasing after the latest pop- Christian fad, and slandering one another while Satan destroys everyone around them. Satan has even intensified his attacks against Christians who have by and large left the faith as taught by the Apostles in favor of theology and structures founded by Reformers, Anti-Popes and even personal opinion. As the End Times approach it is even more important for Christians to understand spiritual warfare as taught by the Sacred Scriptures and Apostolic Tradition.

This know also, that in the last days perilous times shall come. -II Timothy 3:1

But now, since the last times are upon us, evil is spread abroad among men. -Irenaeus

In order to be properly prepared for these very difficult and dangerous spiritual times, Christians who take seriously their faith must place emphasis on the revival of orthodox Catholic theology, practice and polity, as well as principles of spiritual warfare. There is no question that the Christian lifestyle is war. Everything about the faith flies in the face of a culture increasingly hostile to God, ethics, morality and Christ centered life. The sooner we recognize and prepare for it, the sooner we will be able to withstand the persecutions of a world under the strong influence of Satan and his minions. Luke 14:31 says:

"What king, going to make war against another king, sitteth not down first, and consulteth whether he is able with ten thousand to meet him that cometh against him with twenty thousand?"

No ruler worth his weight has ever ventured into a battle without a detailed and thorough examination of his resources and development of his combat strategies. In essence, that is what we are doing in this book. We are making a careful evaluation of the strategy, weapons, and spiritual tools available to us to win the war against our Adversary, Satan. In the military world, "strategy" is the science of forming and carrying out military operations. It is the method which leads to the goal of victory. In this book you will learn to formulate and carry out spiritual strategy which will bring victory in spiritual warfare.

CHAPTER ONE
THIS IS WAR!

For we wrestle not against flesh and blood, but against principalities, against powers, against the rulers of the darkness of this world, against spiritual wickedness in high places. - Ephesians 6:12

To really understand fully the concept of spiritual warfare, you must first understand the material and spiritual worlds, as well as the basic theology behind spiritual warfare. Each of us lives on the precipice between two distinct realms; the material created universe and the immaterial spiritual realm. The material realm is that which can be seen, felt, touched, heard, or tasted. It is the realm of the senses and is known and experienced primarily through our sensory perception. The country, nation, city, or village in which you live is part of the natural material realm. You are a resident in a natural world located on one of the visible continents of the physical world. You can see the people who are part of your environment. You can communicate with them. You can experience the sights, sounds, and smells around you. However there is another realm in which you live, even if unknowingly or imperceptibly. That world is a spiritual world. You cannot normally see it with your physical eyes, but it is just as real as the natural world in which you live. Paul speaks of this division of natural and spiritual:

There is a natural body, and there is a spiritual body.
-I Corinthians 15:40

All of us possesses a natural body which serves as our vehicle of expression in the natural world, but you are also a spiritual being with an eternal soul and spirit. The tripartite constituent parts of humanity are the body, soul, and spirit. Your spiritual self (soul and spirit) is part of a spiritual world just as your natural body is par of the natural world.

The soul dwells in the body, yet is not of the body. The invisible soul is guarded by the visible body.
- Letter to Diognetus

He clothed and covered man's spirit with an earthly body...
- Lactantius

SPIRITUAL DISCERNMENT
Because the warfare we are discussing is of a spiritual nature, it must be understood with a spiritual mind. In our natural, sinful state, we cannot understand spiritual things:

But the natural man receiveth not the things of the Spirit of God: for they are foolishness unto him; neither can he know them, because they are spiritually discerned.
-I Corinthians 2:14

It is imperative that we learn to use "spiritual discernment" to understand spiritual things. Perhaps one of the best examples of natural and spiritual discernment is recorded in II Kings chapter 6. It records the story of a natural battle in which troops of the enemy nation of Syria had surrounded a small town called Dothan where the prophet Elisha was staying. When Elisha's servant, Gehazi, saw the great host of the enemy he became fearful. Elisha prayed that God would open Gehazi's spiritual eyes so he could see the angelic hosts surrounding and protecting them. God actually opened the natural eyes of Gehazi and allowed him to visibly see the superior spiritual forces of God aligned for battle. The story of this battle at Dothan is akin to the current spiritual conditions in the world. There are some (and I do not mean psychics), like Elisha, who see clearly into the spiritual realm. They know there is a conflict occurring, have identified the real Adversary, and recognize the superior forces of God that assure victory. There are others like Gehazi, who with a little encouragement, will be able to open their spiritual eyes and no longer be fearful of and defeated by the Adversary. But sadly, there are many people who, like those in the city of

Dothan, are spiritually blind, sleeping while the Adversary storms the gates.

THE TWO REALMS OF EXISTENCE
Within the natural and spiritual realms there exists two distinct and opposing kingdoms which are ruled by natural and spiritual leaders.

1. **Natural Kingdom**- All of us live in the natural kingdom of this world. We live in and are connected to the natural world and our environment. We live in cities or villages which are part of a nation. That nation is a kingdom of the world. A natural kingdom is a territory or people over which a political leader is the sovereign ruler. The Bible speaks of these natural kingdoms as "kingdoms of the world." The kingdoms of the world have come under the power and influence of Satan.

Again, the Devil taketh Him (Jesus) up into an exceeding high mountain, and sheweth Him all the kingdoms of the world, and the glory of them; And saith unto Him, All these things will I give thee, if you wilt fall down and worship me.
- Matthew 4:8-9

As for you, you are a foreigner in this world, a citizen of Jerusalem, the city above. - Tertullian

John 5:19 further informs us of the sobering fact that *"the whole world is under the control of the evil one."*

From the beginning, He had given the devil power over the earth. - Lactantius

2. **Spiritual Realities**- In addition to the natural kingdom of this world there are two spiritual kingdoms: The realm of the influence of Satan and the Kingdom Of God. Every person alive is a "resident", so to speak, of one of these two realities. The realm of Satan consists of Satan, spiritual beings called demons, and all who live in sin and rebellion to the Gospel.

These are the spiritual forces of evil at work in the world today. The Kingdom of God consists of God the Father, Jesus Christ, the Holy Spirit, spiritual beings called angels, and all who live in righteous obedience to the Gospel. These are the spiritual forces of good. Allow me to clarify here a bit. The Kingdom of God is restricted to a single Church. The Bible speaks of the true Church which is limited. The true Church is composed of all those who have become residents of the Kingdom of God. That Church is "pre-denominational" and is the heir to the promises of the Gospel of Jesus Christ. It is the ancient orthodox Catholic Church. At the present time in the natural world, the Kingdom of God exists individually within every person who has recognized the personal Kingship of Christ. In the future, there will be an actual visible manifestation of God's Kingdom on a new earth.

THE INVISIBLE WAR

The invisible spiritual war is an intense conflict stemming from the very foundations of human existence which involves all men and women. The realm of Satan is a spiritual reality. Thus:

...we wrestle not against flesh and blood, but against principalities, against powers, against the rulers of the darkness of this world, against spiritual wickedness in high places. -Ephesians 6:12

Their great business is the ruin of mankind. So, from the start, spiritual wickedness sought our destruction.

-Tertullian

Spiritual warfare is not a natural war of flesh and blood, guns and tanks, missiles and bombs. It is not a war of nation against nation, or person against person, though it can manifest in these ways. It is not essentially a visible battle. It is an invisible struggle in the spiritual realm. It is a sustained conflict within and around humanity. It is not a visible war is because spirits are involved and we learn in Luke 24:39 that a spirit is by definition not material in any sense that we understand it. Spiritual warfare is "multidimensional," which means it is fought in different dimensions and on many levels. It is...

- A socio-political and cultural war between the Christian and the world: John 15:18-27
- A personal war between the flesh and the spirit: Galatians 5:16-26
- A spiritual battle between Christians and demonic entities: Ephesians 6:10-27

Every person alive is engaged in this warfare, whether they realize or even choose to believe it or not. There is no neutral ground. Those not living the Gospel and in communion with Christ's Church are in bondage to evil to one degree or another and are subject to the influence of demonic forces. They are the real victims of the war. Christians have been freed from the Adversary through Jesus Christ and are victors, but they are still engaged in the war. They can still be wounded and fail and even worse if they are not careful. The verse from Sacred Scripture at the start of this chapter indicates that we fight against evil spiritual forces. "Wrestling" by definition involves close personal contact. No one is exempt from this conflict. No one can view it from a distance. There are no conscientious objectors or pacifists in this war. You are a soldier in it whether you like it or not. You are in the midst of conflict whether you acknowledge it or not. If you believe it will just go away, you are wrong. The Christian warfare never ceases. This invisible warfare is being waged all across the planet.

The thief cometh not but for to steal, and to kill, and to destroy: I am come that they might have life, and that they might have it more abundantly. -John 10:10

....these contaminated and abandoned spirits wander over

the whole earth. - Lactantius

Satan and the forces of evil fight to maintain control of the minds, nations, and institutions of the world. Governments, cultures, and false religions are all a part of the war. The Adversary does not want them to come under God's authority. The war also goes on continually within the hearts, minds, and souls of men and women. Satan blinds the minds of unbelievers. He attacks believers in the areas of worship, the Gospel, their spiritual lives, and their witness for Christ. Even personal finances, relationships, marriage, and family are attacked in an effort to demoralize and humiliate the Christian into defeat.

ORIGINS OF THE CONFLICT

The spiritual war started in Heaven with an angel named Lucifer who was originally a beautiful angel created by God and was part of the Kingdom of God. Lucifer decided he wanted to take over God's Kingdom. You can read about This rebellion in Isaiah 14:12-17 and Ezekiel 28:12-19. You will study about it in detail later in this course. A group of angels joined Lucifer (now called Satan) in this rebellion. Lucifer and the rebellious angels were cast out of Heaven by God. They formed their own kingdom on earth.

And there was war in Heaven: Michael and his angels fought against the dragon (Satan); and the dragon fought and his angels. -Revelation 12:7

And the great dragon was cast out, that old serpent, called the Devil, and Satan, which deceiveth the whole world: he was cast out into the earth, and his angels were cast out with him. - Revelation 12:9

Lucifer is now known as Satan and the angels which followed him in rebellion are now known as demons. Demons, being spiritual beings, can enter, torment, control, and use humans who are subject to Satan's Kingdom. They motivate and encourage evil acts. Satan directs his demons in their evil activities. He combines these powerful forces with the negative forces and institutions of the world and the frailties of the human mind to wage this war against humanity.

From the devil comes the incentive to sin. - Tertullian

There was also a belief in the early church in a second and separate fall of a group of angels known as the Watchers. These angels fell, being in lust after women, and mated with them creating a hybrid offspring known as Nephilim. The full account is contained in the apocryphal Book of Enoch.

.

The angels transgressed this appointment and were captivated by love of women. And they begat children, those who are called demons. - Justin the Martyr

From the seed, giants are said to have been born.
-Commodianus

REASONS FOR THE WAR

Humanity was originally created in the image of God and for the glory of God (Genesis chapter 2). The spiritual war against humanity started with the first temptation in the garden of Eden (Genesis chapter 3) Satan caused Adam and Eve to sin. Eve had infused knowledge that she should not be paying attention to the serpent. Her sin was a bad curiosity- seeking a knowledge not appropriate to her station. This resulted in all men inheriting the fallen nature and committing individual acts of sin due to this nature:

Wherefore, as by one man sin entered into the world, and death by sin; and so death passed upon all men, for that all have sinned. - Romans 5:12

Because she was in the beginning deceived by the serpent, this Eve became the author of sin. Actually it was

the wicked demon, who also is called Satan, who then spoke to her through the serpent. And he works even to this day in those men who are possessed by him.

-Theophilus

It also resulted in the invisible war between man and the demonic forces.

And I will put enmity between thee (Satan) and the woman (humanity), and between thy seed (the demonic) and her seed (humanity)... - Genesis 3:15

From this we learn that this was the apostate angel and the enemy. For he was envious of God's workmanship and took in hand to render this workmanship into something at enmity with God. -Irenaeus

He deceived man because he had envied him. -Tertullian

Because of sin, humanity was separated from God and condemned to experience old age, disease, death and separation from God. But God loved man so much that He made a special plan to save him from sin and the fallen nature.

For God so loved the world, that He gave His only begotten Son, that whosoever believeth in Him should not perish, but have everlasting life. For God sent not His Son into the world to condemn the world; but that the world through Him might be saved. - John 3:16-17

Through belief in and discipleship to Jesus Christ, confession of and repentance from sin, and cleaving to His Church, we can be released from the power of the Adversary. The death and resurrection of Jesus Christ not only resulted in salvation from sin, it also defeated Satan.

...For this purpose the Son of God was manifested, that He might destroy the works of the devil. - I John 3:8

But if Satan is defeated, why does the war still rage? Following any war there are always pockets of enemy resistance, rebellious troops that will not give up until forced to do so. Although Christ defeated Satan, we are living in territory which is still occupied by enemy resistance forces. Understanding spiritual warfare strategies gives us the ability to deal with these evil powers. Satan is trying to keep humanity captive in sin and take down as many of us with him as he can before the final judgment. Through deceptive methods he is enticing men and women to temporary lusts of sinful living. He aims for the affections of the soul and spirit which rightfully belong to God:

The thief (Satan) cometh not, but for to steal, and to kill, and to destroy; I am come that they might have life, and that they might have it more abundantly. - John 10:10

That most stubborn Foe never gives his malice a rest. Indeed, he is then the most savage when he fully feels that a man is freed from his clutches. -Tertullian

Satan still wants to be the supreme ruler and our deity. He is waging an intense battle for the heart, mind, soul, and spirit of every man, woman and child. His strategies are directed at God, His plan, and His people. The battle will continue until the great final conflict which you will learn more about later.

DEFINITION OF SPIRITUAL WARFARE

Spiritual warfare is the analysis of and active participation in the exposure and direct confrontation of demonic forces and their activities. It includes study of the opposing forces of good and evil, the strategies of Satan, and spiritual strategies for overcoming this Adversary. Spiritual warfare is more than a mere analysis of spiritual principles. It includes active participation in warfare by application of these strategies in life and ministry. One of the most effective strategies of Satan is to keep Christians ignorant of his devices. Paul said it is important to know Satan's strategies.

...Lest Satan should get an advantage of us: for we are not ignorant of his devices. - II Corinthians 2:11

We should learn all we can about Satan's strategies of attack. We must also understand the Scriptural basis of victory over Satan and the forces of evil. We are called to intelligent and informed combat.

There is a strong conflict to be waged against the devil. Therefore, we should stand bravely, so that we may be able to conquer. -Cyprian

Basic to the understanding of spiritual warfare is this major principle which you must grasp in its entirety:

You must recognize that all battles of life, whether physical, spiritual, emotional, mental, or with human personalities are only outward manifestations of a spiritual cause.

Although in the natural world problems may seem to occur through the chance circumstances of life, often the basis of these natural battles is in the spirit realm. This is not to say that chance does not play a role in human affairs, only that more often than we would like to admit, spiritual causes are behind most issues. We have tried to correct the evils of this world through education, legislation, and wars. It has not worked because the manifest evils of the world are the results of an underlying spiritual cause. They cannot be corrected by merely human means. In the world of humanity a king is the sovereign ruler of a kingdom. All the lands and people in the kingdom belong to him. He has the power of life and death over his subjects. The same is true in the spiritual realm. You are either part of the Kingdom of God or the Kingdom of Satan. Either you acknowledge God or Satan as the central power over your life. One of the parables told by Christ illustrates that we are either part of the Kingdom of Satan or the Kingdom of God. Jesus compared the world to a field. The good seed in the field were the faithful children of the

Kingdom of God. The bad seed, which resulted in the growth of tares (weeds), were the rebellious children of Satan.

The field is the world; the good seed are the children of the Kingdom; but the tares are the children of the wicked one. - Matthew 13:38

People enter the Kingdom of Satan through natural birth. Sacred Scripture teaches that all are born in sin. This means that we have a basic fallen nature or the "seed" of sin within. Our fallen, self centered inclination then is to do evil.

Behold, I was shapen in iniquity; and in sin did my mother conceive me. - Psalms 51:5

Wherefore, as by one man (Adam) sin entered into the world, and death by sin; and so death passed upon all men, for that all have sinned. - Romans 5:12

For all have sinned and come short of the glory of God. - Romans 3:23

Because we are born with the fallen nature, we have all at one time been part of the Kingdom of Satan, even if unwittingly. All who remain sinners, who refuse to enter into a personal relationship with God through His Son (thus entering the Kingdom of God), remain part of the Kingdom of Satan. The whole message of the Sacred Scriptures, is the appeal to us to leave this evil control of Satan and be partakers of the Kingdom of God. We are born, in a sense, into the Kingdom of Satan through our natural birth. We must be reborn into the Kingdom of God through a spiritual birth. This explained in John chapter 3. There are only two divisions in the invisible war. Christ said, "He that is not with me is against me" (Luke 11:23). You cannot be neutral in this spiritual war. You are on one side or the other. There are no Christians who refuse to recognize the reality of this war. Anyone claiming to be a Christian and yet denies this reality is a demonstrable liar.

Then again, some Christians, because of their fear of confrontation with the Adversary, try to ignore the war and form a truce with the enemy. They think if they ignore Satan and the demonic, he will not bother them. This is one of Satan's main strategies. He tries to render Christians immobile by his terror tactics. But there is no neutrality in this war. Even those who attempt to avoid getting the attention of the demonic will at some point in their lives gain that attention, like it or not. You are either a victim or victor. Are you on the side of good or of evil? Are you part of Satan's rebellion or the Kingdom of God? To which kingdom do you belong? Your response will determine your eternal destiny.

---

1. This course focuses on the spiritual warfare that rages between the forces of Satan and the Kingdom of God. If you are not a Christian you need to receive Christ into your life and change your ways. If you are not attending a church, you should do so immediately, finding a traditional Latin Mass in your area. The community of the Faithful is where soldiers in this war are given support and spiritual sustenance. It is important that you gain understanding of both spiritual kingdoms present in the world today, and the Church as the Body of Christ.
2. Do you feel you have been a "victim" of spiritual attack? In what areas of your life do you sense the battle? Have you been losing the battle in the spiritual realm? Emotional realm? Physical realm? Mental realm? With human personalities? It is important to identify these areas of defeat so you can apply the knowledge you gain in this book to these practical areas of life and ministry.
3. Review the story in II Kings 6 which was discussed in this lesson. Do you know people like Gehazi or those in the city of Dothan? How might you help them?
4. Since spiritual warfare has many dimensions, we must war personally against sin, socially against evil in the world, and supernaturally through prayer, fasting, spiritual disciplines and deliverance ministry.
6. Study the Bible as a spiritual warfare manual. It is the historical record of spiritual warfare, revealing the victories and strategies of past battles.

CHAPTER TWO
THE CHURCH MILITANT

I came not to call the righteous, but sinners to repentance. - Luke 5:32

In the natural world, when a recruit joins an army, he must take an oath of allegiance to his country, to defend it against all enemies. When you join the Church Militant, you must repent of your allegiance to sin and the Kingdom of Satan, and pledge to defend the faith against all enemies. This is done primarily through repentance. Repentance is an inward decision or change of mind resulting in the outward action of turning from sin to God and righteousness. Acts 20:21 calls it "repentance toward God." By the act of repenting you turn away from your sin and leave the realm of Satan. Repentance is a personal decision to change your allegiance from the Kingdom of Satan to the Kingdom of God.

Then God also to the Gentiles granted repentance unto life. - Acts 11:18

Repentance is a gift of God:

Him [Jesus] hath God exalted with His right hand to be a Prince and a Savior, for to give repentance... - Acts 5:31

Repentance is great wisdom. For he who has sinned understands that he acted wickedly in the sight of the Lord. He remembers the actions he has done, and he repents. -Hermas

Although emotions may be involved in repentance, true repentance is an intellectual decision, not just an emotion. Sorrow for sin and the shedding of tears is not enough in itself. This must be accompanied by an inward decision that results in an outward change. Repentance is important because God commands it.

...but [God] now commandeth all men everywhere to repent. - Acts 17:30

Repentance is the price for which the Lord has determined to award pardon... -Tertullian

God especially desires for men to be cleansed of their sins. Therefore, he commands them to repent.
- Lactantius

It is necessary to avoid spiritual destruction.

...but, except ye repent, ye shall all likewise perish.
- Luke 13:3

A sinner avoids destruction by repentance.
- Apostolic Constitutions

It is necessary for eternal life. Through repentance and acceptance of the sacrifice of Christ the penalty of death is removed and eternal life is granted.

When they heard these things, they held their peace, and glorified God, saying, Then hath God also to the Gentiles granted repentance unto life. - Acts 11:18

He who ceases to sin renders the anger of God extinguishable. -Lactantius

It is necessary for forgiveness. God cannot forgive your sins unless you repent.

Then Peter said unto them, Repent, and be baptized every one of you in the name of Jesus Christ for the remission of sins, and ye shall receive the gift of the Holy Ghost.
- Acts 2:38

It is possible if he repents of his actions and makes

satisfaction to God, turning to better things. -Lactantius

It is God's desire that no one experience the spiritual destruction of eternal separation from God in Hell.

The Lord...is long suffering to us-ward, not willing that any should perish, but that all should come to repentance. - II Peter 3:9

He, then, will receive you-His own son-back...-Tertullian

It is one of the reasons Christ came into the world.

I came not to call the righteous, but sinners to repentance. - Luke 5:32

It is necessary to enter God's Kingdom.

From that time Jesus began to preach, and to say, Repent: for the Kingdom of Heaven is at hand. - Matthew 4:17

When you become part of the Church Militant, you are automatically enlisting in the army of God, as it were. When you ask for forgiveness of sins you experience "conversion." Conversion means "to turn." When it is used in connection with repentance, it means to turn from sin and the counsel of Satan to the Church and the Gospel of Jesus Christ. You leave the realm of Satan and join the Kingdom of God.

And many of the children of Israel shall He turn to the Lord their God. - Luke 1:16

And the hand of the Lord was with them; and a great number believed, and turned unto the Lord. - Acts 11:21

Conversion is turning from the darkness of sin to the light of God's righteousness.

...to turn them from darkness to light. - Acts 26:18

It is turning from the influence of Satan to reliance on God.

...to turn them...from the power of Satan unto God.
- Acts 26:18

It is turning from worldly things to spiritual things.

...Ye should turn from these vanities unto the living God.
- Acts 14:15

It is turning from false gods and religions to the true and living God.

...Ye turned to God from idols to serve the living and true God. - I Thessalonians 1:9

Conversion must always accompany repentance. You must turn from the former things, that is, your rebellion, and turn to God and His Church.

Verily I say unto you, except ye be converted, and become as little children, ye shall not enter into the Kingdom of Heaven. - Matthew 18:3

It saves you from spiritual destruction.

He which converteth the sinner from the error of his way shall save a soul from death and shall hide a multitude of sins. - James 5:20

It is required for the removing of your sins. Your sin is written in the records of God until you repent and are converted, then your sins are blotted out.

Repent ye therefore, and be converted, that your sins may be blotted out...- Acts 3:19

Repentance and conversion are best illustrated by a story Christ told about the prodigal son, found in Luke 15:11-24. This young man left his father and home, went to a distant land, and through sinful living and rebellion wasted all of the gifts his father bestowed upon him. Eventually he realized his condition. He was hungry, lonely, filthy, in rags, and tending pigs for a job. It was so bad he was actually eating pig slop. Then he made an important decision. He said, "I will arise and go to my father." This inward decision resulted in a change in his outward actions. He went home to his father to seek forgiveness. The young man realized his sinful condition. He made an intellectual decision to go to his father and repent of his sin. This is an example of true repentance, an inward decision which results in outward action. Luke 15:20 tells us how the young man arose and left his old rebellious life and went to his father to start a new life. This is conversion. All of humanity is like the prodigal son. In our sinful and rebellious state we turned our backs on God our Father and Heaven our intended home, where we can enjoy the Beatific Vision and company of the Saints. Each step we take toward rebellion is a step away from God and one step nearer the spiritual destruction of eternal separation from God. There is a major decision we must make. We must come to our senses and recognize our spiritual condition. We must make an intellectual decision which will result in a change of spiritual destiny.

JUSTIFICATION AND SALVATION

There are two other terms used in the Sacred Scriptures which relate to repentance. These terms are "justification" and "salvation." God is the judge of all mankind. When you are living in sin you are condemned before Him.

...but he that believeth not is condemned already, because he hath not believed in the name of the only begotten Son of God. And this is the condemnation, that light is come into the world, and men loved darkness rather than light, because their deeds were evil. - John 3:18-19

When you repent from sin, confess those sins, and make the decision to turn from your sinful ways, this establishes a righteous relationship with God. This relationship or right standing before God is called "justification".

Know ye not, that to whom ye yield yourselves servants to obey, his servants ye are to whom ye obey; whether of sin unto death, or of obedience unto righteousness? But God be thanked, that ye were the servants of sin but ye have obeyed from the heart that form of doctrine which was delivered you. Being then made free from sin, ye became the servants of righteousness. - Romans 6:16-18

When you are justified by repentance and conversion, you are saved from a life of sin as well as from the penalties of sin. This is possible only through living the Gospel and joining His Church where you can avail yourself of its spiritual riches, such as the Sacraments.

SPIRITUAL WARFARE IS THEOLOGY

The subject of spiritual warfare must be studied within the context of God's total purpose for the redemption of humanity, and thus within the context of Christian theology. Study the parables of the sower and the tares among wheat in Matthew 13. Both parables concern the growth of the Kingdom of God which occurs through the planting of the Gospel. Both parables picture the warfare between the two kingdoms with the battle centering on the redemptive works and plan of God. Learning the principles of spiritual warfare prepares you to enter the arena of this world and fight for souls. This is why authority over Satan was given to the Apostles (and later their successors) before they were sent out to share the Gospel (Matthew 28:18-20). Satan and the hordes of demonic entities will war against you as you seek to win souls to Christ and bring them into His Church. Employing Scriptural strategies of spiritual warfare helps you challenge the principalities and powers who rule over individual human lives, societies, and even nations. This is why we start with the topic of repentance and conversion. Repentance and conversion result in justification and salvation. This is God's plan for humanity.

---

1. Have you repented and been converted? If not, you need to stop right now in this study and do the following:

- Repent of your sins.
- Ask Jesus to forgive you through the Sacrament of Confession.
- Accept Christ as your Lord and Savior.
- Turn from your sinful ways (be converted), and enter His Church.

2. As a believer, when you sin, you must also repent. Study the following Biblical examples:

THE CORINTHIANS:

The believers at a city called Corinth had to repent: Now I rejoice, not that ye were made sorry, but that ye sorrowed to repentance... (II Corinthians 7:9)

For I fear, lest, when I come...that I shall bewail many which have sinned already and have not repented of the uncleanness and fornication and lasciviousness which they have committed. (II Corinthians 12:20-21)

THE EPHESIANS:

The believers at Ephesus were told to repent: Remember therefore from whence thou art fallen and repent and do the first works. (Revelation 2:5)

CHRISTIANS IN PERGAMOS:

God told the Christians in Pergamos: Repent; or else I will come unto thee quickly, and will fight against them with the sword of my mouth. (Revelation 2:16)

CHRISTIANS IN SARDIS:

Remember therefore how thou hast received and heard, and hold fast, and repent. (Revelation 3:3)

CHRISTIANS IN LAODICEA:

As many as I love, I rebuke and chasten; Be zealous therefore, and repent. (Revelation 3:19)

HOW ABOUT YOU?

Is there unconfessed sin in your life? Wherever there is sin, there must be repentance. "If we say that we have no sin, we deceive ourselves and the truth is not in us. If we confess our sins, He is faithful and just to forgive us our sins, and to cleanse us from all unrighteousness." (I John 1:8-9)

3. Because repentance is necessary for salvation, God made a special plan to enable the message of repentance to reach everyone. The call to repentance began in the New Testament with the ministry of John the Baptist: The voice of one crying in the wilderness, Prepare ye the way the Lord, make His path straight. John did baptize in the wilderness, and preach the baptism of repentance for the remission of sins. (Mark 1:3-4) Repentance was the first message Jesus preached: Now after that John was put in prison, Jesus came into Galilee, preaching the Gospel of the Kingdom

of God, And saying, the time is fulfilled, and the Kingdom of God is at hand: repent ye, and believe the Gospel. (Mark 1:14-15) Repentance was preached by the Faithful in the Early Church: And they went out and preached that men should repent. (Mark 6:12) ...Testifying both to the Jews and also to the Greeks, repentance toward God, and faith toward our Lord Jesus Christ. (Acts 20:21) Today, Christians still have the responsibility to spread the message of repentance throughout the world. Jesus gave final instructions to His apostles that......repentance and remission of sins should be preached in His name among all nations, beginning at Jerusalem. (Luke 24:47)

4. If you are responsible to share the message of repentance then you must know how men are persuaded to repent. People repent because of:

THE GOODNESS OF GOD:

The blessings of God in the life of an ungodly person are not to be mistaken as God's approval of his lifestyle. The goodness of God is one way the Lord appeals to men to turn to Him: "Despisest thou the riches of His goodness and forbearance and long suffering; not knowing that the goodness of God leadeth thee to repentance?" (Romans 2:4)

PREACHING:

The preaching of the Gospel causes men to repent. The preaching of Jonah resulted in the whole city of Ninevah repenting: The men of Ninevah shall rise in judgment with this generation and shall condemn it: because they repented at the preaching of Jonas. (Matthew 12:41)

CHRIST'S CALL:

As the Gospel is preached, people hear and respond to the call of Christ which leads to repentance: I am not come to call the righteous, but sinners to repentance. (Matthew 9:13)

GOD, THE FATHER:

Jesus said no one could come to Him except the Father draw him. God draws men to repentance: No man can come to me, except the Father which hath sent me draw him...(John 6:44)

REBUKE:

Rebuke causes men to repent. Rebuke is correction given from the Sacred Scriptures:...If thy brother trespass against thee, rebuke him; and if he repent, forgive him. (Luke 17:3)

GODLY SORROW:

As you learned, repentance may be accompanied by emotion. Emotion alone is not true repentance, but Godly emotion coupled with an intellectual decision leads to true repentance: Godly sorrow [for sin] worketh repentance to salvation. (II Corinthians 7:10)

CHAPTER THREE
GOD

Hear, O Israel: The Lord our God is one Lord.

- Deuteronomy 6:4

THE TRINITY

There are many false gods worshiped throughout the world, but there is only one true God. The Sacred Scriptures contain the revelation of this true God. This one God revealed in three distinct Persons of the Father, the Son Jesus Christ, and the Holy Spirit. God the Father, Jesus Christ, and the Holy Spirit are described in Sacred Scripture in terms of their nature. When we speak of "nature" we mean basic qualities which describe God. These qualities are also known as "attributes" which means "characteristics." The Sacred Scriptures reveal that God is:

TRIUNE:

God has a triune nature. This means He is three distinct Persons, yet He is one God:

Hear, O Israel: The Lord our God is one Lord.

- Deuteronomy 6:4

These are united in essence-the Father, the Son, and the Spirit. -Athenagoras

The three persons of the Trinity of God are called God the Father, Jesus Christ the Son, and God the Holy Spirit. There are several Scriptures which confirm this triune nature of God. When Jesus was being baptized by John the Baptist in the Jordan River, God spoke and the Holy Spirit descended.

And Jesus, when He was baptized, went up straightway out of the water: and, lo, the heavens were opened unto Him, and He saw the Spirit of God descending like a dove, and lighting upon Him: And lo, a voice from Heaven

saying, This is my beloved Son, in whom I am well pleased. - Matthew 3:16-17

Prior to returning to Heaven after His ministry on earth, Christ spoke of the Holy Spirit coming from God the Father.

But when the Comforter is come, whom I will send unto you from the Father, even the Spirit of truth, which proceedeth from the Father, He shall testify of me.
- John 15:26

The Apostle Peter spoke of the triune nature of God.

If ye be reproached for the name of Christ, happy are ye; for the Spirit of glory and of God resteth upon you: on their part He is evil spoken of, but on your part He is glorified. - I Peter 4:14

The Apostle Paul spoke of the Trinity in his writings.

For the law of the Spirit of life in Christ Jesus hath made me free from the law of sin and death. Fo what the law could not do, in that it was weak through the flesh, God sending His own Son, in the likeness of sinful flesh, and for sin, condemned sin in the flesh - Romans 8:2-3

The grace of the Lord Jesus Christ, and the love of God, and the communion of the Holy Ghost, be with you all.
- II Corinthians 13:14

For through Him (the Son) we both have access by one Spirit unto the Father. - Ephesians 2:18

The book of Acts also verifies the triune nature of God.

Therefore being by the right hand of God exalted, and having received of the Father the promise of the Holy

Ghost, He hath shed forth this, which ye now see and hear. - Acts 2:33

ETERNAL:
The Trinity of God is eternal with no beginning and no ending.

Lord, Thou hast been our dwelling place in all generations. Before the mountains were brought forth, or ever Thou hadst formed the earth and the world, even from everlasting to everlasting, Thou art God.
- Psalms 90:1-2

And Abraham planted a grove in Beersheba, and called there on the name of the Lord, the everlasting God.
- Genesis 21:33

A SPIRIT:
God is a spirit. This means He is without flesh and blood and therefore invisible to the natural eyes of man.

God is a Spirit: and they that worship Him must worship Him in spirit and in truth. - John 4:24

SOVEREIGN:
God is the sovereign (greatest) power in all the universe.

Read Ephesians l and Romans 9.

OMNIPRESENT:
This means God is present everywhere.

For the eyes of the Lord run to and fro throughout the whole earth... - II Chronicles 16:9

The eyes of the Lord are in every place, beholding the evil and the good. -Proverbs 15:3

Whither shall I go from Thy Spirit? Or whither shall I flee

from Thy presence? If I ascend up into Heaven, Thou art there: if I make my bed in Hell, behold, Thou art there.
-Psalms 139:7-8

This is the attribute of God, the Highest and Almighty, and the living God; not only to be everywhere present, but to see all things and to hear all things. -Theophilus

OMNISCIENT:
This means God knows all things.

...Thou knowest it altogether. - Psalms 139:4

...God is greater than our heart, and knoweth all things.
-I John 3:20

...But all things are naked and opened unto the eyes of Him with whom we have to do. -Hebrews 4:13

God knows all things. He not only knows those things that presently exist, but also those things that *will* exist. He knows how each thing will be. -Clement of Alexandria

OMNIPOTENT:
This means God is all powerful.

...I am the Almighty God... -Genesis 17:1

...With God all things are possible. -Matthew 19:26

...For the Lord God omnipotent reigneth. -Revelation 19:6

God hath spoken once; twice have I heard this; that power belongeth unto God. -Psalms 62:11

UNCHANGING:
God does not change His person, nature, purpose, or plans are concerned.

For I am the Lord, I change not... -Malachi 3:6

Jesus Christ the same yesterday, to day, and for ever.
-Hebrews 13:8

HOLY:
God is sinless, pure and holy.

...Ye shall be holy: for I the Lord your God am holy.
-Leviticus 19:2

JUST:
God is fair and impartial in judgment.
...A God of truth and without iniquity, just and right is He.
-Deuteronomy 32:4

FAITHFUL:
God keeps His promises and is absolutely trustworthy.

...He abideth faithful: He cannot deny Himself.
-II Timothy 2:13

BENEVOLENT:
God is good, kind, and wants the best for you.

The Lord is good to all: and His tender mercies are over all His works. -Psalms 145:9

MERCIFUL:
God shows mercy to sinful humanity.

...The Lord God, merciful and gracious, long suffering, and abundant in goodness and truth. Keeping mercy for thousands... -Exodus 34:6-7

GRACIOUS:
God shows undeserved kindness to sinful man.
...For I am gracious. -Exodus 22:27

The Lord is gracious, and full of compassion; slow to anger, and of great mercy. -Psalms 145:8

LOVING:
God is love.

**He that loveth not knoweth not God; for God is love.
-I John 4:8**

WISE:
God shows deep understanding and keen discernment.

**The Lord by wisdom hath founded the earth; by understanding hath He established the heavens.
-Proverbs 3:19**

INFINITE:
God is not subject to natural and human limitations. He is not subject to the limitations of space.

But will God indeed dwell on the earth? behold, the heaven and heaven of heavens cannot contain thee: how much less this house that I have builded? -I Kings 8:27

He is not subject to the limitations of time.

The Lord shall reign for ever and ever. -Exodus 15:18

NAMES FOR GOD
The Sacred Scriptures give other names for God which reveal His ministry to you as you are engaged in this great spiritual conflict. The names for God include:

1. Yahweh: Which means Lord. The Bible combines this name with other names for God:
Yahweh-Rapha: "The Lord that healeth" Exodus 15:26
Yahweh-Nissi: "The Lord our banner" Exodus 17:8-15
Yahweh-Shalom: "The Lord our peace" Judges 6:24

Yahweh-Ra'ah: "The Lord my shepherd" Psalms 23:1
Yahweh-Tsidkenu: "The Lord our righteousness" Jeremiah 23:6
Yahweh-Yireh: "The Lord who provides" Genesis 22:14
Yahweh-Shammah: "The Lord is there" Ezekiel 48:35

2. Elohim: Means God and is used wherever the creative power of God is implied.

3. Father: Acts 17:28; John 1:12-13

4. Adonai: Means Lord or Master: Exodus 23:17; Isaiah 10:16,33

5. El: This is often used in combination with other words for God:
El Shaddai: "The God who is sufficient for the needs of His People" Exodus 6:3
Elolam: "The everlasting God" Genesis 21:33
El Elyon: "Most high God who is exalted above other so called gods" Genesis 14:18,22

6. The Lord Of Hosts: In the Biblical record, these different names of God were used when requesting God to move in a specific way on behalf of His people. For example, the name Jehovah- Rapham meaning "the Lord that healeth," was used when seeking healing. The specific name of God which should be used in spiritual warfare is "Yahweh Sabbaoth" which is translated "the Lord of hosts" in the King James version of the Bible. When you call upon that name in warfare, the battle is the Lord's and all the hosts of Heaven come to your aid.

GOD THE SON

God the Son, Jesus Christ, combines the divine and the human natures in one union. God the Father sent Jesus Christ to earth in human form while yet retaining His divine nature. Jesus was sent by God to earth so man could be pardoned from sin.

For God so loved the world, that He gave His only begotten Son, that whosoever believeth in Him should not perish, but have everlasting life. For God sent not His Son into the world to condemn the world; but that the world through Him might be saved. He that believeth on Him is not condemned: but he that believeth not is condemned already, because He hath not believed in the name of the only begotten Son of God. - John 3:16-18

The life of Jesus Christ is recorded in the Sacred Scriptures in the books of Matthew, Mark, Luke, and John. These books provide a detailed record of the birth, life, death, resurrection, teachings, and ministry of Our Lord. As part of the plan of God, Christ came to earth in human form, ministered among us, died for our sins, was resurrected from the dead, and commissioned His Apostles to bear the Gospel to the nations of the world. Following His resurrection from the dead, Jesus appeared to many people, commissioned His Apostles, and then returned to Heaven. Keep in mind that even though He is in Heaven He is still omnipresent. In other words, His presence is everywhere.

SPECIAL FUNCTIONS:
The special functions of Christ in relation to spiritual warfare include the following:

1. Redeeming humanity from sin: It is through the death of Jesus Christ that you are freed from the bondage of sin in which the Adversary has ensnared you.

..for of whom a man is overcome, of the same is he brought in bondage... -II Peter 2:19

Because the creature itself also shall be delivered from the bondage of corruption into the glorious liberty of the children of God. - Romans 8:21

Stand fast therefore in the liberty wherewith Christ hath

made us free, and be not entangled again with the yoke of bondage. -Galatians 5:1

2. Authority over the forces of evil: The death of Jesus not only freed humanity from sin, but also resulted in triumph over the forces of evil. Because of this, priests, bishops, and to a lesser extent laity have authority over the Adversary.

Then He called His twelve disciples together, and gave them power and authority over all devils and to cure diseases. -Luke 9:1

3. Destroying the works of the Devil:

...For this purpose the Son of God was manifested, that He might destroy the works of the Devil. -I John 3:8

4. Intercession for believers: In Heaven Christ is at the right hand of God the Father interceding for the Church Militant engaged in spiritual warfare.

...It is Christ that died, yea rather, that is risen again, who is even at the right hand of God, who also maketh intercession for us. -Romans 8:34

THE TITLES OF JESUS:
The title "Christ" means "the anointed one" (John 4:25-26). Additional names given Jesus Christ in Sacred Scripture include the following:
Adam (the second)- I Corinthians 15:45-47
Advocate- I John 2:1
Almighty- Revelation 1:8
Alpha and Omega -Revelation 21:6
Amen -Revelation 3:14
Ancient of Days- Daniel 7:9
Angel of His Presence- Isaiah 63:9
Anointed Above His Fellows- Psalms 45:7
Anointed (His)- Psalms 2:2

Apostle of our profession- Hebrews 3:1
Arm of the Lord -Isaiah 51:9-10
Author and Finisher of Faith -Hebrews 12:2
Author of Eternal Salvation -Hebrews 5:9
Begotten of God -I John 5:18
Beloved -Ephesians 1:6
Bishop of Souls -I Peter 2:25
Blessed and Only Potentate- I Timothy 6:15
Branch (The) -Zechariah 3:8
Branch (Righteous)- Jeremiah 33:15
Branch of Root Of Jesse -Isaiah 1:1
Bread of Life -John 6:48
Bright and Morning Star -Revelation 22:16
Captain of the Lord's Host -Joshua 5:15
Carpenter's Son -Matthew 13:55
Chief Cornerstone -I Peter 2:6
Chiefest Among 10,000 -Song of Solomon 5:10
Christ (The) -John 1:41
Christ the Lord- Luke 2:11
Christ Jesus Our Lord -Romans 8:39
Christ the Power of God -I Corinthians 1:24
Counselor -Isaiah 9:6
Covenant of the People -Isaiah 42:6
Dayspring -Luke 1:78
Daystar -II Peter 1:19
Deliverer -Romans 11:26
Door (The) -John 10:9
Elect -Isaiah 42:1
Emmanuel -Matthew 1:23
Eternal Life -I John 5:20
Everlasting Father -Isaiah 9:6
Faithful and True -Revelation 19:11
Faithful Witness -Revelation 1:5
First Begotten -Hebrews 1:6
First Born -Psalms 89:27
First Born Among Many -Romans 8:29
First Fruits -I Corinthians 15:23
First and Last -Revelation 22:13

Foundation Laid in Zion -Isaiah 28:16
Glorious Lord -Isaiah 33:21
God of Israel -Isaiah 45:15
God with Us -Matthew 1:23
Great God -Titus 2:13
Great High Priest -Hebrews 4:14
Head of the Body -Colossians 1:18
Head over all Things -Ephesians 1:22
Headstone of the Corner -Psalms 118:22
Heir of all Things -Hebrews 1:2
Holy One of Israel -Isaiah 41:14
Hope of Glory -Colossians 1:27
I Am -John 8:58
Image of the Invisible God -Colossians 1:15
Immanuel -Isaiah 7:14
Jesus Christ Our Lord -Romans 1:3
Judge of Israel -Micah 5:1
King of Glory -Psalms 24:7
King -Zechariah 9:9
King Over all the Earth -Zechariah 14:9
Lamb of God -John 1:29
Light of the World -John 8:12
Lily of the Valley -Song of Solomon 2:1
Living Bread -John 6:51
Lord God Almighty -Revelation 4:8
Lord and Savior -II Peter 2:20
Lord of All -Acts 10:36
Lord our Righteousness- Jeremiah 23:6
Lord (Your Redeemer) -Isaiah 43:14
Love -I John 4:8
Man of Sorrows -Isaiah 53:3
Master -Matthew 23:10
Messiah -Daniel 9:25
Mighty God -Isaiah 9:6
Mighty One of Jacob -Isaiah 60:16
Most Holy -Daniel 9:24
Most Mighty -Psalms 45:3
Nazarene -Matthew 2:23

Only Wise God -I Timothy 1:17
Our Passover -I Corinthians 5:7
Physician -Luke 4:23
Prince of Peace -Isaiah 9:6
Prince of Kings of the Earth -Revelation 1:5
Prophet -Deuteronomy 18:15-18
Propitiation -Romans 3:25
Rabbi -John 1:49
Redeemer -Isaiah 59:20
Resurrection -John 11:25
Righteous Servant -Isaiah 53:11
Rock -I Corinthians 10:4
Root of Jesse -Isaiah 11:10
Rose of Sharon -Song of Solomon 2:1
Savior of the World -I John 4:14
Seed of David -John 7:42
Seed of the Woman -Genesis 3:15
Shepherd (good) -John 10:11
Son of God -Romans 1:4
Son of Man -Acts 7:56
Son of Mary -Mark 6:3
Son of the Highest -Luke 1:32
Star out of Jacob -Numbers 24:17
Stone -Matthew 21:42
Sun of Righteousness -Malachi 4:2
Sure Foundation -Isaiah 28:16
Teacher -John 3:2
Truth -John 14:6
Vine -John 15:1
Way -John 14:6
Wonderful -Isaiah 9:6
Word -John 1:14
Word of God -Revelation 19:13

GOD THE HOLY SPIRIT

The Holy Spirit is part of the triune nature of God, but the Holy Spirit also has an individual personality. Sacred Scripture reveals that the Holy Spirit has a mind.

And He that searcheth the hearts knoweth what is the mind of the Spirit... -Romans 8:27

Searches out the human mind.

But God hath revealed them unto us by His Spirit: for the Spirit searcheth all things, yea, the deep things of God.
-I Corinthians 2:10

Has a will.

But all these worketh that one and the selfsame Spirit, dividing to every man severally as He will.
-I Corinthians 12:11

Speaks.

Then the Spirit said unto Philip, Go near, and join thyself to this chariot. -Acts 8:29

Loves.

Now I beseech you, brethren, for the Lord Jesus Christ's sake, and for the love of the Spirit, that ye strive together with me in your prayers to God for me. -Romans 15:30

The Holy Spirit intercedes on behalf of Christians.

Likewise the Spirit also helpeth our infirmities: for we know not what we should pray for as we ought: but the Spirit itself maketh intercession for us with groanings which cannot be uttered (spoken). -Romans 8:26

From this list of personality traits you can immediately recognize the important functions of the Holy Spirit in spiritual warfare. The Holy Spirit guides your warfare. He reveals spiritual things that cannot be known through our intellectual faculties. The Holy Spirit speaks the will and words of God to you. He also intercedes for you as you are engaged in spiritual warfare.

GIFTS OF THE HOLY SPIRIT:
The Holy Spirit gives special spiritual gifts to believers. Some are in operation in our world today, some are not. The main references listing the gifts of the Holy Spirit are:

Romans 12:1-8
I Corinthians 12:1-31
Ephesians 4:1-16
I Peter 4:7-11

The gifts of the Holy Spirit are given to certain individuals to equip them for Christian life, and others for spiritual combat against the forces of Satan. The gifts of the Holy Spirit include the following:

Special gifts to equip the Church:
Bishops, priests, deacons, deaconess, religious brothers and sisters, all who fulfill the callings of teachers, pastors, evangelists, and apostles.

Speaking gifts to explain the Gospel:
Prophecy, teaching, exhortation, word of wisdom, word of knowledge.

Serving gifts to enable the Church:
Serving, helps, leadership, administration, giving, showing mercy, discerning of spirits, faith, hospitality.

Sign gifts to establish God's authority:
Exorcisms, miracles, healings.

The Holy Spirit also develops spiritual fruit in the life of the believer. The "fruit of the Holy Spirit" refers to the nature of the Spirit revealed in the life of the believer, spiritual qualities which should be evident in the lives of all Christians. The gifts of the Holy Spirit are for the power of the Church. The fruit of the Holy Spirit is for character in the life of a Christian. If you do not develop Christlike character traits then you will become a victim of Satan. Spiritual fruit is evidence of spiritual maturity. Like fruit in the natural world, it is a product which is the result of the process of life. There are two types of spiritual fruit. There is the spiritual fruit of reproduction.

Ye have not chosen me, but I have chosen you, and ordained you, that ye should go and bring forth fruit, and that your fruit should remain... -John 15:16

There is also the inner fruit of Christlike qualities. These qualities are completely opposite of the fallen nature of humanity:

Now the works of the flesh are manifest, which are these; Adultery, fornication, uncleanness, lasciviousness, Idolatry, witchcraft, hatred, variance, emulations, wrath, strife, seditions, heresies, Envyings, murders, drunkenness, revelings, and such like: of the which I tell you before, as I have also told you in time past, that they which do such things shall not inherit the Kingdom of God. But the fruit of the Spirit is love, joy, peace, long suffering, gentleness, goodness, faith, Meekness, temperance: against such there is no law.

-Galatians 5:19-23

Although the power of the fallen nature and Satan was defeated at the cross, as a believer you experience this only to the degree that you practice your Christian faith. Therefore, to be effective in denying the power of the fallen nature, it is necessary that you develop the fruit of the Holy Spirit.

WHERE IS THE HOLY SPIRIT?

Christ promised His Apostles that upon His return to Heaven the Father would send the Holy Spirit to comfort and guide them.

And I will pray the Father, and He shall give you another Comforter, that He may abide with you for ever; Even the Spirit of truth: whom the world cannot receive, because it seeth him not, neither knoweth Him; but ye know Him; for He dwelleth with you, and shall be in you.

-John 14:16-17

One of the main functions of the Holy Spirit is to testify of and bring glory to Jesus Christ.

But when the Comforter is come, whom I will sent unto you from the Father, even the Spirit of truth, which proceedeth from the Father, He shall testify of me.

-John 15:26

God the Holy Spirit, is in the world today through His Church. He is active in convicting us of sin, drawing us to Jesus Christ, empowering the Church Militant for spiritual warfare, guiding them, and testifying of Jesus Christ.

SENSITIVITY OF THE HOLY SPIRIT

The Holy Spirit has a sensitive nature. This means He has feelings that can be affected by the actions of humanity. Because of the sensitive nature of the Holy Spirit the Sacred Scriptures warn that we should not lie to the Holy Spirit (Acts 5:3-4), resist the Spirit (Acts 7:51), quench the Spirit (I Thessalonians 5:19), grieve the Spirit (Psalms 78:40 and Ephesians 4:30), insult the Spirit (Hebrews 6:4-6), blaspheme the Spirit (Matthew 12:31-32), or vex the Spirit (Isaiah 63:10). It is important that you do not offend the sensitive nature of the Holy Spirit. If the Holy Spirit is offended by your actions He will withdraw His presence. You cannot wage effective spiritual warfare without the power of the Holy Spirit.

TITLES OF THE HOLY SPIRIT:

There are several titles used in Sacred Scripture to describe the Holy Spirit It is important that you know the function of the Holy Spirit as you enter spiritual warfare. The Holy Spirit is called:

The Spirit of God: I Corinthians 3:16
The Spirit of Christ: Romans 8:9
The Eternal Spirit: Hebrews 9:14
The Spirit of Truth: John 16:13
The Spirit of Grace: Hebrews 10:29
The Spirit of Life: Romans 8:2
The Spirit of Glory: I Peter 4:14
The Spirit of Wisdom and Revelation: Ephesians 1:17
The Comforter: John 14:26
The Spirit of Promise: Acts 1:4-5
The Spirit of Holiness: Romans 1:4
The Spirit of Faith: II Corinthians 4:13
The Spirit of Adoption: Romans 8:15

Sacred Scripture also uses several symbols to represent the Holy Spirit.

The dove: John 1:32, Song Of Solomon 6:9
Oil: Luke 4:18, Acts 10:38; Hebrews 1:9
Water: John 7:37-39; Isaiah 44:3
A seal: Ephesians 1:13; 4:30; II Corinthians 1:22
Wind: John 3:8; Acts 2:1-2
Fire: Exodus 3:2; 13:21; Leviticus 9:24; Acts 2:3

It is not enough just to understand and recognize these facts regarding God.

Thou believest that there is one God; thou doest well: the devils also believe and tremble. -James 2:19

The demonic entities also believe in God and are fearful of Him, but they are still rebellious, evil and bent on your destruction. To simply believe in God is not enough. You must acknowledge Him as Lord of your life. You must accept the sacrifice of Jesus Christ for your sin, repent, ask forgiveness, and become a new creature in Christ, be baptized and cleave to His Church.

---

1. Are you presently in a spiritual battle? As you pray about your problem, call upon the name of the Lord of Hosts.
2. Think about a battle you are presently facing and study again the functions of God the Father, Jesus Christ, and the Holy Spirit in warfare. How can God the Father assist you in your personal battle? How can Jesus assist you? What is the function of the Holy Spirit in the problem you are facing?

CHAPTER FOUR
ANGELS

The angel of the Lord encampeth round about them that fear Him, and delivereth them. -Psalms 34:7

WHAT ARE ANGELS?

Angels are ministering spirits sent by God to do His will.

Are they not all ministering spirits, sent forth to minister for them who shall be heirs of salvation. -Hebrews 1:14

Let us consider the whole multitude of His angels how they stand ready to minister to His will. -Clement of Rome

The title "angel" means messenger. Angels were created by God.

Praise ye Him, all His angels: praise ye Him, all His hosts. Let them praise the name of the Lord: For He commanded and they were created. -Psalms 148:2 and 5

For by Him were all things created, that are in Heaven, and that are in earth, visible and invisible, whether they be thrones, or dominions, or principalities, or powers: all things were created by Him and for Him. -Colossians 1:16

All the angels were righteous and holy when they were first created. They worshiped and served the one true God. Later, some angels rebelled against God and lost their position as angels. They became part of a force of evil called "demons." There are now two kinds of angels: Good angels, which are the subject of this chapter, and evil angels (demons).

THE ORGANIZATION OF ANGELS

The good Angels have been organized by God in a special order.

For by Him were all things created, that are in Heaven, and that are in earth, visible and invisible, whether they be thrones, or dominions, or principalities, or powers: all things were created by Him and for Him. -Colossians 1:16

We recognize also a multitude of angels and ministers, whom God, the Maker and Framer of the world, distributed and appointed to their various posts by His Logos. -Athenagoras

The other angels were created by Him, and entrusted with the control of matter and the forms of matter.

- Athenagoras

THE ORDERS OF ANGELS

The angels were created in hierarchy. Science tells us that material creation, that which we can see, accounts for only a small percentage of existence. That leaves a vast amount of things we do not see that are very real. This means that, since there is a guardian angel for each person, there must be billions of angels just in the lower hierarchy of angels, and traditionally there are 9 "choirs" of angels. A third of these angels fell. Their fall was a rebellion to Christ- His authority. Satan refused to serve. So when we speak of demonic activity we must keep in mind that in every case it is ultimately rooted in rebellion to Christ. There are literally multitudes of angels (Luke 2:13-15) who are apparently classified according to the duties they perform. We will not explore all nine choirs, but these are a few of the main classifications of angels.

God works through archangels and kindred angels...

-Clement of Alexandria

MESSENGERS- This function of angels is most likely the largest in number. These are the angels composing the innumerable group, visualized by Daniel (Daniel 7:10), who carry out the will of God in Heaven and on earth. This is the group that usually relates to the Christian in terms of spiritual warfare, though this is not to say others do not assist as well. They interpret God's will, protect, provide guidance, bring answers to prayer, announce, warn, instruct, bring judgment, encourage, sustain, deliver, and intercede on behalf of Christians. This order would also encompass guardian angels.

Every believer-although the humblest in the church is said to be attended by an angel, who the Savior declares always beholds the face of God the Father. Now, this angel has the purpose of being his guardian. So if that person is rendered unworthy by his lack of obedience, the angel of God is said to be taken from him. -Origen

CHERUBIM- This order of angels is first mentioned in Genesis 3:24. They are also mentioned as part of the ark of the covenant (Exodus 25:18-22). Ezekiel mentions these beings and describes them as having four appearances; the face of a lion, the face of an ox, the face of a man, and the face of an eagle (Ezekiel 1:3-28; 10:22). This symbolism of the cherubim suggests they are the living creatures surrounding the throne of God in Revelation 4:6. They appear to be the highest order of angels, the guardians of God. Satan was originally a part of this order.

SERAPHIM- This order is mentioned in Isaiah 6:2,6. Their position is above the throne of God in contrast to the position of cherubim who surround His throne. The duty of these angels seems to be to lead Heaven in the worship of God. In addition to the different orders of angels, there are some individual angels mentioned by name in Sacred Scripture.

MICHAEL:

Michael the archangel is mentioned by name in Daniel 10:13,21; 12:1; Jude 9; and Revelation 12:7. He is the only angel who is called an archangel. He is represented as having charge over an army of angels in Revelation 12:7 and is said to be the prince of the people of Israel in Daniel 10:13,21; 12:1.

The great and glorious angel Michael is he who has authority over this people, and governs them. -Hermas

When Michael, the archangel, disputing with the devil, debated about the body of Moses.... - Hippolytus

GABRIEL:

The meaning of his name is "mighty one." He is mentioned in Daniel 8:16; 9:21; and in Luke 1:19,26. He is always used to deliver an important message from God. It is Gabriel who interpreted the vision for Daniel in 8:16; 9:21 and who announced the birth of John and Jesus Luke 1:19,26.

RAPHAEL:

The meaning of his name is "healing of God". He is a key figure in the Book of Tobit.

SPECIAL GROUPS OF ANGELS:

The Bible also mentions special groups of angels which include:

Angels of the seven churches: Revelation 1:20
Four angels who control the winds: Revelation 1:7
Seven angels who stand before God: Revelation 8:2
Seven angels who administrate the seven last plagues: Revelation 15:1,7

THE ATTRIBUTES OF ANGELS

You will remember from the last chapter that attributes are personality traits or characteristics of an individual.

Angels...

- Are spirits: Hebrews 1:14
- Are sexless: Luke 20:34-36
- Are immortal: Matthew 22:28-30
- Have both visible and invisible forms: Numbers 22:22- 35
- Appear with the likeness of human form: Genesis 19:1-22; 18:2,4,8

• Have emotions: Luke 15:1-10 (angels rejoicing).
• Have appetites: Genesis 18:8
• Are glorified beings: Luke 9:26
• Are intelligent: II Samuel 14:20
• Are meek: Jude 9
• Are powerful: Psalms 103:20; II Peter 2:11
• Have no need to rest: Revelation 4:8
• Travel at an unrecorded speed: Revelation 8:13; 9:1
• Speak languages: I Corinthians 13:1
• Are innumerable: Luke 2:13; Hebrews 12:22; Psalms 68:17; Mark 1:13; Revelation 5:19
• Are immortal: Luke 20:34-36
• Do not marry or have children: Luke 20:34-36
• Are obedient: Psalms 103:20
• Are holy: Revelation 14:10; Mark 8:38
• Are reverent: Their highest activity is the worship of God. Nehemiah 9:6; Philippians 2:9-11; Hebrews 1:6

Angels are active in both Heaven and earth. The source of their power is both granted and governed by God. They have access to the presence of God in Heaven.

...In Heaven their angels do always behold the face of my Father which is in Heaven. -Matthew 18:10

Angels minister in many ways in both Heaven and on earth.

The ministry of angels in Heaven includes:
• Worship: Revelation 4:8; 5:11-12; Isaiah 6:3; Psalms 103:20; 148:1-2
• Standing ready to do God's will: Psalms 103:20-21
• Ministering to the godly who have died in Christ Jesus: Jude 9; Luke 16:22
• Representing children in a special way: Matthew 18:10
• Rejoicing over those who accept the Gospel: Luke 15:10

The ministry of angels on earth includes:
• Ruling nations: Daniel 10

- Ministering to believers in times of testing: Matthew 4:11
- Strengthening believers: Luke 22:43
- Interpreting God's will for men: Zechariah 1:9; Daniel 7:16
- Guiding believers: Acts 8:26.
- Bringing judgment on individuals and nations: Acts 12:23; Genesis 19:3; II Samuel 24:16; Revelation 16:1
- Bringing answers to prayer: Daniel 9:21-22
- Announcing: Luke 1:11-20; Matthew 1:20, 21
- Warning: Matthew 2:13;
- Instructing: Matthew 28:2-6; Acts 10:3-6; Daniel 4:13-17
- Encouraging: Acts 27:23; Genesis 28:12
- Revealing: Acts 7:53; Galatians 3:19; Hebrews 2:2; Daniel 9:21-27; Revelation 1:1
- Sustaining: Matthew 4:11; Luke 22:43
- Preserving: Genesis 16:7; 24:7; Exodus 23:20; Revelation 7:1
- Protecting: Psalms 91:11
- Delivering: Numbers 20:16; Psalms 34:7; Isaiah 63:9; Daniel 3:28; 6:22; Genesis 48:16; Matthew 26:53; Acts 12:1-19
- Destroying: Acts 12:20-23
- Interceding: Zechariah 1:12; Revelation 8:3,4

The future activities of angels will include:

- Participating in the return of Jesus: I Thessalonians 4:16
- Gathering the elect: Matthew 24:31
- Warning and preaching during the tribulation: Revelation 14:6-9
- Separating the wicked from the righteous: Matthew 13:39 and 49
- Binding Satan: Revelation 20

ANGELS AND SPIRITUAL WARFARE

Angels usually relate to the Christian in terms of spiritual warfare. They interpret God's will, protect, provide guidance, bring answers to prayer, announce, warn, instruct, bring judgment, encourage, sustain, deliver, and intercede on behalf of priests and laity in battle. Many Christians have not availed themselves of the aid available from angels because they have not been taught regarding their function in spiritual warfare.

They may have rejected the ministry of angels due to poor instruction, or anti-Catholic bias promoted by evangelical Protestant misunderstanding of the subject matter. They are "ministering spirits" and can minister for you as well as to you. You can ask God to dispatch angels to assist you in battle. King David did this. He prayed...

Let the angel of the Lord persecute them...Let the angel of the Lord chase them... -Psalms 35:5-6

Read the following Biblical accounts of angels participating in warring against the enemy: II Kings 19:35; II Chronicles 32:21; Isaiah 37:36; Revelation 12:7.

IMPORTANT WARNINGS

Angels are holy beings with important duties they must carry out on behalf of the Church Militant. But Sacred Scriptures give some warnings concerning angels.

1. You are not to worship angels:

Let no man beguile you of your reward in a voluntary humility and worshiping of angels, intruding into those things which he hath not seen, vainly puffed up by his fleshly mind. -Colossians 2:18

And I John saw these things, and heard them. And when I had heard and seen, I fell down to worship before the feet of the angel which shewed me these things. Then saith he unto me, See thou do it not: for I am thy fellow servant and of thy brethren the prophets, and of them which keep the sayings of this book: Worship God. -Revelation 22:8-9

Some people have claimed to have been visited by angels who gave them a "new revelation" contrary to God's revelation and deposit of Faith given to the Church. Entire religious movements have been founded on such false revelations.

But though we, or an angel from Heaven, preach any other gospel unto you than that which we have preached unto you, let him be accursed. -Galatians 1:8

You are not to listen to a man, an angel, or any other being that would guide you contrary to the teachings of the Church. As you will learn, one of the main strategies of Satan is deception.

And no marvel; for Satan himself is transformed into an angel of light. -II Corinthians 11:14

2. Do not provoke angels- Read the story of Balaam in Numbers 22, a prophet who was acting in disobedience to God. You will note that he was opposed by an angel of the Lord. When you are disobedient to God, the angels may actually hinder you. You will be fighting a battle, but it will not be warfare against the enemy. Be careful that you do not provoke the angels of God (Ecclesiastes 5:1-6).

ANGELS IN THE LIFE OF JESUS:

Announced the birth of John: Luke 1:11-17
Named him: Luke 1:13
Announced the birth of Jesus to Mary: Luke 1:26-37
Announced the birth of Jesus to Joseph: Matthew 1:20-21
Named Jesus: Matthew 1:21
Announced the birth of Jesus to the shepherds: Luke 2:8-15
Sang: Luke 2:13-14
Directed the flight to Egypt: Matthew 2:13,20
Ministered to Jesus at His temptation: Matthew 4:11
Came to Jesus in Gethsemane: Luke 22:43
Rolled away the stone at His tomb: Matthew 28:2
Announced His resurrection: Matthew 28:5-7
Presented Him to Mary Magdalene: John 20:11-14
Angels ascended on Him: John 1:51
He could have twelve legions of angels: Matthew 26:53
Angels will come with Him when He returns to earth: Matthew 25:31; 16:27; Mark 8:38; Luke 9:26
Angels will be the reapers: Matthew 13:39
They will gather the elect: Matthew 24:31
They will divide the wicked from the righteous: Matthew 13:41,49
They carried the beggar to Abraham: Luke 16:22

They rejoice over sinners who repent: Luke 15:10
They represent little children: Matthew 18:10
He will confess His people before angels: Luke 12:8
They have no sex and cannot die: Luke 20:35-36
The Devil has evil angels: Matthew 25:41

ANGELS IN THE BOOK OF ACTS:
Opened prison doors: 5:19
Directed Philip to the Ethiopian: 8:26
Directed Cornelius to send for Peter: Chapter 10
Delivered Peter from prison: 12:7-19
Struck Herod dead: 12:23
Stood by Paul during the storm: 27:23
Also mentioned in: 6:15; 7:30,35,38,53; 11:13; 23:8-9

ANGELS IN THE EPISTLES:
Elect angels: I Timothy 5:21
Angels are innumerable: Hebrews 12:22
Angels minister to heirs of salvation: Hebrews 1:13-14
Angels will return with Jesus: II Thessalonians 1:7
We are not to worship angels: Colossians 2:18

ANGELS IN THE BOOK OF REVELATION:
Dictated the book to John: 1:1-2; 22:16
Presided over the seven churches: Chapters l-2
Were interested in the sealed book: 5:2
Sang praise to the Lamb: 5:11-12
Were given special power on earth: 7:1-4
Sealed the elect: 7:1-4
Fell down before God: 7:11
Were used to answer prayers of the saints: 8:3-5
Sounded the seven trumpets: 8:6
Ruled the locust army: 9:11
Loosed 200,000,000 horsemen: 9:15-16
Announced the end of time: 10:1,2,6
Fought with the dragon and his angels: 12:7
Proclaimed the Gospel to the nations: 14:6
Proclaimed the fall of Babylon: 14:8; 18:2
Pronounced doom of the beast's followers: 14:9-10
Announced the harvest of the earth: 14:15-18
Had the last seven plagues: 15:1
Announced judgment on Babylon: 17:1,5
Participated in destruction of Babylon: 18:21
Showed John the New Jerusalem: 21:9

Forbid John to worship them: 22:8-9
2. Study the appearance of the angel in Judges 13. Note that the angel returns to Heaven through worship which apparently opens the way through the Satanic atmosphere around us to permit angels to operate on our behalf. Review the story of Daniel and note that the hindrance by the prince of Persia (a Satanic power) was broken by prayer and fasting.
3. There is no Biblical support that a believer can command an angel to do whatever he desires, but you can ask God to dispatch them on your behalf. Think about a battle you are facing and then ask God to send His "ministering spirits" to work in that situation.
4. Read Psalms 78:36,40 and Ecclesiastes 5:6. Israel had a special angel caring for them until they provoked him in the wilderness. If God sends an angel to your aid and you provoke him by sin and unbelief, he may depart from you. It is well to take heed to the warning in Exodus 23:20-22. You may also entertain an angel and not be aware of it...See Hebrews 13:2.

CHAPTER FIVE
SATAN

Be sober, be vigilant, because your adversary the devil, as a roaring lion, walketh about, seeking whom he may devour. -I Peter 5:8

THE ORIGIN OF SATAN

Satan was originally created by God.

All things were made by Him; and without Him was not any thing made that was made. -John 1:3

For by Him were all things created, that are in Heaven, and that are in earth, visible and invisible, whether they be thrones, or dominions, or principalities, or powers; all things were created by Him and for Him. -Colossians 1:16

God does not create evil. Satan was perfect when he was originally created by God, but was given a free will to choose good or evil:

Thou was perfect in thy ways from the day that thou wast created till iniquity was found in thee. -Ezekiel 28:15

In respect that he is the devil, he is not the work of God. Yet, he who is the devil is a created being. -Origen

THE FORMER POSITION OF SATAN

Sacred Scripture describes the original position of Satan in Ezekiel 28:12-17. Read this passage in your Bible before proceeding. When Satan was originally created, he was an angel of God. He was one of the Cherubim, holy, wise, beautiful, and perfect. He was the leader among the cherubs and is called a "guardian" or "covering" cherub. His name was originally Lucifer which means "light bearer" (Isaiah 14:12). He was adorned with precious stones set in gold (Ezekiel 28:13; Exodus 28:15-11), and we learn that music itself was part of his being. He was given a position on God's holy mountain and apparently led in worship (Ezekiel 28:13). He is described as a gem of precious stones. But a gem has no light of its own. It is not beautiful in a dark room. Its beauty is in its ability to reflect light from without When God created Lucifer, He made him with a capacity to reflect the glory of God to a greater degree than any other created being. God was the light that made Lucifer radiate beauty.

THE REBELLION OF SATAN

But Satan did not retain this glorious position.

How art thou fallen from Heaven, O Lucifer, son of the morning. How art thou cut down to the ground which didst waken the nations. For thou hast said in thine heart, I will ascend into Heaven, I will exalt my throne above the stars of God: I will sit also upon the mount of the congregation in the sides of the north; I will ascend above the heights of the clouds; I will be like the Most High. Yet thou shalt be brought down to Hell, to the sides of the pit.

-Isaiah 14:12-15

Thine heart was lifted up because of thy beauty, thou hadst corrupted thy wisdom by reason of thy brightness.

-Ezekiel 28:17

Satan's fall from his angelic position occurred because of pride and rebellion demonstrated in five particular applications of the will in rebellion to the will and kingship of his Creator. Satan said:

I WILL ascend unto Heaven: He desired to occupy the abode of God--Heaven--desiring equal recognition.

I WILL exalt my throne above the angels (stars) of God: He not only desired to occupy God's abode, but he also coveted His rule over the angelic hosts.

I WILL sit also upon the mountain of the congregation: According to Isaiah 2:2 and Psalms 48:2, this is the center of God's earthly rule. Satan desired to rule the earth as well as the angels.

I WILL ascend above the heights of the clouds: The clouds speak of the glory of God. Satan wanted God' glory for himself. (The following verses document clouds in relation to the glory of God: Exodus 13:21; 40-28-34; Job 37-15-16; Matthew 26:64; Revelation 14:14- 16).

I WILL be like the Most High: As we learned in Chapter Three of this course, God has many names by which He is called. Why did Satan choose this particular name? He selected this title because it reflects God as "possessor of Heaven and earth." The results of Satan's rebellion are:

1. BANISHMENT FROM HEAVEN:
Because of his rebellion, Satan was cast out of Heaven by God.

...I will cast thee as profane out of the mountain of God...I will cast thee to the ground... -Ezekiel 28:16-17

2. CORRUPTION OF HIS ORIGINAL NATURE:
Lucifer, once created for God's glory, became Satan with a character that opposed all God is and does.

God made another being, in whom the disposition of the divine origin did not remain. Therefore, he was infected with his own envy, as with poison. So he passed from good to evil. -Lactantius

3. ABUSE OF POWER:
Satan's power was once used for the glory of his Creator. Now it is twisted and distorted to disruptive and destructive purposes. According to Isaiah 14 he weakens the nations, causes the earth and governments to tremble, and those taken as his prisoner have no relief.

Satan lays ploys against everyone. Those who know God, he attacks with wiles and craftiness... -Lactantius

The devil, it must be acknowledged, seems indeed to have power-in this case, really his own, over those who do not belong to God. -Tertullian

4. WILL BE CONSIGNED THE LAKE OF FIRE:
Satan is destined to the lake of fire (Isaiah 14:15).

Eternal fire was not originally prepared for man, but for him who beguiled man, and caused him to offend. I say, it was prepared for him, who is the chief of apostasy, and for those angels who became apostates along with him.

-Irenaeus

5. CORRUPTED OTHER ANGELS:
When Satan fell from Heaven he did not fall alone. He took with him a portion of the angelic host of Heaven who participated in his rebellion against God. This group of angels are now part of an evil force of demons which you will study about in the next chapter.

...he induced as many angels as possible to fall away with him. -Origen

6. INTRODUCED SIN:
When Satan rebelled, sin entered the world and infected humanity.

WHERE IS SATAN?
Satan, in spirit form, is present in the world.

And the Lord said unto Satan, Whence comest thou? Then Satan answered the Lord, and said, From going to and fro in the earth, and from walking up and down in it. -Job 1:7

Be sober, be vigilant, because your adversary the devil, as

a roaring lion, walketh about, seeking whom he may devour. -I Peter 5:8

Although Satan is present in the world, he is not omnipresent, which means he cannot be every place in the world at one time as God can. This is why he employs a host of demons to accomplish his plans. His presence everywhere is through the presence of the many demonic entities who do his will.

SATAN'S ACTIVITIES

Satan has access to the presence of God and operates on the earth, including the "air" or region above the earth:

Now there was a day when the sons of God came to present themselves before the Lord, and Satan came also among them. And the Lord said unto Satan, Whence comest thou? Then Satan answered the Lord, and said, From going to and fro in the earth, and from walking up and down in it. -Job 1:6-7

Wherein in time past ye walked according to the course of this world, according to the prince of the power of the air, the spirit that now worketh in the children of disobedience. -Ephesians 2:2

We may summarize the activities of Satan by noting that they are always directed against God, His plan, and His Church. He will attack in the areas of worship of God, the Sacraments, your personal Christian walk, and your attempts to carry out your vocation in righteousness.

THE ATTRIBUTES OF SATAN

As you have already learned, Satan is a spirit, but he also has attributes of a real personality. He is:

INTELLIGENT AND CRAFTY:

But I fear, lest by any means, as the serpent beguiled Eve

through his subtlety, so your minds should be corrupted from the simplicity that is in Christ. -II Corinthians 11:3

CAPABLE OF EMOTION:

And the dragon was wroth with the woman...
-Revelation 12:17

SELF-WILLED:
And that they may recover themselves out of the snare of the devil, who are taken captive by him at his will.
-II Timothy 2:26

POWERFUL:

...Prince of the power of the air... -Ephesians 2:2

DECEITFUL:

Put on the whole armour of God, that ye may be able to stand against the wiles of the devil. -Ephesians 6:11

VIOLENT AND CRUEL:

Be sober, be vigilant; because your adversary the devil, as a roaring lion, walketh about, seeking whom he may devour. -I Peter 5:8

DECEPTIVELY ATTRACTIVE:

And no marvel: For Satan himself is transformed into an angel of light. - II Corinthians 11:14

THE TITLES OF SATAN

Sacred Scripture gives many names for Satan which reveal more about his nature and activities. As you previously learned, Satan was originally called the "anointed cherub" and "Lucifer" before his rebellion. Other names for Satan are:

Abaddon: (Hebrew word for a destroying angel)
Revelation 9:11
Accuser of the Brethren: Revelation 12:10
Adversary: I Peter 5:8
Angel of bottomless pit: Revelation 9:11
Angel of light: II Corinthians 11:4
Apollyon (Greek word for destroyer): Revelation 9;11
Beelzebub: Matthew 12:24; Luke 11:15; Mark 3:22
Belial: II Corinthians 6:15
Deceiver: Revelation 12:9; 20:3
Destroyer: Revelation 9:11;
I Corinthians 10:10
Devil: (Means slanderer) I Peter 5:8; Matthew 4:1
Dragon: Revelation 12:3
Enemy: Matthew 13:39
Evil One: I John 5:19
God of this world: II Corinthians 4:4
King of Tyrus: Ezekiel 28:12-15
Liar, father of lies: John 8:44
Murderer: John 8:44
Prince of the devils: Matthew 12:24
Prince of this world: John 12:31; 14:30; 16:11
Prince of the power of the air: Ephesians 2:2
Satan: (means adversary, opposer) John 13:27
Serpent: Revelation 12:9; II Corinthians 1:3
Tempter: Matthew 4:3; I Thessalonians 3:5
Roaring Lion: I Peter 5:8
Ruler of darkness: Ephesians 6:12
Spirit that works in the children of disobedience:
Ephesians 2:2

WHAT SATAN IS NOT

Unlike God, Satan is not omniscient (knowing all things). If Satan could foresee the future he never would have allowed Christ to die on the cross. He would have known that the death of Jesus would overthrow his power and provide a way of escape from the bondage of sin for all mankind. Satan is not omnipotent (all powerful). Christ said the power of God within you is greater than the power of Satan. For those who submit to the Kingship of Jesus Christ, Satan is already a defeated foe (John 12:31). He is strong only to those who yield to him. His power is limited by the power of God (Job 1:10-12) and he is only able to overcome a Christian as they yield control to him, or as God wills. Because Satan is not omnipresent (present everywhere) he dispatches demonic entities throughout the earth to do his will and accomplish his purposes. You will learn more about them in the following chapter.

---

1. Study the Biblical record of the words of Satan. His words serve as a further introduction to his strategies: Genesis 3:1,4,5; Job 1:7-12; Job 2:1-6; Matthew 4:1-11; Luke 4:1-13.
2. Satan is an exact opposite of the Holy Spirit. The Spirit was sent by God to draw men to Himself. Satan is committed to draw men away from God.
3. Jesus said Satan...
Is an enemy: Matthew 13:39
Is the wicked one: Matthew 13:38
Is the prince of this world: John 12:31; 14:30
Is a liar and the father of lies: John 8:44
Is a murderer: John 8:44
Fell from Heaven: Luke 10:18
Has a kingdom: Matthew 12:26
Sows tares among the wheat: Matthew 13:38-39
Snatches the Word from hearers: Matthew 13:19; Mark 4:15; Luke 8:12
Bound a woman for eighteen years: Luke 13:16
Desired to have Peter: Luke 22:31
Has angels: Matthew 25:41
Is prepared for eternal fire: Matthew 25:41
4. In studying this lesson on Satan, have you identified areas in which the Adversary is active in your life? Has he deceived you and lied to you? Has he subtly crept into your life to destroy and rob you of joy, peace, or your Christian testimony? It is important to determine this, because areas in which Satan is operative in your life are battlefields in which you will apply the strategies you will learn in this course.
5. Satan is compared to a snake or serpent in the natural world. Consider the spiritual application of the following natural principles:
The venom of poisonous snakes falls into three categories:
Neurotorins: Which affect the nerves.
Hemotorins: Which affect the blood.
Cardiotorins: Which affect the heart.
Satan also affects your nerve (courage), your heart (to attack your worship

and service of God), and tries to prevent the work of the blood of Jesus (salvation, healing,deliverance) in your life. Snakes protect themselves by:

• Disguise: Some snakes are very hard to see because they look like the dirt or trees in which they are found.

• Imitation: Some snakes protect themselves by imitation. One example is the African tree viper which "freezes" itself and sticks its neck out like a twig on a tree.

• Increased size: The puff adder protects itself by blowing itself up as big as possible.

• Frightening sounds: Some snakes hiss or rattle, making frightening sounds to scare you away. Your spiritual enemy comes disguised as an "angel of light" and imitates the things of God. He also tries to frighten you by appearing large and threatening. Snakes capture their food in four different ways:

• Strike: A swift attack.

• Constriction: Where the snake wraps itself around the target and slowly squeezes out its life.

• Throwing weight around over the prey to overcome it.

• Biting and holding the target in its fangs while slow poison paralyzes the target. Sometimes the snake's teeth are broken off in the struggle, but snakes are constantly developing new teeth. The most dangerous part of a snake is its mouth. It shoots enough venom to paralyze, then devours its prey. Do you see how these methods parallel those used in attacks of Satan? Sometimes he attacks with swift and deadly strikes. Other times he constricts your spiritual life with the cares of the world and sinful weights and entanglements. He is always trying to terrorize you, and he loves to hold you in bondage while paralyzing you with his deadly venom. Snakes locate their prey by picking up dust on their tongue which relays information to their brain. If you stand still, a snake cannot locate you. Satan spots you best when the dust is stirred up and you are running in confusion and fear. When the dust is settled and you stand against him fearlessly, just like snake, he cannot strike you. This is why the Bible says "stand still."..and "keep on standing." In a panic situation, a snake will shoot all of its venom at once and is then rendered defenseless for awhile until it can produce more venom. It is possible that this is what occurred in the wilderness temptation when Jesus used the Word of God against Satan's attacks and caused Satan to "depart from him for a season." Here are some ways to avoid snake bite in the natural world. Note that they are also applicable in the spiritual realm:

1. Recognize poisonous snakes (know your enemy).
2. Wear protective clothing (your spiritual armor).
3. Avoid known snake territory (do not go into areas of known temptation or Satanic activity).
4. Have a friend with you (this illustrates the importance of being part of the Church).

5. Avoid walking after dark or in darkened areas. Snakes avoid direct sunlight. (as Christians, we no longer walk as children of the dark but as children of light!)
6. Do not put your hands or feet into places you cannot look (guard your fleshly senses).
7. Do not sit down without looking around carefully (stationary targets are easier to hit than moving targets).
8. Do not go out of your way to kill a snake. Thousands of people are bitten each year because they try to kill them without knowing anything of their habits or habitats. (We are to resist the Devil when we encounter him, not go looking for him).
9. Know what to do in case of snakebite (defensive warfare). In case of snakebite, the first thing that is done in the natural world is to make a cut in the shape of a **cross** (+) over each fang mark and then suck the poison out. What an illustration of the work of the cross of Jesus Christ in freeing us from the "poison" of sin. We have authority over serpents. In Genesis 3, God pronounced a curse upon the serpent (Satan). He said that his head would be bruised by the seed of the woman (Jesus) and that the heel of the seed (Jesus) would be bruised by the serpent. The "bruise" on the "heel" of Jesus speaks of the pressure resulting from bruising Satan's head on the cross of Calvary. When Jesus bruised the head of Satan, it was much like severing the head of a poisonous snake in the natural world. A snake's head can be severed from its body, but it still can bite for hours afterward. The heart has been known to keep beating for two days and the snake's body can continue to move. Jesus severed the head of the "serpent" at Calvary, but the serpent still has life. He is still active in the world today and he still has power. But Satan has no authority. The only authority he has in your life is what you give him and the power and authority within you (Jesus) is greater than his power.

CHAPTER SIX
DEMONIC ENTITIES

Now the Spirit speaketh expressly, that in the latter times some shall depart from the faith, giving heed to seducing spirits and doctrines of devils.
-I Timothy 4:1

THE ORIGIN OF DEMONS

God originally created all of the angels, some of which later became demons.

All things were made by Him; and without Him was not any thing made that was made. -John 1:3

For by Him were all things created, that are in Heaven, and that are in earth, visible and invisible, whether they be thrones, or dominions, or principalities, or powers; all things were created by Him and for Him. -Colossians 1:16

THEIR ORIGINAL POSITION AND FALL

Demons were originally like the other angels of God with the same attributes and positions as the good angels described in Chapter Four. When Satan rebelled against God, a portion of the angels participated in his rebellion. God cast them out of Heaven, along with Satan. They were no longer good angels. They became evil spiritual beings (demons):

And there was war in Heaven: Michael and his angels fought against the dragon (Satan); and the dragon fought and his angels. And prevailed not; neither was their place found any more in Heaven. And the great dragon was cast out, that old serpent, called the Devil, and Satan, which deceiveth the whole world: he was cast out into the earth, and his angels were cast out with him. -Revelation 12:7-9

If demons are not "fallen" angels, then we have no other Biblical explanation for their existence. Satan cannot create his own forces, because all things were created by God. There are two groups of these fallen angels. One group is actively opposing God and His people on earth. Another is confined in chains:

For if God spared not the angels that sinned, but cast them down to Hell, and delivered them into chains of darkness to be reserved unto judgment...- II Peter 2:4

And the angels which kept not their first estate, but left their own habitation, he hath reserved in everlasting chains under darkness unto the judgment of the great day. -Jude 6

There are confined demons and active demons. The leader of both groups is Satan, who is called the "prince" of devils (Matthew 12:24). As noted previously, hell is prepared for the Satan and his angels.

Then shall He (Jesus) say also unto them on the left hand, Depart from me, ye cursed, into everlasting fire, prepared for the devil and his angels. -Matthew 25:41

When Christ confronted two men possessed by demons, their response was:

...What have we to do with thee, Jesus, thou Son of God? art thou come hither to torment us before the time?

-Matthew 8:29

The demons in the possessed men knew their final destiny was a place of eternal torment. Since Hell is a place of torment and was prepared for Satan and his angels, then demons must be the fallen angels.

THEIR SPHERE OF ACTIVITY

Throughout Sacred Scripture, demons are shown as active on earth. Since Satan is not omnipresent, he uses demons to do his will and accomplish his purposes throughout the world. They constitute the "powers of the air" (Ephesians 2:2) and the "powers of darkness" (Colossians 1:13) and are all under the control of Satan.

THE ATTRIBUTES OF DEMONS

In their original sinless condition, demons had the same attributes as the good angels. In their present evil and rebellious state these demons:

Are spirits: Matthew 8:16; Luke 10:17, 20
Can appear visibly: Genesis 3:1; Zechariah 3:1; Matthew 4:9-10
Can speak: Mark 5:9, 12; Luke 8:28; Matthew 8:31
Believe: James 2:19
Exercise their wills: Luke 11:24; 8:32
Demonstrate intelligence: Mark 1:24
Have emotions: Luke 8:28; James 2:19
Have recognition: Acts 19:15
Have supernatural strength: Acts 19:16; Mark 5:3
Have supernatural presence: Daniel 9:21-23
Are eternal: Matthew 25:41
Have their own doctrine: I Timothy 4:1-3
Are evil: Matthew 10:1; Mark 1:27; 3:11

THE NAMES OF DEMONS

Demons are called evil spirits six times and unclean spirits 23 times in the New Testament. They are also called devils (Mark 1:32) and the devil's angels (Matthew 25:41). In addition the apocryphal Book of Enoch gives the names of a number of other angels who fell separately from the rebellion of Satan. They are:

1. Shemyaza-Taught the occult science of root cuttings and enchantments.
2. Azaziel-Taught the making of weapons, use of makeups, dyes, precious metals and stones.
3. Amazarak- Taught sorceries
4. Armaros- Taught the occult removal of curses and

enchantments.
5. Baraqel- Taught astrology
6. Kokabel- Taught astronomical calculations for occult purposes
7. Ezeqeel- Taught Hydromancy
8. Arakiel- Taught Geomancy
9. Shamsiel- Taught Solar worship
10.Sariel- Taught Moon Magick
11.Akibeel- Taught symbolism
12.Tamiel- Taught astronomy
13.Penemue- Taught the use of parchments and inks
14.Kasdeja- Taught abortion
15.Gadreel- Taught combat arts

Others mentioned are Ramuel, Danel, Azkeel, Saraknyal, Asael, Batraal, Anane, Zavebe, Samsaveel, Ertael, Turel, Yomvael and Urakabarameel. As you will learn, sometimes it is helpful to know the name of the demon you are confronting. Knowing a name gives one a power over the entity not otherwise held.

THE ORGANIZATION OF DEMONIC FORCES

Satan is an imitator, not an originator. He has organized his demons in a structure similar to that of God's forces.

For we wrestle not against flesh and blood, but against principalities, against powers, against the rulers of the darkness of this world, against spiritual wickedness in high places. -Ephesians 6:12

Satan has organized his forces into:

Principalities: A principality is the territory or jurisdiction of a prince. Satan has placed a prince over each principality. The prince of the power of Persia is mentioned in Daniel 10. This is how Satan works on a national level influencing governments and nations.

Powers and rulers of darkness of this world: These two

categories of demons are at work in the social, political, and cultural systems of the world. You will learn about how to deal with these and the spirits over principalities as we get deeper into the methodology of exorcism.

Spiritual wickedness in high places: High places in the Old Testament were where worship was carried on. This is how Satan works in the religious structures of the world. You will learn more about this as you study about spiritual wickedness in high places. These organized groups vary in size. For example, Mary Magdalene had seven demons in her prior to her deliverance. Luke 8:30 mentions a "legion" of demons. A legion in the Roman army which ruled at the time of Jesus referred to 6,100 foot soldiers and 726 horsemen! In the case of the demon possessed man recorded in Luke 8:30 the demons were united in their purpose, which in this example was possession of the man. The same is true in Matthew 12:45 and in the case of Mary Magdalene who had seven demons (Luke 16:9). Jesus Christ spoke of the unity of demon powers when He said:

And if Satan cast out Satan, he is divided against himself; how shall then his kingdom stand? -Matthew 12:26

Varying Degrees of Wickedness and Ability

That demons have varying levels of power is illustrated by the demon who said he would return with other evil spirits.

When the unclean spirit is gone out of a man, he walketh through dry places, seeking rest, and findeth none. Then he saith, I will return into my house from whence I came out; and when he is come, he findeth it empty, swept, and garnished. Then goeth he and taketh with himself seven other spirits more wicked than himself and they enter in and dwell there: And the last state of that man is worse than the first... -Matthew 12:43-45

Can Change Their Functions
The demon in I Kings 22:21-23 declared he would be a lying spirit. This indicates he was not one previously for he said "I will be...". We often find that demons change their functions during the process of exorcism in order to confuse the priest as to who he is dealing with.

Are Of Different Kinds
Sacred Scriptures teach that man has a body, soul and spirit. There are three major kinds of demons that attack the body and spirit of man.

1. *Evil or unclean spirits:* They are responsible for immoral acts, unclean thoughts, oppression, possession, depression, and other strategies of Satan which we will study later. They afflict the mind and actions. (Matthew 10:1; 12:43; Mark 1:23-26)

2. *Spirits of infirmity:* These spirits afflict the physical body. (Luke 13:11)

3. *Seducing spirits:* Seducing spirits afflict the mind and spirit of man, influencing him to believe false doctrines as indicated in I Timothy 4:1. These spirits seduce people to believe a lie and be damned to eternal punishment. They are spirits of false doctrine, cults, false Christs, and false teachers.

THE VARIOUS ACTIVITIES OF DEMONS
Demons follow orders given by their prince, Satan. We can summarize the activities of demons by noting that they are always directed against God, His plan, and His Church. Satan uses his demons to accomplish this strategy throughout the world. Demons extend Satan's power by promoting deception and wickedness. They affect individuals, governments, nations, and the world system. They promote rebellion and slander both God and men. They promote idolatry, false doctrines, false religions, slanders, and blind people to the truth of the Gospel. These demons attack unbelievers driving them to commit the most vile acts, to murder, injure, commit

suicide, etc. They affect the mind with emotional and psychological problems and the body with physical infirmities. Demons attack Christians by diabolic temptation, obsession, deception, depression, and oppression. They try to keep you in bondage to habits and fear. They accuse and slander you and create division in the Church. They target your spiritual walk with God and fight against the Church. They also attack your physical body. Unbelievers are defenseless against the attacks of demonic powers, but Christians have powerful spiritual weapons on their side in the forms of prayer, the Sacraments and the priesthood. You will learn about these weapons and strategies as you continue this study of spiritual warfare.

---

1. To learn more about the spiritual forces of evil, study the following Biblical references on the subject of demons:
Genesis: 3:1-15; 6:1-4; 41:8; 44:5
Exodus: 7:8-13; 20-24; 8:6-7, 18-19; 9:11; 22:18
Leviticus: 17:7; 19:26,31; 20:6,27
Numbers: 22:7; 23:23
Deuteronomy: 18:9-14, 20-22; 32:17
Judges: 8:21,26
I Samuel: 15:23; 16:14; 18:10; 28:1-15
I Kings: 5:4; 18:28; 22:19-38
II Kings: 9:22; 17:17; 21:1-9; 23:5,24
I Chronicles: 21:1
II Chronicles: 33:1-10
Job: 1:1-12; 2:1
Psalms: 78:49; 91:6; 106:36-38
Isaiah: 3:18-19; 8:19; 14:12-17; 47:11-15
Jeremiah: 27:9
Ezekiel: 21:21; 28:11-19
Daniel: 1:20; 2:2,27; 4:6-9; 5:7, 11, 15
Hosea: 4:12
Micah: 5:12
Zechariah: 3:1,2; 10:2
Malachi: 3:5
Matthew: 4:1-11, 24; 8:16, 28-34; 9:32-34; 10:1, 25: 11:18; 12:22-30, 11:43-45; 13:19, 39: 15:21-28; 17:14-21; 24:24; 25:41
Mark: 1:12-13, 21-28, 32, 34, 39; 3:11-12, 15, 22-30; 5:1-20; 6:7, 13; 7:24-30; 8:33; 9:17-29, 38-40; 13:22; 16:9, 17
Luke: 4:1-13, 33-37; 6:18; 7:21,33; 8:2, 26-39; 9:1, 37-42, 49-50; 10:17-20;

11:14-26; 13:10-17, 32; 22:3, 31; 24:39
John: 6:70; 7:20; 8:44, 48-49; 10:20-21; 12:31; 13:27; 14:30; 16:11; 17:15
Acts: 5:3, 16; 8:7, 9-11, 18:24; 10:38; 13:6-12; 16:16-19; 19:12- 20; 26:18
Romans: 8:38-39; 16:20
I Corinthians: 5:5; 7:5; 10:20-21
II Corinthians: 2:11; 4:4, 6:14, 15, 17; 11:13-14; 12:7
Galatians: 1:4; 3:1; 4:8-9; 5:19-21
Ephesians: 1:21; 2:2; 4:26-27; 6:11, 12, 16
Colossians: 1:13; 2:15
I Thessalonians: 2:18; 3:5
II Thessalonians: 2:1-10; 3:3
I Timothy: 1:20; 3:6; 4:1-3
II Timothy: 1:7; 2:26; 4:18
Hebrews: 2:14
James: 2:19; 3:15; 4:7
I Peter: 5:8
II Peter: 2:4, 19
I John: 2:13, 18; 3:8, 12; 4:1-4, 6; 5:18
Jude: 1:6, 9
Revelation: 2:9, 13, 24; 3:9; 9:1-11, 20-21; 12:1-13; 13:1-18; 16:13-16; 18:2; 19:20; 20:1-14: 21:8

2. Study the Old Testament record of demonic powers: Satan in the form of a serpent is mentioned seven times in Genesis 3:1-24 and Isaiah 27:1. Satan is also mentioned in I Chronicles 21:1; II Samuel 24:1; Psalm 109:6; Zechariah 3:1-2; and 14 times in the book of Job. Evil spirits are mentioned eight times in the record of King Saul: I Samuel 16:14-23; 18:10; 19:9. Lying spirits are mentioned six times in I Kings 22:21-23. Familiar spirits are mentioned six times in Leviticus 20:27 and I Samuel 28. Religious spirits and spirits of physical harlotry are identified in the book of Hosea. Demons are identified with the gods of pagan nations four times: Leviticus 17:7; Deuteronomy 32:17; II Chronicles 11:15; Psalms 106:19-39. Evil princes who rule nations are identified in the Psalms, the prophets, and specifically in Daniel 10:10-21. Unclean perverse spirits are mentioned twice: Isaiah 19:14

3. Think about this: While demonic forces are God's enemies, at the same time they are subject to His will and used by Him to defeat themselves: See I Samuel 16:14; 18:10; 19:9; I Kings 22:20-22; and Isaiah 19:14.

CHAPTER SEVEN
ENEMY TERRITORY

Love not the world, neither the things that are in the world. If any man love the world, the love of the Father is not in him. For all that is in the world, the lust of the flesh, and the lust of the eyes, and the pride of life, is not of the Father, but is of the world. -I John 2:15-16

THE WORLD

The word "world" has different meanings in Scripture. It can mean the earth or universe in its physical order. It is used to refer to Gentiles which are all nations other than the Jewish nation. But the word "world" also is used to refer to the present condition of human affairs in opposition to God. It is the system that runs the inhabited earth, a system that is opposed to God and the Lord Jesus Christ. It is this meaning that is used in this lesson. The "world" is the corporate group of flesh centered individuals who make up the human race. Flesh, in this context, is not referring to the actual flesh of your body. It is a term which describes the basic evil human nature of man which is in willful rebellion against God. As your enemy, the world is the whole organized system of social, economic, materialistic, and religious philosophies which have their expression through organizations, personalities, and governments. It is not a specific government, organization, or person, but the worldly system upon which these are based. The world system is an extension of man's fleshiness. It provides an atmosphere, environment, and system which promotes fleshly sins. It surrounds man with that which appeals to his fleshly desires. Satan is the "prince" or ruler of the world system.

Now is the judgment of this world: now shall the prince of this world be cast out. -John 12:31

Hereafter I will not talk much with you: for the prince of

this world cometh, and hath nothing in me. -John 14:30

Satan is also called the god of this world.

In whom the god of this world hath blinded the minds of them which believed not... -II Corinthians 4:4

The kingdoms of the world are presently influenced by Satan. They are guided by Satanic philosophy and principles. They are self-centered and sin-governed.

Again, the Devil taketh him up into an exceeding high mountain, and sheweth Him all the kingdoms of the world, and the glory of them; And saith unto Him, All these things will I give thee, if thou wilt fall down and worship me. -Matthew 4:8-9

Some day they will become the kingdoms of our Lord.

And the seventh angel sounded: and there were great voices in heaven saying, The kingdoms of this world are become the kingdoms of our Lord and of His Christ; and He shall reign for ever and ever. -Revelation 11:15

Sin is the reason for the present condition of the world. When Adam and Eve were originally created by God, they were given dominion over the world. This meant they had control over the world, to guide its systems and inhabitants according to the plan of God. When they sinned against God, they lost that dominion. (Genesis 1-3) When Jesus was crucified for the sins of all mankind and resurrected from the dead, He reclaimed the world. He pronounced judgment on Satan and those who rebel against His Kingship.

And having spoiled principalities and powers, He made a shew of them openly, triumphing over them in it.

- Colossians 2:15

Although Christ reclaimed the world from the power of the Adversary, Satan does not want to acknowledge that claim. Satan still is at work in the world with his evil powers. Satan will not acknowledge the social and personal Kingship of Christ until the final conflict. The present situation is similar to military conditions that often occur in the natural world. A political or military power will take control of a nation but their claims will not be acknowledged by rebel troops within that nation. The rebel troops continue to war throughout the country. They try to take possession of territory not rightfully theirs and overpower the citizens. They often use tactics of terror to accomplish these purposes. The situation in the spirit world is similar. Christ reclaimed dominion over the world, the enemy, and his evil forces. But the rebel troops of Satan still war throughout the world. They try to take possession of territory not rightfully theirs and influence men and women for evil. As a result, the world structure is in direct opposition to God, His plan, purposes, and people. The present world system is evil.

Who gave Himself for our sins, that He might deliver us from this present evil world, according to the will of God and our Father. -Galatians 1:4

The world system is without God.

...having no hope, and without God in the world.
-Ephesians 2:12

There is much deception in the world to ensnare believers to become part of the world system.

For many deceivers are entered into the world...-II John 7

The world is already judged and under condemnation by God.

But when we are judged, we are chastened of the Lord,

that we should not be condemned with the world.
-I Corinthians 11:32

The "elements of the world" refer to the elementary principles that govern the world. They lead to spiritual bondage.

Even so we, when we were children, were in bondage under the elements of the world. -Galatians 4:3

The "rudiments of the world" are the regulations on which the world structure rests. They are different from the principles upon which God structures His Kingdom.

Wherefore if ye be dead with Christ from the rudiments of the world, why, as though living in the world, are ye subject to ordinances. -Colossians 2:8,20

The spirit of the world is in direct opposition to the Holy Spirit.

Now we have received, not the spirit of the world, but the spirit which is of God; that we might know the things that are freely given to us of God.- I Corinthians 2:12

Vain Philosophies

Philosophies are principles of knowledge. Worldly philosophies are not based on Christ, and are therefore faulty.

Beware lest any man spoil you through philosophy and vain deceit, after the tradition of men, after the rudiments of the world, and not after Christ. -Colossians 2:8

Worldly wisdom is not God's wisdom. Without a recognition and submission to the social and personal Kingship of Christ all intellectual knowledge is foolishness.

For the wisdom of this world is foolishness with God.
-I Corinthians 3:19

The Course Of The World
The "course" of the world is the cycle of the present world, its routine, the way in which it operates.

Wherefore in times past ye walked according to the course of this world, according to the prince of the power of the air, the spirit that now worketh in the children of disobedience. -Ephesians 2:2

The Voices Of The World
The many "voices" in the world are contrary to the voice of God.

There are, it may be, so many kinds of voices in the world, and none of them is without signification.
-I Corinthians 14:10

The Peace Of The World
The peace of the world is temporary, fragile, and sometimes deceptive.

Peace I leave with you, my peace I give unto you: not as the world giveth give I unto you. Let not your heart be troubled, neither let it be afraid. -John 14:27

The Sorrow Of The World
Godly sorrow differs from that of the world.

For godly sorrow worketh repentance to salvation not to be repented of: but the sorrow of the world worketh death. -II Corinthians 7:10

The Rebellious Nature of the World
The world hates God.

...Know ye not that the friendship of the world is enmity with God? Whosoever therefore will be a friend of the world is the enemy of God. -James 4:4

The world hates the Faithful.

If the world hate you, ye know that it hated me before it hated you. If ye were of the world, the world would love his own; but because ye are not of the world, but I have chosen you out of the world, therefore the world hateth you. -John 15:18-19

Since the world is made up of self-centered and sin centered individuals who hate Christians, we need to learn more about this powerful force called "the flesh."

THE FLESH

This world is an evil social force of Satan that works from the outside to attack Christians. It is the corporate organization of rebellious individuals, cultures, people groups and nations in opposition to the Kingship of Christ. The flesh (a way of saying the fallen nature) is an evil force working from within every person. The same "fleshly spirit" that operates in the world will operate in your life if you allow it to do so. The word "flesh" as used in Scripture can also refer to the actual body of man and beast. The flesh (fallen nature) is the center of willful defiance and rebellion against God.

For I know that in me (that is, in my flesh) dwelleth no good thing; for to will (to do good) is present with me; but how to perform that which is good I find not. For the good that I would I do not; but the evil which I would not, that I do. Now if I do that I would not, it is no more I that do it, but sin that dwelleth in me. -Romans 8:18-20

The flesh is a compulsive inner force which expresses itself in rebellion through sin. It is this meaning of flesh which is meant here. The words "carnal" and "old man" are also used to describe the fallen nature of humanity. All have this basic, sinful, fleshly nature.

Wherefore, as by one man sin entered into the world, and death by sin, and so death passed upon all men, for that

all have sinned. -Romans 5:12
For all have sinned and come short of the glory of God. -Romans 3:23

THE LUST OF THE FLESH

This I say then, Walk in the Spirit, and ye shall not fulfill the lust of the flesh. -Galatians 5:16

What is the lust of the flesh? First let us define the word "lust." Lust is "strong desire, the natural tendency of man towards evil." Sacred Scripture warns that we should not lust after evil things.

Now these things were our examples, to the intent we should not lust after evil things, as they also lusted. -I Corinthians 10:6

Lusting after evil things which will please your fallen nature is "lust of the flesh." It is how Satan attacks from within. It is like a civil war within a nation, with your spirit and flesh fighting against each other. Lust, or sinful desire, first enters through the natural senses. The eye sees something evil or the ear hears something wicked. A touch, a taste, or even a smell can even foster lust. This is how Satan uses the environment of the world to tempt the flesh. These natural senses trigger an evil thought or desire in the mind. This is lust. The lustful thought is what tempts you to do evil.

Let no man say when he is tempted, I am tempted of God; for God cannot be tempted with evil, neither tempteth He any man. But every man is tempted, when he is drawn away of his own lust, and enticed. -James 1:13-14

Remember, God never tempts you. You are tempted when you are drawn by your own sinful, fleshly lusts. But you do not have to yield to this temptation. God always provides a way of escape.

There hath no temptation taken you but such as is common to man: But God is faithful, who will not suffer you to be tempted above that ye are able; but will with the temptation also make a way of escape that ye may be able to bear it. -I Corinthians 10:13

Since the mind is used to tempt the flesh, Paul warns:

For to be carnally minded is death; but to be spiritually minded is life and peace. Because the carnal mind is enmity against God: for it is not subject to the law of God, neither indeed can be. -Romans 8:7-8

You will learn later how the mind is one of the main battlefields of spiritual warfare. If you yield to lust, temptation results and if you yield to temptation, it results in sin which leads to death.

Then when lust hath conceived, it bringeth forth sin, and sin, when it is finished, bringeth forth death. -James 1:15

The world is corrupt because of lust.

...having escaped the corruption that is in the world through lust.-II Peter 1:4

Your flesh is corrupt because of lust.

That ye put off concerning the former conversation the old man, which is corrupt according to the deceitful lusts... -Ephesians 4:22

For the flesh lusteth against the Spirit, and the Spirit against the flesh; and these are contrary the one to the other; so that ye cannot do the things that ye would.

-Galatians 5:17

When you are baptized and filled with the Holy Spirit at Confirmation, that Spirit indwells your spirit. The Holy Spirit in your spirit opposes the lusts of the flesh. Your flesh wars against your spirit and the Spirit of God within you. The fallen nature entices you to sinful lusts. This is why you often cannot live the way you desire to live. Paul described this battle between the spirit and the flesh in Romans chapter 7:

I find then a law, that when I would do good, evil is present with me. For I delight in the law of God after the inward man ; But I see another law in my members (the flesh), warring against the law of my mind and bringing me into captivity to the law of sin which is in my members. -Romans 7:21-23

The lusts of the flesh, if not conquered, lead to sinful works of the flesh which result in spiritual death.

Now the works of the flesh are manifest, which are these: Adultery, fornication, uncleanness, lasciviousness, idolatry, witchcraft, hatred, variance, emulations, wrath, strife, seditions, heresies, envyings, murders, drunkenness, revelings, and such like; of the which I tell you before, as I have also told you in time past, that they which do such thing shall not inherit the Kingdom of God.

-Galatians 5:19-21

This list can be divided into four categories of sins:

1. Worship Sins: Idolatry and witchcraft.
2. Sexual Sins: Adultery, fornication, uncleanness, and lasciviousness.
3. Personal Sins: Drunkenness and revelings.
4. Relationship Sins: Hatred, variance, emulations, wrath, strife, seditions, envyings, murders.

They are contrasted to the fruit of the Holy Spirit which should be developed in the lives of believers. The world and the flesh combine with Satan and his demons to war against believers. These are the spiritual forces of evil.

---

1. Study more on the works of the flesh in Galatians 5:19-21.
2. Contrast to these evil works the fruit of the Spirit in Galatians 6:22-23.
3. Read John 1:1-15 and chapter 3. Observe God's great love for the world despite its sinful, fleshly condition. What did God do to show His love? What was the response of the world?
4. Study further about temptation.
• Satan is called the tempter: Matthew 4:3; I Thessalonians 3:15
• God does not tempt men to do evil: James 1:13-14

You are tempted by:
• Men: Matthew 16:1; 19:3; 22:35; Mark 8:11; 10:2; Luke 11:16; John 8:6
• Satan: Matthew 4:1; Mark 1:13; Luke 4:2; I Corinthians 7:5
• Your lusts: James 1:13-14
• Riches: I Timothy 6:9
• You are to pray not to be led into temptation: Matthew 26:41; Luke 11:4; Mark 14:38; 22:46
• Jesus was tempted, but did not sin: Hebrews 2:18; 4:15
• You are blessed if you endure temptation: James 1:12
• God can deliver you from temptation: Hebrews 4:15; II Peter 2:9; I Corinthians 10:13
• Temptation brings heaviness but you should count every temptation a joy James 1:2; I Peter 1:6
5. Are you experiencing lust which has led to temptation and then to sin? Follow the strategy in I John 1:8-9.
6. It is within the context of describing the warfare between the Holy Spirit and the flesh that Paul identifies the works of the flesh which war within believers. See Galatians 5:16-26.

CHAPTER EIGHT
THE ADVERSARY'S STRATEGY

Be sober, be vigilant; because your adversary the Devil, as a roaring lion, walketh about, seeking whom he may devour; Whom resist steadfast in the faith, knowing that the same afflictions are accomplished in your brethren that are in the world.
-I Peter 5:8-9

THE ADVERSARY AND GOD

Satan's original sin was that he wanted to be like God, so his present power and activities are directed primarily against God. All of his other activities and his very nature are viewed as stemming from his original rebellious ambition. For example, Satan's attack on the first man and woman, Adam and Eve, was really an attack on the character and control of God (Genesis 3:1-5). Satan also induced Cain to murder Abel in opposition to God (I John 3:10-12). You can study every attack of Satan recorded in Scripture and you will discover that it is actually an attack on God and His activities and nature. Satan is in direct opposition to God in every activity and quality of nature. For example, God is love whereas Satan is hateful and promotes hatred (I John 3:7-15). God is life and creates life while Satan promotes death and destruction (Hebrews 2:14). Satan not only opposes God and His nature, but he also opposes God's program. He denies the existence of God (Psalms 14:1-3), promotes lies (Ephesians 2:2; II Thessalonians 2:8-ll); and is behind false religions, the occult, and cults with their false doctrines and practices. Satan's religious system results in false teachers, prophets, and "christs." Despite these evil strategies, Satan and his hosts of demonic powers are no threat to our Almighty God.

THE ADVERSARY AND THE NATIONS

Satan is called the "god of this world" which includes men who are not believers and demonic angels. (II Corinthians 4:4) He offered the nations to Jesus during the temptation of

Christ, and our Lord did not dispute the legitimacy of the offer. He simply refused to rebel against God in submitting to Satan's way of obtaining the rule (Matthew 4:8-10).Satan uses his demons to influence and deceive the nations, leading the leaders and people astray from God. This is why there are cruel dictators, anti-Christ laws, and ungodly political systems in many nations. It also accounts for the wars and divisions between the nations. Satan especially influences leaders against the Church and God's chosen people, Israel. He also works through governments to hinder the spread of the Gospel. During the tribulation period Satan will actually direct the affairs of a group of ten nations through the Antichrist. After the second coming of Christ, Satan will be bound for a thousand years (Revelation 20:3). Upon his release, he will deceive the nations one last time to assemble them against Jerusalem and God (Revelation 20:7-10). In the end, every kingdom of earth and the Kingdom of Satan will become the Kingdoms of our Lord and Savior, Jesus Christ.

THE ADVERSARY AND UNBELIEVERS

The enemy has a very powerful strategy operating against unbelievers. He blinds their minds to the Gospel (II Corinthians 4:3-4) and snatches away the truth of the Gospel when they do hear it so that no response will occur (Luke 8:12). As a result, the Gospel sounds foolish and irrelevant to those who are lost in sin (I Corinthians 1:18). Satan also snares many unbelievers in false religions (I Timothy 4:1-3) and leads them to walk according to the "course of the world" which is the philosophy of the age. This is why we see the rise of Modernism, New Age heresies, and see churches empty, while places of sin thrive. That Anti-Christ philosophy may vary from generation to generation and culture to culture, but it is always creature-centered and creature promoting rather than God-centered. Satan is constantly sowing the seeds of rebellion in the hearts and minds of unbelievers. One of the purposes of the Holy Spirit is to war against Satan for the souls of unbelievers. The Holy Spirit works to convict men and women of their sinful rebellion against God (John 16:7- 11).

THE ADVERSARY AND CHRISTIANS

When you accept Jesus Christ as Savior and submit to his social and personal Kingship, it certainly does not mean the battle is over! You have won one major confrontation when you are enter His Church and Kingdom, but in reality, your intense struggle has only begun. You will learn many specific strategies of Satan as you continue to study this course and are armed with spiritual weapons and mobilized to enter enemy territory. But all of these attacks can be summarized in four major areas. In the life of a Christian Satan attacks. Satan will cause you to question the Church, the Sacred Scriptures, the Priesthood, and will add to, take from, or distort the Scriptures. Remember that this same sort of doubt in God's Word and system happened in the very first temptation of Eve. This is why it is important for you to study and understand the ancient Catholic Faith so you will not be deceived by these attacks. Satan's original rebellion involved his desire to be worshiped, so he especially targets the worship of Christians. He will try to prevent you from worshiping or lead you into false or fleshly worship. When you see the manifold changes in the Divine Liturgy and worship, so that it is marred and changed from God centered to human centered, you must understand that you are witnessing the influence of Satan and should cease participation in such false worship. Satan also attacks your personal walk with God. He accuses and slanders you, tempts you to engage in the works of the flesh, to be occupied with the world, and to rely upon your own human wisdom and strength. He encourages you to leave the Church, to abandon the riches of the Faith and the sustaining power of the Sacraments. If Satan can win territory in your personal walk with God, it will make it easier for him to defeat you in the next area. Finally Satan attacks your attempts to carry out your vocation in righteousness. He will try to deter you from accomplishing God's will by persecution, disaster, discouragement, lack of prayer, and busy involvement with the cares of the world. Satan also tries to affect your work for God by infiltrating the Church with false teachers and disciples (II

Corinthians 11:13-15; II Peter 2:1-19; Matthew 13:38-39). While God sows good seed through your vocation and/or ministry, the enemy sows tares which are the "sons of the wicked one." He promotes division within the Body of Christ trying to affect the work of God and His purposes in your life and ministry.

---

1. Analyze the nation in which you live. What strategies of the enemy do you see operative in your nation?
2. Analyze unbelievers around you for whom you are praying. Has the enemy blinded their eyes to the Gospel? Is he snatching away the Gospel message being presented to them? Are they being indoctrinated in false religion? Are they living in the "course of the world" and its lifestyle? Make these items a matter of prayer.
3. Note the fourfold accusations of Satan:
- He accuses God before the believer: Genesis 3:1-5
- He accuses the believer before God: Job l-2; Revelation 12:9 10
- He accuses the believer before his own conscience: Jeremiah 31:34; Romans 8:33-39
- He accuses the believer through other believers: Matthew 16:13-23; Romans 8:33-39.

4. Think about your own life. Analyze how Satan has attacked you in regards to the Word of God, your worship, walk with God, or work for God.

CHAPTER NINE
THE PLAN

He that committeth sin is of the Devil; for the Devil sinneth from the beginning. For this purpose the Son of God was manifested, that He might destroy the works of the Devil. -I John 3:8

THE PURPOSE OF WARFARE

From the beginning, every battle that has been fought always had a purpose for which it was waged. Before we examine God's battle plan, it is important to understand the purpose of spiritual warfare. This involves understanding the purposes of God the Father and Jesus Christ the Son.

THE PLAN OF GOD

It is God's plan that...

...in the dispensation of the fullness of times He might gather together in one all things in Christ, both which are in Heaven, and which are on earth... -Ephesians 1:10

From the beginning of time, Satan has battled against the fulfillment of this purpose. Your own warfare in the spiritual realm is related to this purpose of God. Satan battles to bring your heart, mind, spirit, and soul into allegiance to him instead of paying your allegiance to the Kingship of the Lord Jesus Christ. God works in you to accomplish His purpose.

For it is God which worketh in you both to will and to do His good pleasure. -Philippians 2:13

God also works through your life to accomplish His purposes.

Neither yield ye your members as instruments of unrighteousness unto sin: but yield yourselves unto God, as those that are alive from the dead, and your members as instruments of righteousness unto God. -Romans 6:13

When you submit yourself to Christ the King to become "an instrument of righteousness unto God," it means you bring your life and ministry in harmony with His purpose and plans. By doing this, you become a more intensely focused target for God's enemy, Satan.

THE PURPOSE OF CHRIST

He that committeth sin is of the Devil; for the Devil sinneth from the beginning. For this purpose the Son of God was manifested, that He might destroy the works of the Devil. -I John 3:8

The reason Christ came into the world was to destroy the works of Satan and to save humanity through His sacrifice on the cross. This immediately set Him in opposition to the Adversary.

The thief cometh not, but for to steal, and to kill, and to destroy: I am come that they might have life and that they might have it more abundantly. -John 10:10

From the beginning of His earthly ministry, Christ set about destroying the works of Satan:

- He revealed the bondage of sin (John 8:34).
- He forgave sins (Matthew 9:1-8; Mark 2:1-12,17; Luke 4:17-32).
- He stressed the heart condition rather than the deception of outward appearance (Matthew 15:16-20; Mark 7:20-23; Luke 6:45; 11:39).
- He healed the sick (Matthew 11:5).
- He raised people from the dead (Mark 5:35-43; Luke 8:49-56; John 11).
- He released people from demonic powers (Matthew 8:16).

In summary, He destroyed the works of Satan in the hearts, souls, minds, and bodies of all who accept His Kingship.

The blind receive their sight, and the lame walk, the lepers are cleansed, and the deaf hear, the dead are raised up, and the poor have the Gospel preached to them.

-Matthew 11:5

Christ not only destroyed the works of Satan, He also exposed the devious strategies of the enemy.

- He taught on the deception of Satan which would increase during the last days on earth (Matthew 24-25; Mark 13; Luke 17:22-37; 21:8-36; Matthew 24-25).
- He warned of Satan who was able to destroy the soul (Matthew 10:28).
- He spoke of the necessity of binding the strong man (Satan) before spoiling his goods (Matthew 12:26-30; Mark 3:23-27; Luke 11:17-24).
- He revealed how Satan tries to prevent the Word of God from being effective in the hearts of men and women (Matthew 13:38; Mark 4:15; Luke 8:12).
- He exposed those who were not right with God as being of their "father, the devil" (John 8:44-47).
- He revealed Satan as the "prince of the world" (John 14:30).

A DIVIDED WORLD

Although Christ came to bring the peace of God (John 14:27; Philippians 4:7), and peace with God (Romans 5:1), His coming also brought terrific division.

Think not that I am come to send peace on earth: I came not to send peace, but a sword. For I am come to set a man at variance against his father, and the daughter against her mother, and the daughter in law against her mother in law. And a man's foes shall be they of his own household.

-Matthew 10:34-36

It is not possible to be neutral. We either live in complete submission to the Kingship of Christ, or we are subject to the power of Satan.

No man can serve two masters: for either he will hate the one, and love the other; or else he will hold to the one, and despise the other. Ye cannot serve God and mammon.
-Matthew 6:24

He that is not with me is against me... -Luke 11:23

Christ spoke of this great division in a story about two paths, one which was straight and narrow and one which was broad. He warned of the deception of Satan's broad path which many took (Matthew 7:13-14). Through the account of the rich man and Lazarus (Luke 16:19-31), Jesus removed the veil between life and death. He let men see the end result of choosing the wrong way. Because He destroyed and exposed the works of Satan, Jesus was under assault throughout His earthly life. The Adversary constantly tried to destroy Him or prevent Him from fulfilling the mission for which He had come. The moment He was born, an attempt was made on His life. During His public ministry there were several plots on His life and at least one attempt which was aborted. He met the opposition of demonic powers, religious leaders, His own followers, and Satan. When you align yourself with the plan and purposes of Jesus by accepting Him as your Savior and King, you become part of the army that wars against Satan, whether you like it or not. The purposes of Jesus become your purposes and this sets you in a tactical position of direct opposition to the Adversary.

THE BATTLE PLAN

There are many different Scriptural strategies that can be used in spiritual warfare, but the basic battle plan for Christians is revealed by first and foremost observing how Jesus dealt with the Adversary. The basic battle plan for spiritual warfare is based on six major points. These are:

- The Sacred Scriptures, Sacraments and Traditional Theology of the Church
- Delegated Apostolic Power And Authority in the Priesthood

- Prayer without ceasing
- Fasting according to the Church's direction
- Keys Of The Kingdom bestowed on the Church
- The Holy Name of Jesus Christ, Sovereign King

THE SACRED SCRIPTURES

One direct confrontation between Jesus and Satan came during a special period of temptation by the enemy. In this encounter, one of the major portions of our spiritual battle plan was revealed. Before proceeding with this lesson, read the accounts of this temptation recorded in Matthew 4:1-11, Mark 1:12-13, and Luke 4:1-13. First Satan tried to get Jesus to turn stones into bread. The power of Jesus which soon was to turn water into wine surely could have turned stones into bread. But to do so in this situation would have been acting independently of God and using His power for personal benefit. Next Satan tried to get Jesus to cast Himself down from the top of the temple. Note that Satan said "Cast thyself down." Satan could not cast Him down, because the power of Satan is a limited power. Satan can persuade you to sin, but he cannot cast you down. As you have learned, every man is tempted when he is drawn away by his own lust. He is not forced, but enticed. In this temptation, Satan used God's Word to back up his appeal, but he misapplied it (Matthew 4:6). Misapplication of God's Word is a major strategy of Satan. In both of the first two temptations Satan said "IF you are the Son of God," do these things. For Jesus to have complied would have been admission that the verification of His sonship by God was inadequate. God had already spoken from Heaven confirming this relationship (Matthew 3:17). Satan always centers his attacks on your relationship with God. The final temptation was an appeal by Satan for worship. In return, Satan would deliver to Jesus all the kingdoms of the world. In these three situations of temptation you can see the evil forces of the world, the flesh, and the Devil warring against Jesus. Jesus met the temptations of Satan with the Word of God. The Bible is a very important spiritual weapon and part of the armor of God which you will study about later. It is called "the sword of the Spirit." The Word of God is the only divinely inspired manual of spiritual warfare. Other books are useful only as they are in harmony with God's Word. In meeting the temptations of Satan, Jesus used the Word of God. Jesus quoted specific Scriptures applicable to the immediate battle. He did not quote passages of chronology or history from the Old Testament. Jesus said, "It is written again..." When you use specific Scriptures, be sure they are in balance with the remainder of the Word of God. They must be viewed in their context and applied in harmony with the total revealed Word of God. In order to use the Word of God effectively in spiritual warfare, you must know the Word of God. You must study, meditate on, and memorize it. Many defeats come because we do not know God's Word.

Jesus answered and said unto them, Ye do err, not knowing the scriptures, nor the power of God.
-Matthew 22:29

The Word of God is our manual for warfare and reveals God's spiritual battle plan.

DELEGATED POWER AND AUTHORITY

The second part of the battle plan is based upon the power and authority over Satan which Jesus delegated to His Apostles and their successors. Apostolic authority via the historic succession coming from Christ Himself is a major weapon in spiritual warfare.

Then He called His twelve disciples together and gave them power and authority over all devils, and to cure diseases. -Luke 9:1

In this order, and by this succession, the ecclesiastical tradition from the apostles, and the preaching of the truth, have come down to us. -Irenaeus

It is necessary to obey the presbyters who are in the

church- those who, as I have shown, possess the succession from the apostles. -Irenaeus

Authority and power are two different things. Consider the example of a policeman. He has a badge and a uniform which are symbols of his authority. His authority comes because of the position he holds with the government. But because all people do not respect that authority, the policeman also carries a weapon. The weapon is his power. Your authority over the Adversary comes through Jesus Christ and your position in Him as either laity or priests bestows a measure of authority and power commensurate to your service in His Church. Your power over the enemy comes through the Holy Spirit.

And behold, I send the promise of My Father upon you; but tarry ye in the city of Jerusalem, until ye be endued with power from on high.-Luke 24:49

Like the policeman, you must have both authority and power to be effective. All Christians receive a measure of authority through the new birth, while some are called to Holy Orders and their position in service to His Church affords them the greater portion of authority and power. The power Christ gave the Apostles and their successors is directed power for specific purposes. These include power over the Adversary.

Power over sin:

And when He had said this, He breathed on them, and saith unto them, Receive ye the Holy Ghost: Whosoever sins ye remit, they are remitted unto them; and whose soever sins ye retain, they are retained. -John 20:22-23

Power to Spread the Gospel:

But ye shall receive power, after that the Holy Ghost is come upon you: and ye shall be witnesses unto me both in

Jerusalem, and in all Judaea, and in Samaria, and unto the uttermost part of the earth. -Acts 1:8

PRAYER

Prayer is the third part of the basic battle plan. Here is a detailed outline to assist you in studying prayer. Prayer is communion with God. It takes different forms. Prayer is described as:

Calling upon the name of the Lord: Genesis 12:8
Crying unto God: Psalms 27:7; 34:6
Drawing near to God: Psalms 73:28; Hebrews 10:22
Looking up: Psalms 5:3
Lifting up the soul: Psalms 25:1
Lifting up the heart: Lamentations 3:41
Pouring out the heart: Psalms 62:8
Pouring out the soul: I Samuel 1:15
Crying to Heaven: II Chronicles 32:20
Beseeching the Lord: Exodus 32:11
Seeking God: Job 8:5
Seeking the face of the Lord: Psalms 27:8
Making supplication: Job 8:5; Jeremiah 36:7

THE PRAYER LIFE OF JESUS

Prayer was an important strategy of the Lord Jesus.

Jesus made prayer a priority:

- He prayed any time of the day or night: Luke 6:12-13
- Prayer took priority over eating: John 4:31-32
- Prayer took priority over business: John 4:31-32

Prayer accompanied any event of importance:

- At His baptism: Luke 3:21-22
- During the first ministry tour: Mark 1:35; Luke 5:16
- Before the choice of the disciples: Luke 6:12-13
- Before and after the feeding of the 5,000: Matthew 14:19,23; Mark 6:41,46; John 6:11,14-15
- At the feeding of the 4,000: Matthew 15:36; Mark 8:6,7

- Before the confession of Peter: Luke 9:18
- Before the transfiguration: Luke 9:28,29
- At the return of the seventy: Matthew 11:25; Luke 10:21
- At the grave of Lazarus: John 11:41-42
- At the blessing of the children: Matthew 19:13
- At the coming of certain Greeks: John 12:27-28
- Before the hour of His greatest anguish: Matthew 26:26-27; Mark 14:22-23; Luke 22:17-19
- For Peter: Luke 22:32
- For the giving of the Holy Spirit: John 14:1-6
- On the road to Emmaus: Luke 24:30-31
- Prior to His ascension: Luke 24:50-53
- For His followers: John 17
- The prayer Jesus taught is recorded in Matthew 6:9-13.

THREE KEYS OF PRAYER

There are three keys in effectual prayer: We find them contained in the simple terms asking, seeking, and knocking.

Ask, and it shall be given you; seek, and ye shall find; knock, and it shall be opened unto you: For every one that asketh receiveth; and he that seeketh findeth, and to him that knocketh it shall be opened. -Matthew 7:7-8

Asking is the first level of prayer. It is simply presenting a request to God and receiving an immediate answer. In order to receive, the condition is to ask.

...ye have not, because ye ask not. -James 4:2

We have the powerful spiritual weapon of prayer, and yet many do not use it. They do not ask, and because of this, they do not receive. Seeking is a key of prayer. This is the portion of prayer where answers are not as immediate as we might like. The apostles gathered in the upper room where they continued in prayer is an example of seeking. They sought fulfillment of the promise of the Holy Spirit, that Confirmation, and continued "seeking" until the answer came. (Acts l-2)

Knocking is the next key. It is prayer that is persistent when answers are longer in coming. It is illustrated by the parable Christ told in Luke 11:5-10. This is the most intense key of spiritual warfare in prayer. It is illustrated by the persistence of Daniel who continued to knock despite the fact he saw no visible results as Satan hindered the answer from God. (Daniel 10)

TYPES OF PRAYER:

There are various types of prayer illustrated in the model prayer given by the Lord (Matthew 6:9-13). Types of prayer include:

1. Worship and praise:

You enter into God's presence with worship and praise; singing hymns, Gregorian chant, the Divine Office, and in the Divine Liturgy.

Enter into His gates with thanksgiving, and into His courts with praise; be thankful unto Him, and bless His Name.

-Psalms 100:4

Worship is the giving of honor and devotion. Praise is thanksgiving and an expression of gratitude not only for what God has done but for what He is. You are to worship God in spirit and in truth.

But the hour cometh, and now is, when the true worshipers shall worship the Father in Spirit and in truth: for the Father seeketh such to worship Him. God is a Spirit, and they that worship Him must worship Him in spirit and in truth. -John 4:23-24

Praise and worship can be with:

Singing: Psalms 9:2,11; 40:3; Mark 14:26

Audible praise: Psalms 103:1

Lifting up of the hands: Psalms 63:4; I Timothy 2:8

Musical instruments: Psalms 150:3-5

Standing: II Chronicles 20:19
Bowing: Psalms 95:6
Kneeling: Psalms 95:6
Prostration: Psalms 149:5

...the high praises of God...in their mouth, and a two edged sword in their hand. -Psalms 149:6

2. Consecration:
This is prayer committing your life and will to God. It includes prayers of consecration and dedication to Christ the King and His Church in various ways.

3. Petition:
Prayers of petition are requests. Requests must be made according to the will of God as revealed in His written Word. Petitions may be at the levels of asking, seeking, or knocking. Supplication is another word for this type of prayer. The word supplication means "beseeching God or strongly appealing to Him in behalf of a need."

4. Confession and repentance:
A prayer of confession is repenting and asking forgiveness for sin. This type of prayer is most engaged in after the priest hears your confession and gives a penance. Prayer is the central focus of the confessional and your penance.

If we confess our sins, He is faithful and just to forgive us our sins and to cleanse us from all unrighteousness.

-I John 1:9

5. Intercession:
Intercession is prayer for others. An intercessor is one who takes the place of another or pleads someones case. Sacred Scripture records that at one time God looked on the earth and saw there was no intercessor.

And He saw that there was no man, and wondered that

there was no intercessor: therefore His arm brought salvation unto Him, and His righteousness, it sustained Him. -Isaiah 59:16

When God saw there was no intercessor He supplied the need. He sent Christ.

For there is one God, and one mediator between God and men, the man Christ Jesus. -I Timothy 2:5

...It is Christ that died, yea rather, that is risen again, who is even at the right hand of God, who also maketh intercession for us. -Romans 8:34

Wherefore He is able also to save them to the uttermost that come unto God by Him, seeing He ever liveth to make intercession for them. -Hebrews 7:25

My little children, these things write I unto you, that ye sin not. And if any man sin, we have an advocate with the Father, Jesus Christ, the righteous. -I John 2:1

An advocate in a court of justice is a legal assistant or counselor who pleads another's cause. Intercession in spiritual warfare is prayer to God on behalf of another person. Sometimes this intercession is made with understanding. Most laity involved in exorcism ministry are intercessors. As such your prayer is essential to the process of deliverance from demonic captivity. Your sincerity, focus, righteousness before God, and being in a state free from mortal sin are all imperative to your intercessory abilities. The same applies to the priest, who intercedes on behalf of the possessed. He too must have made a good confession, penance, received the Sacraments and be in fasting and constant supplication for the victim of Satan.

I exhort therefore, that first of all, supplications, prayers, intercessions, and giving of thanks, be made for all men.

For kings, and for all that are in authority..

-I Timothy 2:1-2

THE MODEL PRAYER

During the earthly ministry of Jesus His disciples once came to Him with an interesting request.

... one of His disciples said unto Him, Lord, teach us to pray... -Luke 11:1

The disciples did not ask how to preach or perform miracles. They did not seek lessons on how to build lasting relationships. They did not inquire regarding the wonders of physical healing. They asked to be taught how to pray. What created this desire? It was the visible effects of prayer in the life and ministry of Jesus. The disciples had witnessed the powerful results of this spiritual power in action. Read the Lord's Prayer, which is our model prayer, and observe the various types of prayer we have discussed.

Our Father, which art in Heaven,
Hallowed be thy name.
Thy kingdom come.
Thy will be done in earth, as it is in Heaven.
Give us this day our daily bread.
And forgive us our debts, as we forgive our debtors.
And lead us not into temptation,
but deliver us from evil;
For thine is the Kingdom, and the power
and the glory, forever. Amen.
– Matthew 6:9-13

HOW TO PRAY

Look up each of the following references in your Bible to learn how you should pray:

- Prayer is to be made to God: Psalms 5:2
- Empty repetition is forbidden, but earnest repetition is not: Matthew 6:7; Daniel 6:10;

Luke 11:5-13; 18:1-8

- You sin by neglecting to pray for others: I Samuel 12:23
- Pray with understanding (in a known tongue): Ephesians 6:18
- Pray in the Spirit: Romans 8:26; Jude 20
- Pray according to the will of God: I John 5:14-15
- Pray in secret: Matthew 6:6
- Quality rather than quantity is stressed. Prayer is not successful because of "much speaking": Matthew 6:7
- Pray always: Luke 21:36; Ephesians 6:18
- Pray continually: Romans 12:12
- Pray without ceasing: I Thessalonians 5:17
- Pray to the Father in the name of Jesus: John 15:16
- With a watchful attitude: I Peter 4:7
- Pray according to the example of the model prayer: Matthew 6:9-13
- Pray with a forgiving spirit: Mark 11:25
- Pray with humility: Matthew 6:7
- Sometimes accompany prayer with fasting: Matthew 17:21
- Pray fervently: James 5:16; Colossians 4:12
- Pray with submission to God: Luke 22:42
- Use the strategies of binding and loosing in prayer: Matthew 16:19

WHAT YOU SHOULD PRAY FOR:

- The peace of Jerusalem: Psalms 122:6
- Laborers in the harvest: Matthew 9:38
- That you enter not into temptation: Luke 22:40-46
- Them that spitefully use you (your enemies): Luke 6:28
- All the saints: Ephesians 6:18
- The sick: James 5:14
- One for another (bearing each others burdens): James 5:16
- For all men, kings, and those in authority: I Timothy 2:1-4

• For daily needs: Matthew 6:11
• For wisdom: James 1:5
• For healing: James 5:14-15
• For forgiveness: Matthew 6:12
• For God's will and Kingdom to be established: Matthew 6:10
• For relief from affliction: James 5:13

HINDRANCES TO PRAYER

• Sin of any kind: Isaiah 59:1-2; Psalm 66:18; Isaiah 1:15; Proverbs 28:9
• Idols in the heart: Ezekiel 14:1-3
• An unforgiving spirit: Mark 11:25; Matthew 5:23
• Selfishness, wrong motives: Proverbs 21:13; James 4:3
• Power hungry, manipulative prayers: James 4:2-3
• Wrong treatment of marriage partner: I Peter 3:7
• Self-righteousness: Luke 18:10-14
• Unbelief: James 1:6-7
• Not abiding in Christ and His Word: John 15:7
• Lack of compassion: Proverbs 21:13
• Hypocrisy, pride, meaningless repetition: Matthew 6:5; Job 35:12-13
• Not asking according to the will of God: James 4:2-3
• Not asking in Jesus' name: John 16:24
• Satanic demonic hindrances: Daniel 10:10-13; Ephesians 6:12
• Not seeking first the Kingdom: It is only when you seek first the Kingdom of God that you are promised the "other things": Matthew 6:33
• God has a higher purpose in denying your request: II Corinthians 12:8-9
• When you do not know how to pray as you should, prayer is hindered. This is why it is important to let the Holy Spirit pray through you: Romans 8:26

WHEN NOT TO PRAY

It is important to learn how to wait before the Lord in prayer for His guidance and direction before acting. But it is equally important to know when not to pray. When God calls you to action, you must act, not continue to pray. For example, at the bitter waters of Marah when Moses cried unto the Lord, God showed him exactly what to do to sweeten the waters. There was no need to wait further on the Lord in prayer. Moses was to act upon what God had revealed. The same was true of Joshua when he prayed about the terrible defeat of Israel at Ai. God revealed there was sin among the people of Israel. He actually told Joshua...

Get thee up; wherefore liest thou thus upon thy face? Israel hath sinned...Up, sanctify the people...
-Joshua 7: portions of 10, 12, and 13

It was not the time to pray. It was the time to act upon the direction given in prayer. Some people use prayer as an excuse to avoid involvement and acting upon what God has told them to do. Others continue to pray when God has already answered but they did not like the answer. Review the story of Balaam in Numbers 22. Note especially verses 18-19. Balaam had no right to go to God with the same matter for God had clearly forbidden him to have anything to do with it (see verse 12).

FASTING

Fasting is the fourth part of our battle plan. It is combined with prayer to wage effective warfare in the spiritual realm. Fasting, in the most simple definition, is going without food. According to Sacred Scripture there are two types of fasts. The total fast is when you do not eat or drink at all. An example of this is found in Acts 9:9. The partial fast is when the diet is restricted. An example of this is in Daniel 10:3. Fasting is a personal matter between an individual and God. It is to be done in private and not boasted about.

Moreover when ye fast, be not as the hypocrites, of a sad countenance; for they disfigure their faces, that they may

appear unto men to fast. Verily I say unto you, they have their reward. But thou, when thou fastest, anoint thine head, and wash thy face; That thou appear not unto men to fast, but unto thy Father which is in secret and thy Father which seeth in secret shall reward thee openly.

- Matthew 6:16-18

Church authorities may call a public fast and request the whole church fellowship to fast.

Blow the trumpet in Zion, sanctify a fast, call a solemn assembly.-Joel 2:15

THE PURPOSES OF FASTING

There are definite spiritual purposes for fasting. It is important that you understand these, for if you fast for the wrong reasons it will be ineffective. Study each of the following references regarding the purposes of fasting. They reveal the great power of fasting in spiritual warfare. You fast:

- To humble yourself: Psalms 35:13; 69:10
- To repent of sin: Joel 2:12
- For revelation: Daniel 9:2; 3:21-22
- To loose bands of wickedness, lift heavy burdens, set the oppressed free, and break every bondage: Isaiah 58:6
- To feed the poor, both physically and spiritually: Isaiah 58:7
- To be heard of God: II Samuel 12:16,22; Jonah 3:5,10

Fasting does not change God. It changes you. God relates to you on the basis of your relationship to Him. When you change, then the way God deals with you is affected. You do not fast to change God, because God does not change. Read the book of Jonah for an example of how this occurred in the city of Ninevah.

LENGTH OF THE FAST

How long you fast depends upon what God speaks into your spirit, or the needs of the Church. He may lead you to fast a short or lengthy time. Remember the story of Esau and Jacob? Jacob was originally making a meal for himself but denied himself in order to obtain the birthright. How much better if Esau had fasted that one meal!

KEYS OF THE KINGDOM

Jesus gave to His apostles and their successors the keys of the Kingdom. Those keys include the power to bind and loose and they are the fifth part of our basic battle plan.

And I will give unto thee the keys of the Kingdom of Heaven; and whatsoever thou shalt bind on earth shall be bound in Heaven; and whatsoever thou shalt loose on earth shall be loosed in Heaven. -Matthew 16:19

Christ taught the importance of binding evil spirits before casting them out, but the principle of binding and loosing is more than casting out demons. You can bind the power of the enemy to work in your life, home, community, and in the Church. You can loose men and women from the bondage of sin, depression, and discouragement of the Adversary. The principle of binding and loosing is an important strategy to overcome the power of Satan. It is a key to the Kingdom of God. In every situation with which you are confronted...every problem, every challenge...there is a spiritual key. That key is in exercising the principle of binding and loosing. When you recognize what to bind and what to loose and act upon this discovery, the Adversary will be defeated.

THE NAME OF JESUS

The final part of the basic battle plan is found in the Holy Name of Jesus. The Word of God is to be applied in His name, we pray, fast, and we priests use our delegated power and authority and the keys of the Kingdom in His Holy Name.

If ye shall ask any thing in my name, I will do it.

-John 14:14

...Verily, verily, I say unto you, Whatsoever ye shall ask the Father in my name, He will give it you. -John 16:23

And these signs shall follow them that believe, in my name shall they cast out devils; they shall speak with new tongues; They shall take up serpents; and if they drink any deadly thing, it shall not hurt them: they shall lay hands on the sick, and they shall recover.-Mark 16:17-18

And Jesus came and spake unto them, saying, All power is given unto me in Heaven and in earth. Go ye therefore, and teach all nations, baptizing them in the name of the Father, and of the Son, and of the Holy Ghost; Teaching them to observe all things, whatsoever I have commanded you; and, lo, I am with you always, even unto the end of the world. - Matthew 28:18-20

The Church is to teach, baptize, cast out demons, heal the sick, and overcome every power of the Adversary through the Holy Name of Jesus. It is more powerful than any other name.

Far above all principality, and power, and might, and dominion, and every name that is named, not only in this world, but also in that which is to come. -Ephesians 1:21

Wherefore God also hath highly exalted Him, and given Him a name which is above every name; That at the name of Jesus every knee should bow, of things in Heaven, and things in earth, and things under the earth; And that every tongue should confess that Jesus Christ is Lord, to the glory of God the Father. -Philippians 2:9-11

NO NEED FOR FAILURE

Christ faced every temptation of Satan which we face, but He overcame these temptations without sin. Because He entered the arena of spiritual warfare, He understands your battles and strengthens you.

For we have not an high priest which cannot be touched with the feeling of our infirmities; but was in all points tempted like as we are, yet without sin. -Hebrews 4:15

Because He emerged victorious, you can also be a victor.

For in that He Himself hath suffered being tempted, He is able to succor them that are tempted. -Hebrews 2:18

Read the story of the death and resurrection of Christ in Matthew 26-28; Mark 14-16; Luke 22- 24; and John 18- 21. The death and resurrection of Jesus Christ was the greatest confrontation that ever occurred between the power of Satan and the power of God. Through the death of Jesus, Satan thought he had destroyed God's plan. He had killed God's only Son. He had destroyed the King who was to reign over God's Kingdom. But Jesus said:

Thinkest thou that I cannot now pray to my Father, and He shall presently give me more than twelve legions of angels? But how then shall the Scriptures be fulfilled, that thus it must be?-Matthew 26:53-54

...My Kingdom is not of this world: if my Kingdom were of this world, then would my servants fight, that I should not be delivered to the Jews: but now is my Kingdom not from hence. -John 18:36

...Thou couldest have no power at all against me, except it were given thee from above...-John 19:11

Jesus did not die because His power was less than that of Satan. His death did not end the plan for God's Kingdom. It was not time for His Kingdom to be visibly established in the world. The death of Jesus actually fulfilled the plan of God. Humanity could now be saved from the bondage of sin and the penalty of sin (eternal separation from God because of sin). Great though it was, salvation from sin was not the only victory gained by Christ through His death on the cross. Through His death and resurrection, Jesus defeated all the power of the enemy.

...When He ascended up on high (was resurrected) He led captivity captive, and gave gifts unto men. (Now that He ascended, what is it but that He also descended first into the lower parts of the earth? He that descended is the same also that ascended up far above all Heavens, that He might fill all things.) (Ephesians 4:8-10)

And having spoiled principalities and powers. He made a shew of them openly, triumphing over them in it.

-Colossians 2:15

Jesus defeated every power of the Adversary, including death. He also passed judgment upon Satan.

Now is the judgment of this world: now shall the prince of this world be cast out. -John 12:31

Christ made a way of salvation. He defeated death and the principalities and powers of Satan. He pronounced judgment on Satan which will be fulfilled in the future. As you have learned, the present situation is similar to conditions which have existed in certain countries in the natural world. The powers of rebel forces will be overthrown by the government. The rebel leader will be under judgment, but still at large. Resistance forces under his direction still war in the land. Jesus has conquered Satan and set his judgment, but he is still at large and his forces of demonic powers, the fallen nature, and the world are still at war all around and in us. They attempt to control territory that is rightfully that of the Conqueror. They try to blind men to the fact Satan has been defeated and is under judgment. They try to control homes, churches, and nations. That is where the warfare of the Christian comes into focus. Jesus has defeated the enemy but Satan remains at large in the world. It is our task to open the eyes of men and women to his deception. Your personal battle will continue until judgment on Satan is executed or until you go to be with Christ through death, which ever comes first.

To the intent that now unto the principalities and powers in heavenly places might be known by the church the manifold wisdom of God.-Ephesians 3:10

Through Christ, your are a victor over Satan rather than a victim.

And hath put all things under His feet, and gave Him to be the head over all things to the Church. Which is His body, the fullness of Him that filleth all in all.

-Ephesians 1:22-23

All things are "under the feet" of Christ the King. This means He has conquered them. He is the head of the Church, and we are the body. It is stated that all things are under His feet, which means under His body, the Church. This means we are victors, not victims. You can be kept from the power of Satan. Our King Himself prayed for us to be kept from the power of the Adversary.

I pray not that thou shouldest take them out of the world, but that thou shouldest keep them from the evil. Neither pray I for these alone, but for them also which shall believe on me through their word. -John 17:15,20

You are a conqueror, not through your own power, but through the powers of a greater One.

...In all these things we are more than conquerors through Him that loved us. -Romans 8:37

When the spiritual battle gets rough, just remember that Sacred Scripture assures us that God's purposes will be accomplished.

The Lord of hosts hath sworn, saying, Surely as I have thought, so shall it come to pass; and as I have purposed so shall it stand. -Isaiah 15:24

This is the purpose that is purposed upon the whole earth; and this is the hand that is stretched out upon all the nations. For the Lord of hosts hath purposed and who shall disannul it? and his hand is stretched out, and who shall turn it back? -Isaiah 15:26-27

The Lord of Hosts has a purpose, and no force of the world, flesh, demons, Hell, or Satan himself will ever stand in its way.

---

1. In this lesson you learned of the importance of the Word of God in spiritual warfare. *How often do you study the Word?*
2. In this lesson you learned that Jesus came to destroy the works of Satan. Read more about the purposes of Jesus in the following verses: Luke 4:18-19; 4:43; 19:10; 24:46-49; John 6:38; 9:4; 12:46; 18:37. Read the statement of God's purpose as it relates to Jesus: John 3:16-18; Ephesians 1:9-10.
3. Jesus had many encounters with evil spirits. But evil spirits and temptation by Satan were not the only battles Jesus fought. Satan also used men who were close to Jesus to war against Him:

Peter: Simon Peter was one of the twelve disciples chosen by Jesus, yet at times Peter was used by Satan to war against Jesus. When Jesus had revealed His forthcoming death, Peter began to rebuke Him for saying such things (Mark 8:32). Jesus said to Peter...

...Get thee behind me, Satan; for thou savourest not the things that be of God, but the things that be of men. (Mark 8:33)

Jesus did not mean Peter was actually Satan, rather that Peter was being used by Satan at that particular moment. One of the chief strategies of Satan is to use those close to you to try to keep you from doing God's will. As Jesus, you must put their persuasions behind you. Is Satan using someone close to you to try to keep you from doing God's will? At a later time, when Peter pledged loyalty to the Lord, Jesus said to him:

...Simon, Simon, behold, Satan hath desired to have you, that he may sift you as wheat; But I have prayed for thee, that thy faith fail not: and when thou art converted, strengthen thy brethren. (Luke 22:31-32)

Jesus knew that when the time of crucifixion drew near Peter would deny Him. He saw how the enemy desired to sift everything good out of Peter's life. But Jesus also could see the great potential in Peter. He realized that someday he would emerge as the first pope of the early church.

Judas: Judas was one of the original twelve disciples chosen by Jesus. Jesus knew from the beginning how the enemy would use this man:

Jesus answered them, Have not I chosen you twelve, and one of you is a devil? He spake of Judas Iscariot, the son of Simon; for he it was that should betray Him, being one of the twelve. (John 6:70-71)

Read of Jesus' betrayal by Judas in Matthew 26:20-25 and John 13:21-30. Has Satan used close associates to betray and wound you? As Jesus, you cannot let that deter you from the purpose God has set for you.

4. Read Malachi 1:13. The prophet reports that in his time some were so bored with their religious observances that they said, "Behold, what a weariness." Perhaps these people never had learned how to worship? Study more about worship: Psalms 5:7; 22:27; 29:2; 45:11; 66:4; 86:9; 95:6; 96:9 97:7; 99:5,9; Exodus 34:14; I Chronicles 16:29; Matthew 15:9; Mark 7:7; John 4:23-24; Philippians 3:3.

5. Study more about praise in the book of Psalms. Mark the word "praise" every time it occurs in Psalms then go back and study all the verses you have marked.

6. Here are some more facts about prayer:

Answers to prayer are granted:

Immediately at times: Isaiah 65:24; Daniel 9:21-23
Delayed at times: Luke 18:7
At times, different from our desires: II Corinthians 12:8-9
Beyond our expectations: Jeremiah 33:3; Ephesians 3:20

Different postures may be used in prayer:

Standing: I Kings 8:22; Mark 11:25
Bowing down: Psalms 95:6
Kneeling: II Chronicles 6:13; Psalms 95:6; Luke 22:41; Acts 20:36
Falling on the face: Numbers 16:22; Joshua 5:14; I Chronicles 21:16; Matthew 26:39
Spreading forth the hands: Isaiah 1:15; II Chronicles 6:13
Lifting up the hands: Psalms 28:2; Lamentations 2:19; I Timothy 2:8

Common problems you will need to overcome in order to pray:

Lack of time
Distractions
Tiredness
Lack of desire

Organizing The Prayer Forces:

Prayer is one of the most powerful weapons of spiritual warfare. The New

Testament reveals the following structure for organizing prayer forces to wage warfare more effectively:
Personal prayer: Prayer is to be made on an individual basis in private: Matthew 6:6
Two praying together: Praying of two together is the smallest unit of corporate prayer: Matthew 18:19
Small groups: Small group cells consist of more than two individuals joining together in prayer. There is great power when two or three people join together for this purpose: Matthew 18:20
Liturgical congregational prayer: The entire church should join together in times of Liturgical prayer: Acts 1:14-15

Prayer Promises:
Study the following promises regarding prayer. They reveal the great power of this weapon in spiritual warfare:
- The Father knows what you need even before you ask: Matthew 6:8
- If any two agree in prayer, it will be answered: Matthew 18:19
- All things are possible with God: Matthew 19:26; Luke 18:27
- Prayer combined with faith is effective: Matthew 21:22; Mark 11:24
- The effectual fervent prayer of the righteous availeth much: James 5:16
- If you ask in the name of Jesus, it will be done: John 14:14

7. Study further on fasting:
- Fasting is one of the things that approves us as ministers of God: II Corinthians 6:3-10
- Prayer with fasting was used in organizing the Church: Acts 14:23
- We are to "give ourselves" to fasting: I Corinthians 7:5

8. Jesus said you would have power to tread on "serpents and scorpions." In Chapter Five you studied the natural and spiritual parallels of a serpent. Here are some facts about scorpions that can be applied spiritually: Scorpions avoid others. A scorpion will fight to the death. It will seize its prey, crush it, and then inject deadly poison from its stinger. If you are stung by a scorpion, you may experience pain, speech difficulties, restlessness, weakness, and numbness. Scorpions live in dark places and die when exposed to the heat (light). First the scorpion will try to escape, then it begins to strike frantically with its tail. In the natural world, army ants are the main enemy of the scorpion. Can you apply these truths spiritually as we did with the facts about snakes in Chapter Five?

CHAPTER TEN
OFFENSE AND DEFENSE

Neither give place to the Devil. -Ephesians 4:27

DEFENSIVE WARFARE

Defensive warfare is battle waged to defend territory. It is warfare that waits for the enemy to strike, then pulls its forces together in defensive response. The defender must respond to his opponent and his decisions are forced on him by the attacker. This type of warfare does not advance into enemy territory. It defends territory already claimed. It is important, however, because the spiritual forces of Satan are constantly attacking you as a Christian. If you do not know how to defend yourself, you will become a victim of these attacks.

OFFENSIVE WARFARE

Offensive warfare is aggressive warfare. It is not a warfare of waiting and responding in defense. It is warfare which takes the initiative of attack. The enemy is identified, his strategy recognized, and offensive advances against him are made in the spirit world. In offensive warfare the attacker has the advantage of making decisions first. Offensive warfare gains territory rather than defends it. Offensive advances are the only type of spiritual warfare which will reach the world with the Gospel of Jesus Christ. We cannot remain in our comfortable homes and churches and practice defensive strategies only. The Church Militant must advance into enemy territory. It must go to the strongholds of Satan with the power of the Gospel message. We must wage aggressive offensive spiritual battle. There is one thing in common about offensive and defensive warfare. Both involve personal action by the Christian. In natural warfare, unused weapons do not inflict causalities on the enemy nor win wars. The same is true in the spiritual realm. Your spiritual weapons are affected by your will to use them. It is true that God empowers for battle, but you have a personal responsibility in both defensive and offensive spiritual strategies. In Old Testament battles, the

Lord fought for and with His people, Israel. But first, they had to position themselves on the battlefield. When God sees a spiritual weapon being used in His name and a man or woman on the battlefield daring to attempt the impossible, the Lord of Hosts is moved to action. Read the story of Elisha in II Kings 13:14-19. In this object lesson using the bow and arrows, there are some spiritual parallels that will help you understand your part in the battle. Elisha told King Joash, "Take up the bow and arrows." Paul said, "Take the sword of the Spirit" and declare war. By taking up your offensive and defensive weapons, you are demonstrating your intention to fight. Elisha told the king to put his hands upon the bow, then Elisha laid his hands upon the king's hands. The strategy for victory is your hand upon the weapon and His hand over yours. Open up the window of the place where the enemy is victorious. Israel's foe was to the east, so Elisha told the king to open the window eastward. God wants you to open up the "windows" of every area of your life to expose the failure, defeat, and bondage of the enemy. Elisha told the king, "Shoot," and the king shot. Then Elisha said, "The Lord's arrow of victory over Syria." The open window is not enough. The weapon in your hand is not sufficient. Even God's hand upon your hand will not win the battle. You must follow the command of the Lord of Host to "Shoot!" This is your part in the warfare; to actually use the weapon that is in your hand which is guided by the hand of the Lord. Elisha told the King to take the arrows and hit them upon the ground as a symbol of his victory over Syria. The king did so, but he "smote thrice and stayed (stopped)." Elisha told him that because he limited God by hitting the ground only three times, his military victory would be limited. This happened because the King did not understand the objective of warfare. Elisha had said the Lord wanted to totally consume the enemy (verse 17). By striking the ground only three times, the King settled for only partial victory. The Lord's objective for you is total victory. If you fail to understand this objective then your victory will be limited. What happened between Elisha and King Joash in the secret chamber that day determined the outcome of the battle with Syria. It is what happens in the secret chamber with the Lord that determines your victories in the actual battles of life.

DEVICES OF SATAN

Basic to both offensive and defensive warfare is knowledge of the strategies of Satan.

Lest Satan should get an advantage of us: for we are not ignorant of his devices. -II Corinthians 2:11

The word "devices" means a scheme, project, plot or underhanded plan of evil character. Satan can gain advantage over you when you are ignorant of his devices and fail to respond in offensive and defensive battle. One of the most powerful verses on offensive spiritual combat is:

For we wrestle not against flesh and blood, but against principalities, against powers, against the rulers of the darkness of this world, against spiritual wickedness in high places. -Ephesians 6:12

God's choice of the word "wrestle" is significant. Wrestling, or martial arts, is a natural parallel of a great spiritual truth. Martial arts is an experience of mastery and strength. To wrestle means "to contend in struggle for power over an opponent." Consider these facts about wrestling in the natural world as applied to your spiritual warfare:

1. PREPARATION AND TRAINING: A wrestler in the natural world must train to be successful at his sport. He must practice wrestling. He must have a proper diet. He must learn the rules of wrestling and they must be carefully followed to win the match. Laity and priest alike must learn the rules of spiritual warfare in order to be victorious. A proper "diet" of Scripture, Sacraments, Confession, and prayer is necessary for successful spiritual wrestling. As in wrestling in the natural world, skill is gained through practice. The primary purpose of training in the natural world is to prepare the wrestler to perform at peak efficiency while experiencing the least amount of fatigue. This is true also in the spiritual realm. Some people are easily fatigued and defeated spiritually because they are not properly trained for spiritual warfare.

2. THE NATURE OF COMBAT: Individual championship wrestling is not a team sport. When a wrestler tires there is no substitute team member to send in. Wrestling involves intimate, face to face, personal contact with the opponent. The same is true in exorcism ministry. Priests are involved in intimate, face to face combat with the Adversary. No other Christian can take his place in this spiritual combat. There are no "time outs" in wrestling as in other sports. There are no "time outs" in the spiritual realm either. Satan never rests from this war. The priest must never be off guard.

3. STRATEGY: There are both offensive and defensive strategies in natural wrestling which are applicable in the spiritual realm. Stalling is one technique used in wrestling. Stalling is avoiding confrontation with an opponent. Points are lost in the judging system for stalling. You also "lose points" when you "stall" spiritually and do not aggressively wrestle your enemy. Some priests and lay persons spend their entire lives stalled in confrontation with the Adversary. They never aggressively wrestle and gain the victory.

4. LOSING BALANCE: Another important strategy in natural wrestling is to upset the balance of the opponent. Once an opponent's balance has been destroyed, he is kept struggling to regain it. Sacred Scripture speaks much of the importance of balance or "temperance." One of the strategies of Satan in the spiritual realm is to try to upset balance. Many cults have resulted because of improper balance on doctrinal issues. Homes, churches, and even nations have been defeated because of improper balance by wrong emphasis or lack of emphasis in certain areas. A priest or layperson called to the area of exorcism ministry can fall prey to a lack of balance in studied focus. Many have fallen prey to Satan simply because they became obsessed with the subject of Satan and the demonic. It must never become a major focus of your life or ministry. There are two types of balance involved in wrestling: Physical and mental balance. Before physical balance can be destroyed, mental balance must first be attacked. To accomplish this, a strategy of surprise is used. A move is initiated that is distracting and a surprising. While the wrestler focuses on this, the intended technique is applied. By leading an opponent to believe some move is about to be attempted, he will try to avoid the imagined danger and leave himself open to the actual attack. Satan upsets balance through the strategy of surprise. He upsets your mental balance by distracting attacks and while you are focused on these, he launches his intended assault in another area of your life.

5. ANTICIPATION: Anticipation is important in natural wrestling. A wrestler who can discern when a particular move is going to be made is usually able to block or counter attack. When the intended move is made it is not as likely to be successful since it is anticipated and the wrestler is prepared. The same is true in the spiritual realm. If you are not ignorant of Satan's devices and anticipate his strategies, then you are prepared. You are not thrown off balance when attacks occur.

6. BAITING: There are moves in wrestling which are made to "bait" an opponent, to tempt and entice him into making a move which will weaken his position. In the spirit world Satan is constantly tempting you to moves which will weaken your spiritual position. In natural wrestling, moves are planned to place an opponent in a position that leaves him open to attack. Situations are purposely created to do this and advantage is taken of an opponent's weakened position at the instant it occurs. Spiritually, Satan creates situations which leave you open to attack, then he immediately takes advantage of your weakened position. When engaged in exorcism it is essential to remain focused on the task at hand. Don't respond to insight into your personal life being exposed, to offers of speaking to deceased relatives, or of having your spiritual questions answered. Don't respond to hearing the voices of deceased family or loved ones, or to taunts daring you to open yourself to the demon in order to relieve its victim of its presence. All of these tactics (and many more) of baiting have been used. You must remember as you wrestle that it is Satan who holds the weakened position. The power within you is greater than his power. He has already been dealt the final weakening blow by the Lord Jesus Christ. But you must exercise the advantage given you by the Lord in order to win the match.

7. ATTACK AND COUNTERATTACK: In natural wrestling, every move you make sets you up for a response from the opponent. The same is true in the spiritual realm. When you make a move for God, Satan will always counterattack with a move of his own. Keep in mind that Satan and the demons have been around for the entire history of humanity. They have an intimate knowledge of human frailties, proclivities and decision making processes. They are very good at determining what your response to any given situation will be. You must be sure to make decisions based solely on proven truths and not the whims or fancies of the day, or those who are not a part of the Kingdom of God.

8. MOBILITY: In wrestling, a mobile opponent is considered dangerous. This is why you want to pin your opponent down. In the spiritual realm, Satan and the demons are mobile opponents. He goes "to and fro" as a lion seeking to devour. You must be on guard for his constant mobility. Satan also recognizes the effectiveness of your mobility. He wants to prevent you from being on the move for God. This is why he strives to throw you and pin you down spiritually. With specifics to exorcism, the priest must be certain to bind the demon during each and every session. In addition, he must become adept at recognizing when one demon subsides while another comes to the forefront, so that he may bind him as well. It is also important that you not allow the demon to keep you focused on one area of questioning for too long. This is a stall tactic and is meant to keep you immobile and your prayer ceases.

9. RECOVERY: Any error made in wrestling results in an action that can be taken advantage of by the opponent. Any error you make in spiritual warfare is quickly taken advantage of by the enemy. It is important in wrestling to learn how to recover from a fall. It is necessary to be able to convert the bottom position into an advantage. There are moves of escape and reversal which will enable this. In spiritual wrestling you may at times experience a fall and be temporarily pinned by the enemy. But you do not have to remain in this position. God has given strategies in which, if followed, will convert your disadvantage into an advantage. He has provided strategies for escape and reversal spiritually just as are used in natural wrestling. The life of Joseph is an excellent example of this. He had the disadvantages of being sold into slavery and put in prison. But he converted disadvantages to advantages. In the end, he triumphed over the enemy. There are other moves in wrestling which result in taking an opponent down from behind, dragging, pinning, throwing, and pulling him. The exorcist may find his personal areas of sin or struggle with sin exposed before everyone interceding on behalf of the victim. This is meant to demoralize the priest and force him to fight from the bottom position, as it were. It is essential that the priest not show emotional responses to the information being exposed, but continue to pray the ritual of exorcism without ceasing. Though inwardly you may be startled, ashamed and even fearful, you must not allow these emotions to show.

10. THE OBJECTIVE: The objective of wrestling in the natural world is to defeat the opponent by causing him to fall or pinning him to the ground. This results from a series of strategic moves and/or by wearing the opponent down. Satan constantly wars against believers trying to wear them down. His objective is to cause believers to fall, throw them, and trap in the bondage of sin. His goal is to destroy your supportive points, just as a wrestler does to his opponent in the natural world. The goal is to make you prostrate spiritually. Exorcism is a very emotionally and physically draining experience for everyone involved. It can be the most devastating of all areas of ministry, making on even mentally exhausted. It is always advisable that a priest have another priest present who can at times take the lead, to remove some of the pressure of this rite. Priests must become sensitive enough to recognize when his fellow priest is wearing down, and if necessary, intervene without being asked. However, this must never be done in the presence of the possessed, but only privately and with the prayerful support of the intercessory team.

11.MENTAL ATTITUDE: Mental attitude is very important in wrestling. In a study on the subject, the following attitudes were said to be necessary for championship wrestling in the natural world. These attitudes also are true in the spiritual realm:

Desire: To wish and want to win is not enough. The champion wrestler must have a will to win. Desire is an emotion which transcends all else in life.

Persistence: Sustained effort is required for championship wrestling. A champion wrestler will not accept defeat.

Purpose: Winning is the goal and purpose of wrestling. To achieve this goal he must not only know he is master of the situation, but he must also let his opponent know.

---

1. You are not to trust in "chariots" (natural weapons) of men: Psalms 20:7. God has "spiritual" chariots. Read about them in Psalms 68:17; 104:3; Isaiah 19:1; and II Kings 2:11.
2. You need to wage both offensive and defensive warfare because Satan is a destroyer: John 10:10; I Corinthians 10:10; Matthew 10:28.
• If you obey God, He will not let the destroyer come in: Exodus 12:23
• God keeps you from the destruction of Satan: Psalms 17:4
• Satan is your adversary, the one you fight against: I Peter 5:8.

You are not to give him room to operate against you: I Timothy 5:14. If you obey God, He will be an enemy to your adversaries: Exodus 23:22.

3. You do not have to be defeated by Satan. Study the following references:

You can chase the enemy: Leviticus 26:7-8; Deuteronomy 32:30; Joshua 23:10

You can have victory: Deuteronomy 7:21; I Chronicles 29:11; Psalms 5:11; 18:29; 24:8; 91:1; Isaiah 49:19; I Corinthians 15:57; I John 5:4

The Lord is your fortress: II Samuel 22:2; Psalms 18:2; 31:3; 71:3; 91:2; 144:2; Jeremiah 16:19

You have dominion over the enemy: Psalms 8:6; 49:14; 72:8; 119:133; Daniel 7:27; Ephesians 1:21

Safety comes from the Lord: Proverbs 18:10; 21:31; 29:25. Psalms 91 is the Psalm of safety.

God delivers you from distress: Psalms 25:17; 107:6,13; 19:28

You can capture enemy thoughts: II Corinthians 10:5

God looses bonds of the enemy: Psalms 116:16; Romans 8:15-21; Galatians 5:1

4. When Paul speaks of wrestling, he is talking about wrestling with the enemy, not with God as did Jacob. Be sure when you are wrestling it is not God grappling with you to break the spirit of self-sufficiency in order to transform you from a "Jacob" to an "Israel."

5. Review Chapter Three of this book and list the functions of the Holy Spirit in both offensive and defensive warfare.

CHAPTER ELEVEN
DEFENSIVE WEAPONS

Put on the whole Armor of God, that ye may be able to stand against the wiles of the Devil. -Ephesians 6:11

The Bible teaches the following defensive actions which must be taken by the believer.

Submit yourselves therefore to God. Resist the Devil, and he will flee from you. -James 4:7

Note the order in this verse: First submit, then resist. Many people skip over the first step of submission and try resisting Satan, only to discover it does not work. Defeat results when you act independently of God. It is the humble, not the arrogant and self-confident, who overcome the enemy. You will be able to resist Satan only as you submit to the Kingship of Christ and enter His Church. To "resist" means to "stand firm against and oppose the enemy at every point." Sacred Scripture does not teach us to go looking for demons, but to resist them when they approach us.

Be sober, be vigilant; because your adversary the Devil, as a roaring lion, walketh about, seeking whom he may devour. Whom resist steadfast in the faith, knowing that the same afflictions are accomplished in you brethren that are in the world. -I Peter 5:8-9

To resist "in the faith" means to resist on the authority of the Gospel of Christ the King, and the Apostolic power of the Church. Do not leave room for Satan to operate in your life or the lives of those entrusted to your spiritual care.

Neither give place to the Devil. -Ephesians 4:27

You must recover souls from Satan's snare by applying Biblical strategies.

And that they may recover themselves out of the snare of the devil, who are taken captive by him at his will.

-II Timothy 2:26

ABSTAIN FROM FLESHLY LUSTS

To "abstain" means to keep yourself from something and refuse to do it.

Dearly beloved, I beseech you as strangers and pilgrims, abstain from fleshly lusts which war against the soul.

-I Peter 2:11

For this is the will of God, even your sanctification, that ye should abstain from fornication. -I Thessalonians 4:3

Abstain from all appearance of evil. -I Thessalonians 5:22

Wherefore take unto you the whole Armor of God, that ye may be able to withstand in the evil day, and having done all, to stand...Stand therefore.. -Ephesians 6:13-14

When you "stand your ground" you are defending that which rightfully belongs to Christ the King.

PUT OFF EVIL

Study Ephesians 4:17-32. The "putting off" of all the evil behavior listed there is defensive warfare. Don't be led aware by the error of the wicked.

Ye therefore, beloved, seeing ye know these things before, beware lest ye also being led away with the error of the wicked, fall from your own steadfastness. -II Peter 3:17

But shun profane and vain babblings; for they will increase unto more ungodliness. -II Timothy 2:16

To "shun" means to avoid or turn away from. You should avoid every evil thing related to the Adversary.

TEST THE SPIRITS

Testing the spirits prevents deception.

Beloved, believe not every spirit whether they are of God: because many false prophets are gone out into the world. -I John 4:1

You are not operating in unbelief when you try the "spirits" of those with whom you come in contact or in operation in and around you. If they are true, they will pass the test. Priests must, more than anyone else, be capable of testing the spirits and recognizing the ploys of the demonic realm. There are many heretical teachings floating around the Christian world today that have caused tremendous damage to the spiritual lives of Christians. The changes of the Second Vatican Council is an example of modern heresy that destroyed a vibrant body. By the councils literal rejection of everything of ancient Christian tradition, the churches are now nearly empty, convents and monasteries closed, vocations are at an all time low, seminaries closed or are filled with homosexuals, pedophiles, and an assortment of heretics ranging from the New Age to the Buddhist, to the Hindu oriented. Priests must guard their flock as if they were, each and every one, his very own children. Guard against Modernism and the spirit of the age in which we live, that caters to the vanities of man more than demanding fidelity to Christ the King and Sovereign High Priest. When you receive false teachers into your home or parish you become partakers of their evil. Defend your home and your parishioners from enemy attack.

If there come any unto you, and bring not this doctrine, receive him not into your house, neither bid him God speed; For he that biddeth him God speed is partaker of his evil deeds.-II John 10-11

Keep yourselves away from those evil plants that Jesus Christ does not tend. -Ignatius

Therefore, it is fitting that you remain aloof from such persons and not speak of them either in public or private.-Ignatius

We call those heretics "empty", for they are destitute of the counsels of God and the traditions of Christ.

-Clement of Alexandria

It is incumbent to obey the presbyters who are in the church-those who, as I have shown, possess the succession from the apostles. -Irenaeus

LAY ASIDE WORLDLY AFFAIRS

You are to lay aside worldly affairs which prevent you from being a good soldier. To "lay aside" is a defensive action you must take.

Thou therefore endure hardness, as a good soldier of Jesus Christ. No man that warreth entangleth himself with the affairs of this life; that he may please him who hath chosen him to be a soldier. -II Timothy 2:3-4

Wherefore seeing we also are compassed about with so great a cloud of witnesses, let us lay aside every weight, and the sin which doth so easily beset us, and let us run with patience the race that is set before us. -Hebrews 12:1

Wherefore lay apart all filthiness and superfluity of naughtiness, and receive with meekness the engrafted word, which is able to save your souls. - James 1:21

THE ARMOR OF GOD

Put on the whole Armor of God, that ye may be able to stand against the wiles of the Devil. -Ephesians 6:11

"Put on" indicates action you must take. The basic description of the armor of God is given in Ephesians 6:10-17. Read this passage in your Bible. Paul introduces the subject of warfare by emphasizing that the battle is not a natural one and natural weapons are ineffective. Spiritual battles must be fought with spiritual weapons. Paul describes the armor to be used in spiritual warfare.

Wherefore take unto you the whole Armor of God, that ye may be able to withstand in the evil day, and having done all, to stand. Stand therefore, having your loins girt about with truth, and having on the breastplate of righteousness; And your feet shod with the preparation of the Gospel of peace. Above all, taking the shield of faith, wherewith ye shall be able to quench all the fiery darts of the wicked. And take the helmet of salvation and the sword of the Spirit, which is the Word of God.

-Ephesians 6:13-17

The purpose of the armor is to be able to stand against the wiles (deceit, cunning, craftiness) of the enemy, Satan. It is your responsibility to put on the armor.

But put ye on the Lord Jesus Christ, and make not provision for the flesh, to fulfill the lusts thereof.

-Romans 13:14

The night is far spent, the day is at hand: let us therefore cast off the works of darkness, and let us put on the armor of light. -Romans 13:12

The phrase "put on" means to "put on once and for all." Your spiritual armor is not like an athletic uniform you put on at game time. You put on the armor once and for all and leave it on the rest of your life. Just as a soldier on the battlefield does not take his armor off and on, you will not lay down your armor until you attain the Beatific Vision. If you do not have your armor on at all times, you are vulnerable to the attacks of the demonic entities. It is wise to check often that each "piece" of your spiritual armor is still in place. The first division of armor covers three things you have done in the past. "Having put" indicates something you have already done if you are a Christian.

• Having your loins girt about with truth (verse 14)
• Having on the breastplate of righteousness (verse 14)
• Having your feet shod with the preparation of the Gospel of peace (verse 15)

The second division includes things which are to be put on in the present.

• Taking the shield of faith (verse 16)
• Taking the helmet of salvation (verse 17)
• Taking the sword of the Spirit (verse 17)

In Ephesians 6:11 Paul emphasizes putting on the whole armor of God. Some of us are preoccupied with but one piece of God's armor to the extent that others are neglected. You must have on the whole armor or you may find yourself being an expert in the use of the "sword of the Spirit" and still defeated because you have forgotten the shield of faith.

The Belt
The first piece of armor to be buckled on is the girdle or belt of truth. In the natural world, a suit of armor was attached to the belt which held the other pieces of armor in place. The truth of God's Word is the spiritual belt to which all other pieces of armor are attached. Satan's first attack on man was on truth.

And the woman said unto the serpent...God hath said, Ye shall not eat of it, neither shall ye touch it, lest ye die. And the serpent said unto the woman, Ye shall not surely die
.-Genesis 3:2-4

The truth will protect you from lies and doctrinal errors of the enemy. Truth is the under girding of your spiritual armor. You are to have your loins (your spiritual vital organs) girt (covered) with truth. This requires you to understand the teachings of the Church, the Sacred Scriptures and to be capable of explaining them to others. A priest or intercessor not firmly grounded in the truths of the Gospel, and in complete faith in the teachings and traditions of the Church should never engage in exorcism ministry. If there is even the slightest doubt as to the absolute truth of the Gospel and Church you are open to vicious attacks from the demonic realm.

Stand therefore, having your loins girt about with truth...
-Ephesians 6:14

What is the truth?

- Jesus said, "I am the truth."John 14:6
- The Holy Spirit is the "Spirit of truth."John 14:17
- God is truth. Romans 3:4
- God's Word is truth. Psalms 119:151
- The Gospel is truth. Colossians 1:5

The Breastplate
In the natural world, the breastplate covered the upper body of the warrior to protect vital organs such as his heart, lungs, etc. The spiritual breastplate of righteousness does not refer to your righteousness, but to the covering of the righteousness of Christ. This is imputed righteousness. That is, it is bestowed upon us vicariously through the merits of Christ. This state of righteousness is achieved only when we are without unconfessed sin, have received the Sacraments, and are in good standing with the Church.

And be found in Him, not having mine own righteousness, which is of the law, but that which is through the faith of

Christ, the righteousness which is of God by faith.

-Philippians 3:9

You do not stand on your own merits. You stand in Christ. You can not face the demonic hordes without the protection of the righteousness of Christ. This goes for priest and laity alike.

By the word of truth, by the power of God, by the Armor of righteousness on the right hand and on the left.

-II Corinthians 6:7

The righteousness of Christ protects your spiritual "vital organs" from attacks of Satan and from unrighteousness. The breastplate of righteousness must be buckled on to the belt of truth.

The Shoes

There are many types of shoes for different purposes. Some are for walking, others for specific sports activities. A soldier's shoes are another kind. They are shoes designed for warfare. A soldier who cannot advance on the battlefield is disabled in warfare. "Feet shod with the preparation of the Gospel of peace" indicate a readiness to advance in the spiritual realm. These spiritual shoes protect your will from the temptation of the enemy who would lead you in wrong paths. They indicate your willingness to do every good work and to spread the Gospel to all nations. These spiritual shoes will also enable you to stand against the enemy as Paul encourages you to do (Ephesians 6:14).

The Shield

In the natural world, the shield was used to provide protection to the warrior's entire body. Your spiritual shield is called the "shield of faith." There are several types of faith mentioned in Sacred Scripture. There is saving faith, the gift of faith, and the spiritual fruit of faith. But the word "faith" when used in relation to the "shield of faith" speaks of defensive faith. This faith is a firm trust and confidence in Christ the King which protects your whole being. It protects you from flaming missiles of doubt and unbelief sent by the Adversary. This shield of faith is a calm and confident trust in God which deflects all the fiery arrows of the enemy from their target. The shield of faith is the constant application of the Gospel of Christ to the issues of life. It is a faith that enables you to overcome the evil forces at work in the world.

For whatsoever is born of God overcometh the world; and this is the victory that overcometh the world, even our faith. -I John 5:4

Faith is voluntary anticipation, the assent of piety.
-Clement of Alexandria

Faith is something superior to knowledge and its criterion.- Clement of Alexandria

Combined with love of God, faith is most effective.

...putting on the breastplate of faith and love...
-I Thessalonians 5:8

And he loves Christ Jesus who does His will and keeps His commandments. -Clement of Alexandria

It is faith based on truth.

He shall cover thee with His feathers, and under His wings shalt thou trust: His truth shall be thy shield and buckler.
- Psalms 91:14

It is faith based on salvation.

Thou hast also given me the shield of thy salvation: and thy right hand hath holden me up, and thy gentleness hath made me great. -Psalms 18:35

He seeks all and desires to save all. He seeks to make everyone the children of God. -Hippolytus

Without faith, you have no grasp of truth. Without faith you cannot receive salvation. Without faith you cannot go forth with the Gospel of peace. Without faith you cannot claim the righteousness of Christ and effectively use the sword of the Spirit which is the Word of God. Faith is not an assumption or presumption. It is a fact based upon God's Word. You can increase your faith by hearing God's Word (Romans 10:17), acting upon your present faith (Romans 1:17), and seeking God (Hebrews 12:2).

The Helmet

The helmet of salvation is not something you put on when you get saved. Remember, we are dealing with spiritual armor here, and it is assumed that you are a Christian and a member of the Church Militant before you start putting on the armor. The helmet of salvation represents a regenerated mind. It represents a transformed and renewed thought life. You will learn later that Satan desperately fights for control of them mind. An undisciplined mind makes the Christian warrior easy prey to sinful deceptions of the enemy. Paul speaks of the helmet as the "hope of salvation" in I Thessalonians 5:8. Salvation, when properly experienced and understood, protects your mind. Salvation embraces the past, present, and future. You have been saved from the guilt and penalty of past sin. You are being saved from the power of sin in the present through the sacrament of Confession. The "hope of salvation" refers to salvation in the future tense. It is final salvation from the presence of sin when Christ returns. The hope of this future salvation strengthens your mind against the attacks of Satan. You have a confident hope in the future because God is working out His purpose.

...according to His good pleasure, which He hath purposed in Himself; That in the dispensation of the fullness of times He might gather together in one all things in Christ,

both which are in Heaven, and which are on earth; even in Him. -Ephesians 1:9-10

The Sword Of The Spirit
The "sword of the Spirit" is the Word of God. It is both a defensive and offensive weapon. You already learned how Christ used the Word in defense against the attacks of Satan.

Prayer: After describing the Christian soldier's armor, Paul comments "**Praying always with all prayer and supplication in the Spirit, and watching thereunto with all perseverance and supplication for all saints."**

-Ephesians 6:18

We are the true worshipers, and the true priests who praying in the spirit, offer a sacrifice in spirit; prayer, a victim that is proper and acceptable to God. -Tertullian

For who of you does not know that the prayer of one who accompanies it with lamentation and tears, with the body prostrate, or with bended knees, propitiates God most of all? -Justin the Martyr

As you learned, prayer and its associated practice of fasting are also powerful spiritual weapons. These two weapons can be used both offensively and defensively. Briefly examine the summary of the armor of God and its purposes which follows:

THE ARMOR OF GOD
Ephesians 6:10-18
TRUTH (girdle)
Protects from...
DECEPTION Sword of the Spirit
RIGHTEOUSNESS (breastplate)
Protects from...
UNRIGHTEOUSNESS
PEACE (shoes)
Protects from...

CONFUSION
FAITH (shield)
Protects from...
UNBELIEF
SALVATION (helmet)
Protects from...
BONDAGE

• The girdle or belt of truth protects from the deception of Satan which can lead to unrighteousness (sin).
• The breastplate of righteousness protects from unrighteousness (sin) which leads to confusion.
• Feet shod with the preparation of the Gospel of peace protects from spiritual confusion which results in unbelief.
• The shield of faith protects against unbelief which results in bondage. The helmet of salvation protects from bondage.
• The sword of the spirit, the Word of God, is used as both an offensive and defensive weapon.

Note the downward progression of one not protected by the armor of God: Deception leads to unrighteousness (sin) which always results in confusion. Confusion results in unbelief, and unbelief always results in spiritual bondage.

---

1. Read Psalms 45:3 and Isaiah 59:17. Both passages describe God putting on spiritual armor. What two pieces of armor does God put on that are not included in our spiritual armor? (Isaiah 59:17)
2. David mentions spiritual armor as he recalls how God has helped him in battle. Study Psalms 18:29-50.
3. It is important that you have experience using your spiritual armor. In I Samuel 17 read about what happened when David tried to use armor with which he was not familiar.
4. The Lord uses spiritual armor to protect you from your enemies: Psalms 35:1-3 David had much to say about his enemies: Psalms 5:8; 6:10; 8:2; 9:3; 11:2; 15:5; 17:9; 18:3, 17, 20, 26, 34, 37; 27:2; 30:1 31:23; 44:5-6; 56:9; 60:12; 61:3; 95:6; 108:13. Read what God says about your enemies: Exodus 15:6; Matthew 10:36; 13:39; Luke 1:11; 10:19; Acts 2:35; I Corinthians 15:25-26; Colossians 1:21.
5. God is your shield. See Genesis 15:1; Psalms 3:3; 5:12; 28:7; 33:20;

59:11; 84:9,11; 115:9-11; 119:114; 144:2.

6. Read Exodus 17. Israel was under attack and God told Moses to stretch forth his rod. Previously, Moses had used the rod as a shepherd's staff and to provide water for God's people. Now, for the first time, he stretches forth the rod to resist the principalities and powers of the hosts of wicked spirits responsible for the Amalekite attack. There is a great spiritual lesson in this story. The leaders of God's people are not only responsible to shepherd, feed, and water the flock, but when an attack from the enemy comes it is their responsibility to use the "rod of God" to defend God's Church.

7. How do you respond to these fiery darts of Satan? Think about how you would use the shield of faith to defend yourself from each of these attacks. Record your answers to use them in the next attack:

Selfishness:

Covetousness:

Pride:

Doubt:

Fear:

Depression:

Discouragement:

Lust:

Greed:

Anger:

8. Examine yourself: Is all your spiritual armor in place?

9. Study how the Lord is revealed as a shield in the book of Psalms:

- He is surrounding shield: Psalms 5:12
- He is a saving shield: Psalms 18:35
- He is a personal shield: Psalms 3:3
- He is a shield to those who trust in Him: Psalms 18:30
- His shield is a gift: Psalms 18:35
- He is a tested shield: Psalms 28:7
- He is a trusted shield: Psalms 144:2
- He is a victorious shield: Psalms 59:11
- He is a protecting shield: Psalms 84:11
- He is an anointed shield: Psalms 84:9
- He is a sheltering shield: Psalms 119:114
- He is a helping shield: Psalms 116:11

CHAPTER TWELVE
OFFENSIVE WEAPONS

The Lord hath opened his armory, and hath brought forth the weapons of his indignation: for this is the work of the Lord God of hosts...
-Jeremiah 50:25

This charge I commit unto thee, son Timothy, according to the prophecies which went before on thee, that thou by them mightest war a good warfare.
-I Timothy 1:18

Fight the good fight of faith, lay hold on eternal life, whereunto thou art also called, and has professed a good profession before many witnesses.
-I Timothy 6:12

You are to fight this battle intelligently with purpose.

I therefore so run, not as uncertainly; so fight I, not as one that beateth the air. -I Corinthians 9:26

Knowing your offensive weapons can give you the ability to fight with purpose instead of uncertainty.

OFFENSIVE STRATEGIES

Here are the weapons you use to wage offensive spiritual warfare:

PRAYER

You already studied prayer and fasting as defensive weapons. But prayer is also a powerful offensive weapon. When you use it to wage offensive warfare you do not just pray only for your own personal wants, needs, and problems. You intercede for people, leaders, and nations, pulling down strongholds of Satan and his demonic forces. All Christians are to intercede at times, but there is a special calling to intercession for some.

This powerful ministry brings the intercessor before the Lord to wage mighty battles in the unseen realm. The value of praise and worship was also mentioned. Praise and worship are powerful offensive weapons. In II Chronicles 20 when Israel faced a mighty enemy, they began to sing and praise God and He set an ambush to defeat their army.

THE SWORD OF THE SPIRIT

The "sword of the Spirit," which is the Word of God, is a weapon that can be used both defensively and offensively. Sacred Scripture is a defensive weapon when you use it to defend against the attacks of Satan. It is offensive when you use it to claim territory for the Lord by sharing the Gospel message and engage in intercessory prayer and exorcism. There are two different words used in Scripture for the "Word of God." One word is "logos" which refers to the total utterance of God. This refers to the complete revelation of what God has said. The second word, "rhema," refers to a specific saying of God that has special application to a specific situation. This is the word used in this passage calling the "sword of the Spirit" the Word of God. You will remember that Christ used specific ("rhema") sayings of God, applicable to the immediate temptation. To be able to do this implies familiarity with the total Word of God. If you are to use specific Scriptures applicable to immediate battles, you must have knowledge of God's total revelation.

THE MIND OF CHRIST

For as much then as Christ hath suffered for us in the flesh, arm yourselves likewise with the same mind...

-I Peter 4:1

Let this mind be in you, which was also in Christ Jesus.

-Philippians 2:5

To "let" means to permit or embrace. You are to arm yourself with the same mind that Jesus had, a mind set to wage aggressive warfare.

...For this purpose the Son of God was manifested, that He might destroy the works of the Devil. -I John 3:8

You must "let" or permit this mind to be developed. You must take aggressive action to "arm yourself" with a similar mental attitude.

And be not conformed to this world; but be ye transformed by the renewing of your mind, that ye may prove what is that good, and acceptable, and perfect will of God. -Romans 12:2

To be "transformed" means to experience a complete change which will be expressed in character and conduct. Renewing and arming your mind with Christlikeness results in such a transformation. Reviewing the lives of Christ and His Saints is a good way to begin this process. You can gain incredible insights and begin to emulate the Christlike qualities you see reflected in the various Saints of the Faith.

PULLING AND CASTING DOWN

The goal of offensive warfare is to pull and cast down the strongholds of the enemy.

For the weapons of our warfare are not carnal, but mighty through God, to the PULLING DOWN OF STRONG HOLDS; CASTING DOWN imaginations and every high thing that exalteth itself against the knowledge of God, and bringing into captivity every thought to the obedience of Christ.

-II Corinthians 10:4-5

To "pull down" means to take down by effort or force. To "cast" means to throw or hurl. You are told to cast off the works of darkness (Romans 13:12) and cast out demon powers (Matthew 10:8). When you pull and cast down strongholds of Satan you are waging offensive warfare. You are not waiting to defend against an attack of Satan but you are attacking strongholds of the enemy's power.

BINDING AND LOOSING

Priests have the power to bind the forces of evil and loose the forces of good.

And I will give unto thee the keys of the Kingdom of Heaven: and whatsoever thou shalt bind on earth shall be bound in Heaven: and whatsoever thou shalt loose on earth shall be loosed in Heaven. -Matthew 16:19

Through delegation of power and authority via Apostolic Succession from Christ, priests can bind and loose spiritual forces. Note that this weapon works together: It is binding and loosing.

THE BLOOD OF CHRIST

When Jesus died on the cross of Calvary, He loosed us from the dominion of sin and the power of the enemy. His blood secures our access to God and release from the bondage of Satan. Sacred Scripture indicates that "they (Christians) overcame him (Satan) by the blood of the Lamb (Jesus Christ)" (Revelation 12:11). Salvation, healing, and deliverance are all available because of the blood of Christ. His blood enables you to wage offensive warfare for the souls of men and women and bring deliverance and healing in the name of Jesus. Your power to "overcome" the Adversary is because of the "blood of the lamb." As a priest (and as a lay intercessor) you will often recite prayers which invoke the blood of Christ. Demonic entities hate all mention of the blood of Christ and the victory of the cross. When you see the response to these prayers it should strengthen your faith and embolden you to push harder against the demon in the Holy Name of Jesus and continually invoke the blood of Christ in and over the life, spirit and soul of the Adversary's intended victim.

YOUR TESTIMONY

Revelation 12:11 indicates the Adversary is defeated by the "word of your testimony." The word "testimony" means "evidence or record" like that used in a legal case in a court of law. You will recall that Jesus often commanded people who had been delivered to go and tell others what God had done for them. As you "testify" or give evidence to the power of God in your life, you wage offensive spiritual warfare. To be effective, your testimony must be based upon the testimony of the Gospel and His Church, just as a lawyer in a court bases his arguments on the law of the land.

THE HOLY NAME

You already learned that the name of Jesus is part of your arsenal. The Holy Name of Jesus is a powerful offensive weapon also. Jesus said that "in My name" you will cast out demons, heal the sick, and overcome all the power of the enemy (Mark 16:17). Review the various titles of Christ as well to see how many of them reflect offensive action against the Adversary. Also read through the book of Acts and note the miracles done "in His name." The Holy Name of Jesus is not some magical phrase with which we conclude our prayers. It is a symbol of the authority and power He has given His Church. However, not everyone can operate with the same degree of authority in His name. Priests and bishops hold the highest authority in His Holy Name, through Apostolic Succession. You had better be authorized to use His power and authority before you start using His Holy Name to war against Satanic powers. Review the story in Acts 19:13-17 and note what happened to the sons of Sceva.

---

1. Study these references on the offensive action of "casting": Matthew 5:29-30; 7:5; 8:16; Mark 16:17; Romans 13:12; II Corinthians 10:5; I Peter 5:7
2. Study these references on the offensive action of "putting": Romans 13:12, 14; I Corinthians 5:13; 13:11; Galatians 3:27; Ephesians 4:22-24; 6:11; Colossians 3:8-14

3. Study these references on the offensive action of "taking": I Corinthians 3:10; 8:9; 10:12; Galatians 5:15; Ephesians 6:13,17; I Timothy 4:16; Hebrews 3:12.

4. As you learned in this chapter, you must participate in aggressive warfare to defeat the enemy. You must "let" or permit certain things in your spiritual life if you are to be victorious. Study the following references:

Matthew 5:16
John 4:1,27
Romans 13:1,12-13
Romans 14:5,13,16,19
I Corinthians 3:18-21
I Corinthians 10:8-9
II Corinthians 7:1
II Corinthians 10:17
Galatians 5:26
Ephesians 4:26-31
Ephesians 5:3,6,33
Philippians 1:27
Philippians 2:3,5
Philippians 3:15-16
Philippians 4:5-6
Colossians 3:15-16
Colossians 4:6
I Thessalonians 5:6-8
II Timothy 2:19
Hebrews 4:1,14,16
Hebrews 6:1
Hebrews 10:22-24
Hebrews 12:1
Hebrews 13:1,5,15

References What We Are To "Let"

James 1:5-9
James 3:13
James 4:9
James 5:13
I Peter 3:3-4,10-11
I Peter 4:11,15,16,19
I John 2:24
I John 3:7,18
I John 4:7

CHAPTER THIRTEEN
THE PSYCHOLOGY OF EXORCISM

For though we walk in the flesh, we do not war after the flesh: For the weapons of our warfare are not carnal, but mighty through God to the pulling down of strong holds; Casting down imaginations, and every high thing that exalteth itself against the knowledge of God, and bringing into captivity every thought to the obedience of Christ.
-II Corinthians 10:3-5

Paul warned the Corinthian church not to be ignorant of Satan's "wiles." the Greek word for wiles means "schemes" and is from the same word used for "mind." Basically, Satan's primary focus of attacks occur in our thought and emotional/mental life. Thus it is no stretch to say that the mind is the central spiritual battlefield. Each and every attack of Satan involves the human mind in some form or fashion. This does not mean that everyone suffering from the various emotional and mental ailments is possessed. The exorcist should NEVER assume such. These are far more often organic issues best dealt with trained medical professionals. However such emotional/mental states can also be indicative of diabolic oppression. Oppression is not the same as possession and should not be treated as such. Oppression is best treated through a combination of medical, psychological, and pastoral counseling working symbiotically to heal the whole person. The battle for the mind is easily summarized In Sacred Scripture.

For to be carnally minded is death; but to be spiritually minded is life and peace. Because the carnal mind is enmity against God: for it is not subject to the law of God, neither indeed can be. -Romans 8:6-7

Satan wants to make the human mind carnal (sinful, worldly, fleshly). God wants the human mind to be spiritually inclined.

The mind is a key element in spiritual life and spiritual warfare. The greatest commandment given to humanity includes loving God with all your mind. This is one of the main reasons why Satan battles for your mind.

Jesus said unto him, Thou shalt love the Lord thy God with all thy heart, and with all thy soul, and with all thy mind; This is the first and great commandment.

-Matthew 22:37-38

Satan battles for your mind because it is closely tied spiritually to the spirit and to the essence of who we are.

But those things which proceed out of the mouth come forth from the heart; and they defile the man. For out of the heart proceed evil thoughts... -Matthew 15:18-19

Satan battles so strongly for the mind because the way you think affects the way you act.

For as he thinketh in his heart, so is he...- Proverbs 23:7

Satan knows if he can simply control the human mind, twist the thoughts and pervert the mental life, he can control the victims body, his actions, and, if left unchallenged, a demonic entity can enter into the body and possess the victim. Science demonstrates that the mind is one of the most complex and least understood parts of the human body. Because it is so complex, Satan has many subtle methods of attacking the mind. Though it would be impossible to list them all, the following list summarizes the main strategies of attack Satan uses in the battle for the mind.

1. QUESTION THE AUTHORITY OF GOD- The first temptation of humanity started in the mind. It started with this mind game: Questioning the authority of God. Satan said to Eve, "Yea, hath God said?..." Did God really say that you could not eat of the tree of knowledge of good and evil? Questioning

God, His Word and His Church leads to doubt, unbelief, and skepticism.

2. DECEPTION AND SEDUCTION- Deception was also part of the Adversary's strategy. When Satan confronted Eve, he was disguised as a beautiful serpent. Satan uses lies, cults, and "religious spirits" to deceive millions in our world today. Some of the deceptions Satan utilizes include the following lies:

- "You can become a god."
- "You can know the future."
- "You future, including eternity, is predestined. There is nothing you can do about it."
- "Everyone is a child of God."
- "There are more ways to Heaven than by Jesus."
- "God is too good to send anyone to Hell."
- "All God expects you to do is live a good life and do the best you can."
- "The Bible should not be taken literally."
- "The Bible contains many errors."

The lying spirits of Satan attack the mind to confuse you and distort the truth of God's Word.

Now the Spirit speaketh expressly, that in the latter times some shall depart from the faith, giving heed to seducing spirits and doctrines of devils. -I Timothy 4:1

3. THE FLESH- In volume one of this work we examined the flesh as a potential spiritual force of evil. Demonic entities will use the flesh to attack the mind.

But I see another law in my members, warring against the law of my mind, and bringing me into captivity to the law of sin which is in my members. -Romans 7:23

The demonic will manipulate speech, sight, sound, and even the senses of touch and smell to foster wicked thoughts in the human mind.

4. DEPRESSION- To be depressed is to be downcast, sad, discouraged, or in a very low spiritual and mental state. It includes feelings of despair, despondency, and dejection. Depression can lead to suicidal thoughts or actual suicide because of the hopeless feelings which produces uncontrollable mental grief, sorrow, heartache, and crying. Sometimes demons use circumstances of life to lead to depression. For examples, a great loss or fear of loss, suppressed anger, a low self concept, unfulfilled expectations, and a negative attitude can all be used to cause depression. In Proverbs 24:10 we are warned about "fainting in the day of adversity" (troubled or distressed circumstances). Sometimes depression is caused by the negative attitudes of those around us through which Satan works. In Deuteronomy 1:28 God's people admitted, "our brethren have discouraged our hearts." We read in Numbers 21:4 that the soul of God's people was much discouraged. King David often reflected discouragement in his Psalms (see Psalms 69 for an example). The Apostle Paul also had times of deep depression.

For we would not, brethren, have you ignorant of our trouble which came to us in Asia, that we were pressed out of measure, above strength, insomuch that we despaired even of life... -II Corinthians 1:8

If you do not conquer depression it can also lead to oppression by Satanic spirits. This is a deeper form of depression where Satan gains more restrictive power over the mind.

5. DISCOURAGEMENT- Discouragement means to be "without courage." Demonic entities want to discourage you because if you are "without courage," you are ineffective in spiritual warfare.

6. WITHDRAWAL- Another way demons attack the mind is

through withdrawal. The purpose of this strategy is to isolate you from the rest of the Body of Christ. Such withdrawal isolates you from the source of sacramental grace, community prayer and healing.

7. NEGATIVE ATTITUDES AND EMOTIONS- Demons cause negative attitudes towards others. They instill envy, jealousy, suspicion, unforgiving attitudes, distrust, anger, hatred, intolerance, prejudice, competition, impatience, judging, criticism, covetousness, and selfishness. They also try to cause greed, discontent, pride, vanity, ego, importance, arrogance, intellectualism, and self-righteousness. These negative outlooks lead to negative emotions and both stem from your thought life. These attitudes and emotions render you ineffective in spiritual warfare.

8. REBELLION- Demons also influence rebellious thoughts. Rebellion is willful disobedience of God's authority and the authority of His Church. Rebellion includes self-will, stubbornness, and disobedience. Remember that rebellion was the original sin of Satan. His five statements of "I will" demonstrated his rebellion (Isaiah 14:12-14). The "I will" spirit is a way to recognize the operation of the demonic through rebellion.

9. ACCUSATION AND CONDEMNATION- Satan is called "the accuser of the brethren" (Revelation 12:10). He influences accusation to enter your mind, makes you feel inferior, and condemns you. He will give you guilty feelings of shame, unworthiness, and embarrassment.

10.SEXUAL IMPURITY- Demons will insert thoughts of sexual impurity, lust, and mental sexual fantasies. Christ said:

But I say unto you, That whosoever looketh on a woman to lust after her hath committed adultery with her already in his heart. -Matthew 5:28

11. CONFUSION- Demons also cause indecision, confusion, and frustration in your mind. When you are confused, indecisive, and frustrated, you obviously cannot be a strong and powerful witness for Christ.

12. TORMENTING THOUGHTS- Worry, anxiety, dread, apprehension, and nervousness are all used to attack the mind. Mental torment can also come through an overactive mind that will not "shut off" or an under active mind that cannot function properly. Tormenting thoughts also include fear, and bitter memories of events that should be forgiven and forgotten.

13.COMPROMISE- To "compromise" is to settle conflicting principles by adjustment. The principles of God and Satan are in opposition. Satan tries to get you to compromise your spiritual principles. For example, he will tell you it is not necessary to attend the Divine Liturgy each Sunday, to believe the Bible literally, to support the work of the Church, to study the Sacred Scriptures, to pray daily, etc.

MENTAL CONDITIONS

If the demonic is allowed to persist with thoughts of depression, suicide, torment, accusation, etc., it can lead to mental illness. This could include a nervous or mental breakdown and various medically recognized mental conditions. It is essential that investigators and priests have a basic understanding of the types of mental health issues that can be mistaken for demonic activity. The following information is provided purely for informational purposes and not for diagnosis. Investigators and priests are not mental health professionals and are never to diagnose or act as if they are medical or mental health professionals. The fact that someone is suffering from depression or any other mental illness should never be used as a determining factor for demonic activity or to proceed with an exorcism. Nor should an investigator or priest at any time suggest anything resembling demonic imagery.

Temporal Lobe Epilepsy

Temporal lobe epilepsy (TLE) was defined in 1985 by the International League Against Epilepsy (ILAE) as a condition characterized by recurrent unprovoked seizures originating from the medial or lateral temporal lobe. The seizures associated with temporal lobe epilepsy consist of simple partial seizures without loss of awareness and complex partial seizures (ie, with loss of awareness). The individual loses awareness during a complex partial seizure because the seizure spreads to involve both temporal lobes, which causes impairment of memory. The partial seizures may secondarily generalize. Temporal lobe epilepsy was first recognized in 1881 by John Hughlings Jackson, who described "uncinate fits" seizures arising from the uncal part of temporal lobe and the "dreamy state." In the 1940s, Gibbs et al introduced the term *psychomotor epilepsy*. The international classification of epileptic seizures (1981) replaced the term *psychomotor seizures* with *complex partial seizures*. The ILAE classification of the epilepsies uses the term *temporal lobe epilepsy* and divides the etiologies into cryptogenic (presumed unidentified etiology), idiopathic (genetic), and symptomatic (cause known, eg, tumor). Although the causes of temporal lobe epilepsy are widely varied, hippocampal sclerosis is the most common pathologic finding. Hippocampal sclerosis involves hippocampal cell loss in the CA1 and CA3 regions and the dentate hilus. The CA2 region is relatively spared. The clinical correlate on neuroimaging on MRI is called mesial temporal lobe sclerosis.Approximately 50% of patients with epilepsy have partial epilepsy. Partial epilepsy is often of temporal lobe origin. However, the true prevalence of temporal lobe epilepsy is not known, since not all cases of presumed temporal lobe epilepsy are confirmed by video-EEG and most cases are classified by clinical history and interictal EEG findings alone. The temporal lobe is the most epileptogenic region of the brain. In fact, 90% of patients with temporal interictal epileptiform abnormalities on their EEG have a history of seizures. Temporal lobe epilepsy is not more common in one sex but female patients may experience catamenial epilepsy, which is an increase of seizures during the menstrual period. Epilepsy occurs in all age groups, but a group where it was under recognized is in elderly persons. Epilepsy in elderly persons may not be as dramatic and often may present as confusion or memory lapses. The index for suspicion should be low as patients are often misdiagnosed and not treated appropriately.

- Auras occur in approximately 80% of temporal lobe seizures. They are a common feature of simple partial seizures and usually precede complex partial seizures of temporal lobe origin.
- Auras may be classified by symptom type; the types comprise somatosensory, special sensory, autonomic, or psychic symptoms.
- Somatosensory and special sensory phenomena
- Olfactory and gustatory illusions and hallucinations may occur. Acharya et al found that olfactory auras are more commonly associated with temporal lobe tumors than with other causes of temporal lobe epilepsy.
- Auditory hallucinations consist of a buzzing sound, a voice or voices, or muffling of ambient sounds. This type of aura is more common with neocortical temporal lobe epilepsy than with other types of temporal lobe epilepsy.
- Patients may report distortions of shape, size, and distance of objects.
- These visual illusions are unlike the visual hallucinations associated with occipital lobe seizure in that no formed elementary visual image is noted, such as the visual image of a face that may be seen with seizures arising from the fusiform or the inferior temporal gyrus.
- Things may appear shrunken (micropsia) or larger (macropsia) than usual.
- Tilting of structures has been reported. Vertigo has been described with seizures in the posterior superior temporal gyrus.
- Psychic phenomena
- Patients may have a feeling of déjà vu or jamais vu, a sense of

familiarity or unfamiliarity, respectively.
• Patients may experience depersonalization (ie, feeling of detachment from oneself) or derealization (ie, surroundings appear unreal).
• Fear or anxiety usually is associated with seizures arising from the amygdala. Sometimes, the fear is strong, described as an "impending sense of doom."
• Patients may describe a sense of dissociation or autoscopy, in which they report seeing their own body from outside.
• Autonomic phenomena are characterized by changes in heart rate, piloerection, and sweating. Patients may experience an epigastric "rising" sensation or nausea.

Physical
• Following the aura, a temporal lobe complex partial seizure begins with a wide-eyed, motionless stare, dilated pupils, and behavioral arrest. Oral alimentary automatisms such as lip smacking, chewing, and swallowing may be noted. Manual automatisms or unilateral dystonic posturing of a limb also may be observed.
• Patients may continue their ongoing motor activity or react to their surroundings in a semi-purposeful manner (ie, reactive automatisms). They can have repetitive stereotyped manual automatisms.
• A complex partial seizure may evolve to a secondarily generalized tonic-clonic seizure. Often, the documentation of a seizure only notes the generalized tonic-clonic component of the seizure. A careful history from the patient or an observer is needed to elicit the partial features of either a simple seizure or a complex partial seizure before the secondarily generalized seizure is important.
• Patients usually experience a postictal period of confusion, which distinguishes temporal lobe epilepsy from absence seizures, which are not associated with postictal confusion. In addition, absence seizures are not associated with auras nor with complex automatisms. Postictal aphasia suggests onset in the language-dominant temporal lobe.
• Most auras and automatisms last a very short period—

seconds or 1-2 minutes. The postictal phase may last for a longer period (several minutes). By definition, amnesia occurs during a complex partial seizure because of bilateral hemispheric involvement.

Causes

• Approximately two thirds of patients with temporal lobe epilepsy treated surgically have hippocampal sclerosis as the pathologic substrate.

• The etiologies of temporal lobe epilepsy include the following:

- Infections, eg, herpes encephalitis, bacterial meningitis, neurocysticercosis
- Trauma producing contusion or hemorrhage that results in encephalomalacia or cortical scarring; difficult traumatic delivery such as forceps deliveries
- Hamartomas
- Malignancies (eg, meningiomas, gliomas, gangliomas)
- Vascular malformations (ie, arteriovenous malformation, cavernous angioma)
- Cryptogenic: A cause is presumed but has not been identified.
- Idiopathic (genetic): This is rare. Familial temporal lobe epilepsy was described by Berkovic and colleagues, and partial epilepsy with auditory features was described by Scheffer and colleagues.
- Hippocampal sclerosis produces a clinical syndrome called mesial temporal lobe epilepsy (MTLE).
- Febrile seizures: The association of simple febrile seizure with temporal lobe epilepsy has been controversial. However, a subset of children with complex febrile convulsions appear to be at risk of developing temporal lobe epilepsy in later life. Complex febrile seizures are febrile seizures that

last longer than 15 minutes, have focal features, or recur within 24 hours.

Schizophrenia

Schizophrenia is a mental disorder that makes it difficult to tell the difference between real and unreal experiences, to think logically, to have normal emotional responses, and to behave normally in social situations. Schizophrenia is a complex illness. Even experts in the field are not sure what causes it. Some doctors think that the brain may not be able to process information correctly. Genetic factors appear to play a role. People who have family members with schizophrenia may be more likely to get the disease themselves. Some researchers believe that events in a person's environment may trigger schizophrenia. For example, problems (infection) during development in the mother's womb and at birth may increase the risk for developing schizophrenia later in life. Psychological and social factors may also affect its development. However, the level of social and family support appears to affect the course of illness and may protect against the condition returning. There are 5 types of schizophrenia:

- Catatonic
- Disorganized
- Paranoid
- Residual
- Undifferentiated

Schizophrenia usually begins before the age of 45, symptoms last for 6 months or more, and people start to lose their ability to socialize and work. Schizophrenia is thought to affect about 1% of people worldwide. Schizophrenia appears to occur in equal rates among men and women, but in women it begins later. For this reason, males tend to account for more than half of patients in services with high numbers of young adults. Although schizophrenia usually begins in young adulthood, there are cases in which the disorder begins later (over 45 years). Childhood-onset schizophrenia begins after the age of

5 and, in most cases, after normal development. Childhood schizophrenia is rare and can be difficult to tell apart from other developmental disorders of childhood, such as autism. Schizophrenia may have a variety of symptoms. Usually the illness develops slowly over months or even years. At first, the symptoms may not be noticeable. For example, you may feel tense, or have trouble sleeping or concentrating. You can become isolated and withdrawn, and have trouble making or keeping friends. As the illness continues, symptoms develop:

- An appearance or mood that shows no emotion (flat affect)
- Bizarre motor behavior in which there is less reaction to the environment (catatonic behavior)
- False beliefs or thoughts that have nothing to do with reality (delusions)
- Hearing, seeing, or feeling things that are not there (hallucinations)
- Thoughts "jump" between unrelated topics (disordered thinking)

Symptoms can be different depending on the type of schizophrenia.

Catatonic type:

- Agitation
- Decreased sensitivity to pain
- Inability to take care of personal needs
- Negative feelings
- Motor disturbances
- Rigid muscles
- Stupor

Paranoid type:

- Anger
- Anxiety
- Argumentativeness
- Delusions of persecution or grandeur

Disorganized type:

- Child-like (regressive) behavior
- Delusions
- Flat affect
- Hallucinations
- Inappropriate laughter
- Not understandable (incoherence)
- Repetitive behaviors
- Social withdrawal

Undifferentiated type may include symptoms of more than one type of schizophrenia. Residual type - symptoms of the illness have gone away, but some features, such as hallucinations and flat affect, may remain.

Dissociative Identity Disorder

Dissociative identity disorder (previously known as multiple personality disorder) is a fairly common effect of severe trauma during early childhood, usually extreme, repetitive physical, sexual, and/or emotional abuse. Most of us have experienced mild dissociation, which is like daydreaming or getting lost in the moment while working on a project. However, dissociative identity disorder is a severe form of dissociation, a mental process, which produces a lack of connection in a person's thoughts, memories, feelings, actions, or sense of identity. Dissociative identity disorder is thought to stem from trauma experienced by the person with the disorder. The dissociative aspect is thought to be a coping mechanism -- the person literally dissociates himself from a situation or experience that's too violent, traumatic, or painful to assimilate with his conscious self. Dissociative identity disorder is characterized by the presence of two or more distinct or split identities or personality states that continually have power over the person's behavior. With dissociative identity disorder, there's also an inability to recall key personal information that is too far-reaching to be explained as mere forgetfulness. With dissociative identity disorder, there are also highly distinct memory variations, which fluctuate with the person's split personality. The "alters" or different identities have their own age, sex, or race. Each has his or her own postures, gestures, and distinct way of talking. Sometimes the alters are imaginary people; sometimes they are animals. As each personality reveals itself and controls the individuals' behavior and thoughts, it's called "switching." Switching can take seconds to minutes to days. When under hypnosis, the person's different "alters" or identities may be very responsive to the therapist's requests. Along with the dissociation and multiple or split personalities, people with dissociative disorders may experience any of the following symptoms:

- Depression
- Mood swings
- Suicidal tendencies
- Sleep disorders (insomnia, night terrors)
- Anxiety and phobias (flashbacks, reactions to stimuli or "triggers")
- Alcohol and drug abuse
- Compulsions and rituals
- Psychotic-like symptoms (including auditory and visual hallucinations)
- Eating disorders

Other symptoms of dissociative identity disorder may include headache, amnesia, time loss, trances, and "out of body experiences." Some people with dissociative disorders have a tendency toward self-persecution, self sabotage, and even violence (both self-inflicted and outwardly directed). As an example, someone with dissociative identity disorder may find themselves doing things they wouldn't normally do such as speeding, reckless driving, or stealing money from their employer or friend, yet they feel they are being compelled to do it. Some describe this feeling as being a passenger in their body rather than the driver. In other words, they truly believe they have no choice. There are several main ways in which the psychological processes of dissociative identity disorder change the way a person experiences living, including the following:

- **Depersonalization.** This is a sense of being detached from one's body and is often referred to as an "out-of-body" experience.

- **Derealization.** This is the feeling that the world is not real or looking foggy or far away.

- **Amnesia.** This is the failure to recall significant personal information that is so extensive it cannot be blamed on ordinary forgetfulness. There can also be micro-amnesias where the discussion engaged in is not remembered, or the content of a meaningful conversation is forgotten from one second to the next.

- **Identity confusion** or **identity alteration.** Both of these involve a sense of confusion about who a person is. An example of identity confusion is when a person sometimes feels a thrill while engaged in an activity (such as reckless driving, DUI, alcohol or drug abuse) which at other times would be revolting. In addition to these apparent alterations, the person may experience distortions in time, place, and situation.

It is now acknowledged that these dissociated states are not fully-mature personalities, but rather they represent a disjointed sense of identity. With the amnesia typically associated with dissociative identity disorder, different identity states remember different aspects of autobiographical information. There is usually a host personality within the individual, who identifies with the person's real name. Ironically, the host personality is usually unaware of the presence of other personalities. The distinct personalities may serve diverse roles in helping the individual cope with life's dilemmas. For instance, there's an average of two to four personalities present when the patient is initially diagnosed. Then there's an average of 13 to 15 personalities that can become known over the course of treatment. While unusual, there have been instances of dissociative identity disorder with more than 100 personalities. Environmental triggers or life events cause a sudden shift from one alter or personality to another. While the causes of dissociative identity disorder are still vague, research indicates that a combination of environmental and biological factors work together to cause it. As many as 98% to 99% of individuals who develop dissociative disorders have recognized personal histories of recurring, overpowering, and often life-threatening disturbances at a sensitive developmental stage of childhood (usually before age 9). Dissociation may also happen when there has been insistent neglect or emotional abuse, even when there has been no overt physical or sexual abuse. Findings show that in families where parents are frightening and unpredictable, the children may become dissociative. Statistics show the rate of dissociative identity disorder is .01% to 1% of the general population. Still, more than 1/3 of people say they feel as if they're watching themselves in a movie at times, and 7% percent of the population may have undiagnosed dissociative disorder. The point of examining such mental health issues is to demonstrate the very serious need for exorcists to be absolutely certain that the client has undergone a complete mental health evaluation and is not diagnosed with or being treated for any mental health issues. If indeed the client is, the exorcist should proceed with pastoral counseling under the guidance of the clients mental health professional.

New Age Techniques in Psychology

"Meditation, if properly understood and taught, is a powerful complement to the biopsychosocial model of psychiatric treatment" - Joseph Arpaia, M.D., (2000)

It is important that the exorcist be aware of the potential dangers of New Age techniques found in some psychological circles. The newest literature of psychology and psychiatry is replete with references to the beneficial effects of New Age meditation techniques in its various forms on the psychological well being of patients. This "meditation" includes within its scope various forms ranging from Yoga to Rebirthing, Mantra repetition (often described as "concentration meditation," which supposedly blocks out negative thoughts), and *"open meditation"* which *"allows one to keep one's awareness on whatever changing phenomena arise in the mind, thus lowering psychological defenses to formerly repressed material."* (Boorstein, Seymour 2000) These methods are often accompanied by breathing techniques and in some of the more radical of the New Age psychological circles, even with the use of psychedelic drugs, though of a natural variety so as to assure us of their safety. What characterizes these efforts is that such techniques, drawn from various religious traditions, are used in a setting that fails to acknowledge their origins, and which pose a spiritual, moral and ethical dilemma for the Christian patient and practitioner. This is not to deny their apparent therapeutic value in certain situations, but to point out that their use is in many cases similar to the symptomatic relief of a cancer patient without truly treating the underlying disease, and which introduce individuals to spiritual practices not in harmony with the Gospel under the guise of therapy. Therapeutically they may relieve some of the symptoms, but hide the underlying condition which continues untreated. Instead, prayer should be offered as it truly aligns the tripartite constituent parts of man with their Source (God), leading to healing.

The fundamental reason for the use of New Age approaches in psychology is that the average therapist, having no basis in Biblical theology and Christian approaches to meditative prayer and contemplation, has a different vision of the nature of man - what man is. Indeed many have an atheistic/humanistic view of man that says he is nothing more than a highly evolved animal, while others have a more ecumenical or New Age approach that seeks out Eastern "wisdom" and it's view of man to the exclusion of Christianity, which is viewed as repressive and therefore somehow insufficient to meet the therapeutic needs of a patient. In fact, these same therapists often have different views of the nature of man than the Eastern religions in which these New Age meditative techniques were developed. Generally most atheistic/humanistic therapists will view man as being of two parts: mind (psyche) and body. For them health is a holistic approach to the healing and integration of these two parts. If one has a view of man based on this Descartian duality of mind (psyche) and body, such techniques will inevitably be applied to the psyche (and in part to the body as in yoga), and be thought of as therapeutically beneficial. However, Christianity generally takes a tripartite view of man which holds that above both body and psyche (which includes our thinking and emotive processes), there is in man a soul, a spiritual center which is of divine origin. This fact, coupled with the fall, demonstrates why we are often at contention with the inner self. This apparently allows Paul to say that there is a law in his members as opposed to the law of the Spirit.(Rom. 7:23) If this is true, any therapeutic effort towards healing must take into consideration not only the body and the psyche, but also this soul and it's absolute need for communion with God as part of the *wholistic* healing process. One of the purposes of Christian prayer, over and against New Age techniques, is to integrate all three and not just the lower two, connecting them to the ultimate Source of wellness- God. Secular psychologists may be uncomfortable with the concept of a soul within every human being, but experience tells us that there is in every person a *supra-individual self* which goes beyond the classical super-ego category, and indeed, it is clear to the Christian that one's problems may revolve around their inability to resolve conflicts between this inner self ultimately seeking it's Source (God), and the negative desires and thoughts that arise in their psyche. The only hope of bringing happiness and contentment to the patient is to line up these three components, the Spirit, the Psyche and the Body in such a manner that what is "higher" controls what is lower. In simpler terms, if the body runs the show - gluttony or sexual drives for example- than chaos results. Similarly, if anger, greed or the other passions are the center of one's life, chaos once again reigns. Only if the Holy Spirit controls the psyche (as part of the indwelling presence), and the psyche in turn the body, is there any hope of healing. Though it must be added that it is not just a matter of aligning these constituent parts of man to their Source. They must be aligned to some purpose. In this respect one of the purposes of prayer in psychology is not just to create a contented couch potato, blissful in some Eastern mystical way, but rather to align these components for a higher purpose - namely to know, love and serve God - and not simply in some internal vague way, but also an external vibrant way.

Spiritual Nature of New Age Techniques

The practice of New Age meditation as understood by secular psychologists is not necessarily deemed to be connected to what is spiritual, though the word may be used to loosely refer to emotional well-being. For the secular psychologist it is merely one useful psychological technique among many to bring about a sense of wellness, regardless of the fact that the techniques draw from a spiritual tradition. Indeed it can be fairly said that the use of such New Age techniques introduces a spiritual life to the patient. Of course, Christians cannot completely agree with this approach. For the Christian the fact that one may feel better is not at issue. Though Christian theology informs us that spiritual life does not aim at making us feel better (indeed there are times where it can makes us quite uncomfortable), this of course may be one of its results. The Christian spiritual life, which aims at transforming the individual, has as its ultimate aim the sanctification of the individual. This is not of course an easy process. As Perry Whitall has noted, "Only the temple of God can receive God, namely, a soul predisposed by grace, grounded in doctrine, purified of sin, transformed in will, established in virtue.." (1996) This requires more than individual effort because our natural instincts, as a result of our fallen nature, are fixed upon the things of this world. Without the guidance of the Holy Spirit and proper Biblical accountability, one cannot hope to interrupt the self centeredness of the fallen nature which drags us down and prevents our healing. This is one of the problems with New Age psychological therapy. New Age techniques largely promote a ***self will, self healing*** and "power of the mind" approach that ignores the need for divine guidance. This is not to suggest that our will plays no part in healing, but that will must be subordinated to that of God and informed by His Word. The fragmentary nature of these New Age spiritual practices previously mentioned, is not without significant spiritual dangers. One hears little of the psychological consequences that have occurred to people who become deeply involved in such New Age practices such as repeating mantras, the meaning of which they almost never comprehend, to say nothing of the possibility of self-hypnosis with consequent delusions. The emptying of the mind as advocated by some clearly allows for negative forces (demonic entities) and influences to enter and dominate the thinking of those who engage in such activity. The fact that there may be some short term psychological benefits in no way avoids the possibility that such individuals can be demonically influenced to a greater degree than normal temptations and damn their souls for eternity. Of course, these same secular psychologists would deny the existence of a soul, never mind judgment, hell and eternal suffering.

Meditation

What is meditation? Webster's Dictionary defines meditation as *"to keep the mind or attention fixed upon"* something. It is defined by the Catholic Encyclopedia as *"a form of mental prayer consisting in the application of the various faculties of the soul, memory, imagination, intellect and will, to the consideration of some mystery, principle, truth or fact...."* This is an adequate definition from the Christian perspective. As many New Age techniques are drawn from Hinduism we will look briefly at the Hindu approach to these techniques and what they are really designed to do. The word *dhyana* is used for meditation in the Hindu tradition, and the literal meaning is "concentration." It should of course be remembered, that the Catholic Encyclopedia says, *"the control of attention is the vital point in the education of the will."* This gets to the heart of Christian meditation, which is the study of God's Word with the goal of allowing it to speak to us on a personal level, transforming our lives with the goal of sanctification in mind. Hinduism however has a very different definition. Swami Sivananda tells us *"it is a continuous flow of oil. All worldly thoughts are shut out of the mind. The mind is filled or saturated with Divine thoughts, Divine glory and Divine presence."* (2012) While a Hindu would have no problem accepting the definition of meditation in Christianity, the Christian cannot embrace that of the Hindu, as their definition carries a very different meaning regardless of how this may sound compatible. The techniques themselves demonstrate this definition is antithetical to that of Christianity. Take for instance the repeating of a mantra. Most mantras are based on, or include the repetition of the name of one of many Hindu deities. The purpose is not to understand God's will and be guided by the Holy Spirit on the journey of sanctification, but rather to have the individual be permeated with the essence of the false deity's name which, as it vibrates through the psyche and body, has a transformative effect. One becomes united with the deity who is being called upon in the mantra. Meditation then is not a means to know God's will for us, but rather of being absorbed in the nature of the deity as the name is repeated. The problems that arise from the use of mantra's, even those proposed as "non-sectarian", are obvious. The Bhagavad Gita, the most popular Hindu scripture, states:

"The yogi should then sit.....very firmly and practice yoga to purify the heart by controlling his mind, senses and activities and fixing the mind on one point." (A.C. Bhaktivedanta Swami Prabhupada;1972.)

The notion that man can purify himself of the problems of the fallen self leads to a very anti-Biblical theological approach, and as previously noted is one of the driving philosophies behind this type of approach to psychology. It denies the central Christian teachings of the fall, depravity, and of salvation and true wellness only in and through Jesus Christ. It is ***self will*** that saves the Hindu and that is the active agent of healing for the New Age psychologist, not the grace, condescension and intercession of a loving, personal God.

The Central Problem

"Nothing," says William Law, "hath separated us from God but our own will, or rather our own will is our separation from God... the fall of man brought forth the kingdom of this world; sin in all shapes is nothing else but the will of man driving on in a state of self-motion and self-government, following the workings of a nature broken off from dependency upon and union with, the divine will. All the evil and misery in the creation arises only and solely from this one cause." (2013) "It is a question," asks Meister Eckhart, "what burns in hell? Christians reply with one accord: 'self will'." (2010) As Dr. Allen Brown, Professor of Theology at God's Bible School and College writes, the problem with man is "inherited depravity", which he describes thus, *"This is what I consider the best definition of "inherited depravity." It is **self-centeredness**."* (Brown, Allen; 2010) In other words, a fallen self-will directed toward selfish purposes to the exclusion of the will of God is the central problem for man and out of it arises many of the psychological problems plaguing man . As such the self-will cannot be relied upon as a means of wholistic healing. Furthermore, for the Christian, giving up self will is not a process found merely in a passive meditative state, but rather a highly active one that seeks to subordinate the will to the higher will of God revealed in His Word. Self will is the source of sin, and arises out of man centering his reality solely in himself. Pride, arrogance, and rebellion are all a concentrated self will removed from the counsel of God. This means we need to recognize those elements in our own lives - the passions etc., -which are opposed to the Will of God, for these are the "illnesses" to be overcome and an unrecognized illness can hardly be healed. Thus, prayer, as opposed to New Age meditation, is one of the Christian means to follow the footprints of Christ crucified, and thus, by desire and affection, and in union with love, reflect His Image by surrendering self will to God's will. Prayer then can be a means by which we can say with Paul, "Yet not I, but Christ lives in me." Prayer then is the better means of complimenting psychological counseling as it meets the ultimate needs of the fallen self.

CONCLUSION

It should be clear that New Age techniques in psychology, are not in any way "scientific" as the term is currently understood and that the exorcist should avoid the services of psychologists who use such methodologies. The use of New Age techniques is a spiritual practice disguised as therapy that may indeed send very spiritually dangerous messages that ultimately do more harm than good. Christians in the field of psychology must understand the source of such meditative techniques, New Age Techniques, hypnotic regression, cranial-sacral therapy, etc. Their use can in no way be reconciled with Biblical theology. Rather the Christian psychologist should urge prayer. In sincere and mindful prayer with the goal of sanctification, the restraining of our sinful impulses allows the intellect to curb the negative aspects of anger, loss, rejection, and inordinate desire. In connection the tripartite constituent parts of man to their Source (God), that vacuum mentioned earlier is filled and the mind better equipped to receive healing while dealing with personal emotional and mental anguish, since one is no longer seeking the answer in the fallen self will. Then coming to God, one recognizes one's proper dignity - to allow God to be master of mind and body - and is able to see things as they truly are, for its eye, made blind through the illness of the fallen psyche, is opened by the transformative grace of God.

---

1. In the battle for the mind, Satan tries attempts to cause
• A carnal mind: Romans 8:6-7

• A mind alienated from God by wicked works: Colossians 1:21
• A defiled mind: Titus 1:15
• A fleshly mind: Ephesians 2:3
• A hardened mind: Daniel 5:20
• A doubtful mind: Luke 12:29
• A vain mind: Ephesians 4:17
• A blinded mind: II Corinthians 3:14
• A seared mind and conscience: Titus 1:15
• A despiteful mind: Ezekiel 36:5
• An evil mind: Acts 14:2
• An unbelieving mind: II Corinthians 4:4
• A fainting mind: Hebrews 12:3
• A reprobate mind: II Timothy 3:8
• Double mindedness: James 1:8; 4:8
• A corrupt mind: I Timothy 6:5; II Timothy 3:8; II Corinthians 11:3

2. Positive mental qualities you should develop:

• A ready mind: II Corinthians 8:19; I Peter 5:2; Acts 17:11
• A pure mind: II Peter 3:1
• A stayed mind: Isaiah 26:3
• A renewed mind: Ephesians 4:23; Romans 12:2
• A humble mind: Colossians 3:12; Acts 20:19
• A sober mind: Titus 2:6
• A sound mind: II Timothy 1:7
• A mind of love: Matthew 22:37
• A serving mind: Romans 7:25
• A fully persuaded mind: Romans 14:5
• A fervent mind: II Corinthians 7:7
• A willing mind: II Corinthians 8:12

3. Because of continued sin, men can be turned over to a reprobate mind. See Romans 1:28- 32. A reprobate mind is the most evil kind of mind you can imagine.

4. As you learned in this chapter, one of the strategies for victory in the mind is to let the same mind that was in Jesus be in you. Study the New Testament further to discover just what the mind of Jesus was like. What mental attitudes were reflected in His actions? How did His ministry reflect His thought life? How did His words reflect His thoughts?

5. Jesus knows even the thoughts of your mind: See Luke 5:22; 6:8; 11:17.

CHAPTER FOURTEEN
PHYSICAL ATTACKS

The thief cometh not, but for to steal, and to kill, and to destroy: I am come that they might have life, and that they might have it more abundantly.
-John 10:10

The body of the Christian is a temple of the Holy Spirit.

Know ye not that ye are the temple of God, and that the Spirit of God dwelleth in you? If any man defile the temple of God, him shall God destroy; for the temple of God is holy, which temple ye are. -I Corinthians 3:16-17

Because the body of the Christian is a temple of the Holy Spirit, and because we were created in God's Image, it is often attacked by demonic entities through various means.

ILLNESS- Illness exists because of the original sin of Adam and Eve. Although all illness is in the world because of sin, it does not mean everyone who is suffering is doing so because of personal sins. Sacred Scripture reveals various reasons for illness. The first is illness caused by the demonic. Demons attempt to afflict the body just as they attempt to afflict the spirit. The body is no more immune to attack than the spirit is to discouragement, condemnation, etc. But illness can also be used as a way for God to deal with personal sin. For an example see the story of Miriam in Numbers 12. In one healing Christ performed during His earthly ministry He said to the person:

...Behold, thou art made whole: sin no more, lest a worse thing come unto thee. -John 5:14

The illness of this man was apparently a result of sin. In another case, Christ made it clear that the illness was not the result of sin but for the glory of God:

And as Jesus passed by, He saw a man which was blind from his birth. And His disciples asked Him, saying, Master, who did sin, this man, or his parents, that he was born blind? Jesus answered, Neither hath this man sinned, nor his parents; but that the works of God should be made manifest in him. -John 9:1-3

An illness for the glory of God is one which God allows for His glory when physical healing comes through prayer. There have also been cases of possession and oppression where this has been true. All illness however is not caused by sin, the demonic or as a chastisement. Illness is far more often the result of natural laws. For example, you may become ill because you do not eat properly.

EXTREME FATIGUE- Demons will also attack the body through fatigue which results from being too busy or overworked. When a victim is extremely tired physically, demons may take advantage and spiritually assault the victim. Satan came to Christ when He was exhausted from 40 days of fasting (Matthew 4:2). When Elijah was tired from great spiritual exploits he became so discouraged that he wanted to die (I Kings 19:4).

DEATH- Although physical death is a part of the natural scheme of human life until the return of Christ, demonic entities will attempt to cause premature death. They often tempt their victims to commit suicide.

ABUSE- Demonic entities also encourage their victims to abuse their bodies by putting toxic substances into them such as drugs and alcoholic beverages, or in cutting, piercing and scratching their bodies. In regards to physical attacks caused by demonic entities it is important that the exorcist counsel the victim that they, as a Christian, must understand that God is in control of their life and the Holy Spirit is a protective covering over them. Demons cannot harm them nor take their life without the knowledge of God. The power of Christ the

King is greater than that of Satan. The God who made the human body has the power to heal that body.

But unto you that fear my name, shall the Sun of righteousness arise with healing in His wings...

-Malachi 4:2

Who His own self bare our sins in His own body on the tree, that we, being dead to sins should live unto righteousness; by whose stripes ye were healed.

-I Peter 2:24

But He was wounded for our transgressions, He was bruised for our iniquities; the chastisement of our peace was upon Him, and with His stripes we are healed.

-Isaiah 53:5

Beloved, I wish above all things that thou mayest prosper and be in health, even as thy soul prospereth. -III John 1:2

Often when a demon attacks a client physically, this can be a sign of oppression. The priest and intercessors should pray for the client and family, bless the home and arrange for long term pastoral counseling.

Is any sick among you? Let him call for the elders of the church; and let them pray over him, anointing him with oil in the name of the Lord: And the prayer of faith shall save the sick, and the Lord shall raise him up; and if he have committed sins, they shall be forgiven him.

-James 5:14-15

In addition, the priest and lay investigator may witness such physical abuse against the victim (and sometimes the exorcist) as:

- Scratches and claw marks
- Words scratched into the flesh

- Shoving and pushing
- Spontaneous bruising
- Contortion of limbs and soft flesh areas
- Lifting of the body
- Throwing of the body
- Burning sensations often accompanied by red marks
- Violent itching and rashing
- Vomiting profusely (sometimes objects)

And there are many more physical manifestations of this sort. This is by no means an exhaustive list, but merely designed to give the reader a basic idea of the scope of activity to be expected.

ATTACKS ON THE FAMILY

The family is the basic unit of society established by God in the beginning of the world when He first created man. God has always emphasized the family and it is a divine institution. The Almighty raised up a nation of chosen people from the family of one man, Abraham. He selected the physical union of a man and his wife to describe the spiritual union between Christ and the Church. Throughout the Scriptures, God stressed the importance of the family in His will for humanity. Because of the importance of the family in society, the family is a primary target for attack by the demonic forces. Demons undermine the union between a man and his wife in Holy Matrimony. Demons influence people to engage in improper sexual relationships which result in grave mortal sin (I Corinthians 7:5). They are behind the sin of adultery (Galatians 5:19). The spiritual forces of Satan destroy and divide the home. This can range from arguments through divorce and even into legislation and laws which undermine the family unit.

...Every kingdom divided against itself is brought to desolation; and every city or house divided against itself shall not stand. -Matthew 12:25

Once the demonic forces establish division and destroy the homes of a nation, they can gradually erode and undermine the entire nation itself. (This is a good point to keep in mind. Every spiritual battle is connected to a greater spiritual goal.) God established a chain of command in the home. The man is to be the head of the home and love his wife. The wife is to follow his leadership and the children are to be in submission to their parents (I Corinthians 7; Ephesians 5:1-6:1). Demonic forces often attack the man of the home and tempt him to act in unloving or even abusive ways. This results in a loss of respect, trust and obedience from the wife and children. The demons then tempt the wife to act in rebellion against the husband. Demons will also target the children. They will create an atmosphere of lack of discipline which results in rebellion. Read the story of Eli's sons in I Samuel 2 and of David's son, Absalom, in II Samuel 13-19. When a family unit is composed of Christians and unbelievers, spiritual division exists. This division is not a conflict between flesh and blood. It is a spiritual conflict. It cannot be won by harsh words or through debate and argument. The forces of hell fight the unity of the family because it is a natural parallel of the unity between Christ and His Church. Christian families must recognize this and declare with Sacred Scripture:

...but as for me and my house, we will serve the Lord.
-Joshua 24:15

The priest and investigator should be careful to observe the family dynamic. How do they interact? Do they eat meals together? Pray together? Take recreation together? Is there an abnormal amount of familial bickering and argumentation? Is there a member of the family who is not a Christian? In some cases of oppression and possession the demonic entity will manifest to other family members, cause objects to fly at them, frighten them with sounds, foul odors, etc. Be certain to interview each family member separately, and then the family together as a unit. Pay attention to any apparent inconsistencies as these may be indicative of demonic doorways that allow the oppression to continue.

---

1. Read the book of Job. Job was attacked in the physical, material, and family realms. He was also attacked through human personalities. Behind each of these circumstances and areas of attack there was a spiritual reason. See Job.1:6-12; 2:1-6; 42:5.

CHAPTER FIFTEEN
CULTS AND THE OCCULT

In the investigation process of demonic claims it is not infrequent to come into contact with individuals involved in a variety of religious cults and/or the occult. It is important for both the lay investigator and priest to be aware of some basics regarding this area of investigation. Lets start by answering some basic questions.

Don't cultists wear weird clothing and live in communes?

While it is true that some cults do require communal living and adopting different clothing and dietary habits, many are nearly undetectable. Cults are becoming more sophisticated in their approach, and so dress, talk and act in ways that allow them to assimilate easily while subtly promoting their teachings.

Aren't most cult members mentally ill?

Absolutely not. Many cult members are very intelligent, educated, sharp minded and skilled. The reality is that all sorts of people are involved in cults. The usual way in which they are attracted to a cult is through contact during a crisis period of their personal life.

Types of Cults

Religious- Cults that maintain a religious belief system as their base are the most common. Their belief system could be standard Christianity, Hinduism, Islam or any other of the world religions, or they may have invented their own belief system. What makes them a cult is the fact that they use techniques of mind control to modify the behavior and thinking of cult members, not what they believe.

Business- Cults that use commercial gain as their base are called "cults of greed". They will promise their special program will help you become very wealthy. Often they will hold up their leader as an example and explain that if you do what he or she says then you will be successful too. Business cults use mind control to get you working for them for free, and to sell you motivational tapes, videos, books and seminars all of which are supposedly designed to help you succeed, but in reality are designed to enhance the cult's mind control environment and keep you believing in their almost impossible dream of success. Of course they never mention that the primary way the leaders make money are by selling these motivation materials to their group!

Self Help Cults- Cults that use "self help" or counseling or self improvement as their base often target business people and corporations. By doing their courses and seminars they claim you and your staff will become more successful. Business people locked away in hotel rooms are subjected to quasi-religious indoctrination as they play strange games, join in group activities, and share their innermost thoughts with the group. Once you have completed one course you are told you need to do the more advanced course, which naturally costs more than the last. These cults will sometimes request that you do volunteer work and that you help recruit your friends, family and work mates. These groups specialize in creating powerful emotional experiences which are then used to validate your involvement in the cult. The religious overtones are couched in terms which don't sound religious. They usually come to the surface as you near the end of a seminar and are typically New Age oriented.

Political- Cults that use political ideals as their base are well known throughout history. The National Socialist Party, Communist Party, and various racially oriented and nationalistic oriented groups are examples of mind control on a very large scale. On smaller scales white and black supremacists, terrorists, and rebel groups commonly use forms of mind control to recruit and dominate their members.

The Occult- It is also not infrequent for exorcists to encounter the occult. The most common forms encountered are:

Wicca- Wicca is an eclectic occult belief system centering around gods, goddesses, and nature worship. Gary Cantrell, a Wiccan author says Wicca is based on "harmony with nature and all aspects of the god and goddess divinity." Wiccan practice involves the manipulation of nature through various rituals in attempts to gain power, prestige, love, or whatever it is a Wiccan seeks. Wicca utilizes symbols in its ceremonies and follows various pagan calendars in reference to Wiccan festivals. Its roots are in ancient agrarian Celtic Society. Wicca does not have a structure of clergy and/or congregations in the sense that Christians understand the terms. It does have priests and priestesses who are in leadership positions within covens that have witches. The varying traditions of Wicca have different requirements for attaining the level of priest and priestess. Some of the more common varieties of Wicca are Alexandrian, Celtic, Dianic, Dicordian, Eclectic, Gardnerian, and Georgian. Wicca is a recognized as a religion in the military. Some Wiccans practice their rituals “skyclad” (nude). One of the most common aspects of Wiccan belief is the teaching of reincarnation and karma. The purpose of reincarnation is to learn lessons through the various lives. “This process of reincarnation is repeated for numerous lifetimes until a development of the Spirit is reached where the Spirit can truly merge with the male and female balanced creator/creatrix entity. We are returned to the God and to the Goddess.” Karma is the law of cause and effect that "does not punish nor reward. It is simply a universal law that reacts to causation until disharmony is illuminated." Wicca does not claim to be the only way but says that all spiritual traditions and paths are valid to those who practice them. It accepts "the fact that all life is sacred, including plant, animal, and human." Generally, Wiccans do not believe in the existence of Satan and should not be confused with Satanists. They have no orgies or public displays of sexuality in their rituals, no bestiality, and no blood sacrifices. They do not practice spells with the intention to harm people. They deny that there are moral absolutes, believe that nature is divine, and seek to be in harmony with the earth/nature.

Satanism-Satanism has been around in one form or another for as long as Satan has had direct influence in the lives of the rebellious. The modern expressions of Satanism are quite diverse, ranging from philosophical (denying a literal Satan), to religious (accepting the literal Satan as their god). The oldest of the modern organizations is the Church of Satan, founded by Anton LaVey in 1969. The following beliefs are taken from this particular organization.

The Nine Satanic Statements

1. Satan represents indulgence instead of abstinence!
2. Satan represents vital existence instead of spiritual pipe dreams!
3. Satan represents undefiled wisdom instead of hypocritical self-deceit!
4. Satan represents kindness to those who deserve it instead of love wasted on ingrates!
5. Satan represents vengeance instead of turning the other cheek!
6. Satan represents responsibility to the responsible instead of concern for psychic vampires!
7. Satan represents man as just another animal, sometimes better, more often worse than those that walk on all-fours, who, because of his "divine spiritual and intellectual development," has become the most vicious animal of all!
8. Satan represents all of the so-called sins, as they all lead to physical, mental, or emotional gratification!
9. Satan has been the best friend the Church has ever had, as He has kept it in business all these years!

(*From the Satanic Bible)

The Eleven Satanic Rules of the Earth

1. Do not give opinions or advice unless you are asked.
2. Do not tell your troubles to others unless you are sure they want to hear them.
3. When in anothers lair, show him respect or else do not go there.
4. If a guest in your lair annoys you, treat him cruelly and without mercy.
5. Do not make sexual advances unless you are given the mating signal.
6. Do not take that which does not belong to you unless it is a burden to the other person and he cries out to be relieved.
7. Acknowledge the power of magic if you have employed it successfully to obtain your desires. If you deny the power of magic after having called upon it with success, you will lose all you have obtained.
8. Do not complain about anything to which you need not subject yourself.
9. Do not harm little children.
10. Do not kill non-human animals unless you are attacked or for your food.
11. When walking in open territory, bother no one. If someone bothers you, ask him to stop. If he does not stop, destroy him.

The Nine Satanic Sins

1. Stupidity—The top of the list for Satanic Sins. The Cardinal Sin of Satanism. It's too bad that stupidity isn't painful. Ignorance is one thing, but our society thrives increasingly on stupidity. It depends on people going along with whatever they are told. The media promotes a cultivated stupidity as a posture that is not only acceptable but laudable. Satanists must learn to see through the tricks and cannot afford to be stupid.

2. Pretentiousness—Empty posturing can be most irritating and isn't applying the cardinal rules of Lesser Magic. On equal footing with stupidity for what keeps the money in circulation these days. Everyone's made to feel like a big shot, whether they can come up with the goods or not.

3. Solipsism—Can be very dangerous for Satanists. Projecting your reactions, responses and sensibilities onto someone who is probably far less attuned than you are. It is the mistake of expecting people to give you the same consideration, courtesy and respect that you naturally give them. They won't. Instead, Satanists must strive to apply the dictum of "Do unto others as they do unto you." It's work for most of us and requires constant vigilance lest you slip into a comfortable illusion of everyone being like you. As has been said, certain utopias would be ideal in a nation of philosophers, but unfortunately (or perhaps fortunately, from a Machiavellian standpoint) we are far from that point.

4. Self-deceit—It's in the "Nine Satanic Statements" but deserves to be repeated here. Another cardinal sin. We must not pay homage to any of the sacred cows presented to us, including the roles we are expected to play ourselves. The only time self-deceit should be entered into is when it's fun, and with awareness. But then, it's not self-deceit!

5. Herd Conformity—That's obvious from a Satanic stance. It's all right to conform to a person's wishes, if it ultimately benefits you. But only fools follow along with the herd, letting an impersonal entity dictate to you. The key is to choose a master wisely instead of being enslaved by the whims of the many.

6. Lack of Perspective—Again, this one can lead to a lot of pain for a Satanist. You must never lose sight of who and what you are, and what a threat you can be, by your very existence. We are making history right now, every day. Always keep the wider historical and social picture in mind. That is an important key to both Lesser and Greater Magic. See the patterns and fit things together as you want the pieces to fall into place. Do not be swayed by herd constraints—know that you are working on another level entirely from the rest of the world.

7. Forgetfulness of Past Orthodoxies—Be aware that this is one of the keys to brainwashing people into accepting something new and different, when in reality it's something that was once widely accepted but is now presented in a new package. We are expected to rave about the genius of the creator and forget the original. This makes for a disposable society.

8. Counterproductive Pride—That first word is important. Pride is great up to the point you begin to throw out the baby with the bathwater. The rule of Satanism is: if it works for you, great. When it stops working for you, when you've painted yourself into a corner and the only way out is to say, I'm sorry, I made a mistake, I wish we could compromise somehow, then do it.

9. Lack of Aesthetics—This is the physical application of the Balance Factor. Aesthetics is important in Lesser Magic and should be cultivated. It is obvious that no one can collect any money off classical standards of beauty and form most of the time so they are discouraged in a consumer society, but an eye for beauty, for balance, is an essential Satanic tool and must be applied for greatest magical effectiveness. It's not what's supposed to be pleasing—it's what is. Aesthetics is a personal thing, reflective of one's own nature, but there are universally pleasing and harmonious configurations that should not be denied. The investigator and priest should look for signs of occult involvement. Books, jewelry, artwork, ouija boards, crystal wands, statues, idols, symbols, etc. should all be watched for and if found taken from the premises and burned elsewhere by the priest himself. This should never be done on the same property as the client's residence. The purpose of this book is not to explore every cult or aspect of the occult. The investigator and priest is encouraged to engage in an independent study of the subject matter.

---

1. Study the warnings of God to Israel regarding Satan and the occult: Deuteronomy 18:10- 12; Leviticus 17:7; 19:31; 20:16.
2. Study more about sacrifices made to devils: Deuteronomy 32:17; II Chronicles 11:15;Psalms 106:37.
3. The following are common characteristics of cults:
• Dictatorial Leadership: Cults cluster around domineering, charismatic personalities who have absolute authority and are accountable to no one.
• Exclusive: Cults adopt the attitude that they are the only group with divine truth. They exclude from fellowship others who disagree with them.
• Legalistic: Cults usually have strict rules of belief and behavior which have no Scriptural basis.
• Defensive: Cult members are usually led to believe that society, organized religion, and government are against them. This causes a reactionary attitude towards religion, government, and society.
• Oppressive: Cult members are usually manipulated and oppressed by the leadership.
• Secretive: Many things about the cult are kept secret from "outsiders".
• Higher Revelation: Cults often claim "higher revelation" from God. They will always have a source of authority beyond the Scriptures. It may be the writings or revelation of the founder or another person. In some cases it may be the founder's peculiar interpretation of the Bible. Their doctrines will not currently represent Biblical teachings.
• Anti-church: Cults vigorously oppose organized churches and their clergy.
• Anti-family: Cults are sometimes anti-family, which means they want their members to break ties with family who are not members. They try to break biological family ties in order to retain their disciples.
4. There are so many cults world-wide that it is impossible to identify them all, but because of the increasing growth of what is called the "new age movement" major publishing houses in the United States now have "new age departments" because there is such a demand for their materials. The New Age movement has its roots in the ancient occultism. It has historical ties to Sumerian, Indian, Egyptian, Chaldean, Babylonian, and Persian religious practices. The "new age" is a fresh title, but the occult involved in it is nothing new. Jesus is considered just one of many "gods" or revealers of "truth" along with Buddha, Mohammed, Confucius, Zoroaster, Krishna, and many others. The deity of Jesus is denied. While the Church teaches man was separated from God by sin, the New Age movement believes man is born inherently good. They believe he is separated from God only in his consciousness and is the victim of a false sense of separate

identity that blinds him to his essential unity with God. Because of this, the new age movement advocates various methods of altering the consciousness such as yoga, meditation, chanting, ecstatic dancing, drugs, etc. They consider these a means to salvation. Because of these practices and involvement with witchcraft, sorcery, mediums, etc., new age practices open the door to demonic influences. Because they believe there is no evil, therefore there is no crime and no victim. Death is considered an illusion and because they believe a person is continually reincarnated, there are no victims of murder or abortion. The new age methods of spreading propaganda include infiltration (even of the Church) and unification through worldwide networking. New Age members speak of a coming "purging" which will cleanse the world of all those "lesser evolved souls" who do not see themselves as gods. They are working towards the centralizing of power on a global level, an ungodly unity with man as the sole authority. The new age movement may be one of several forces through which Satan will culminate his plans for global unification. It could very possibly could be the platform upon which the antichrist will rise to world-wide domination.

5. Study II Peter chapter 2 and the book of Jude. List characteristics that will help you detect Satan's messengers in the church.

CHAPTER SIXTEEN
FIGHTING THE DEMONIC

How God anointed Jesus of Nazareth with the Holy Ghost and with power: who went about doing good, and healing all that were oppressed of the Devil; for God was with Him. -Acts 10:38

The life of Christ clearly demonstrated that demonic entities are a reality. What Christ taught about demons and how He dealt with them yields valuable information about the strategies of Satan. Christ taught that Satan is the ruler of demons. He taught of the reality and power of demons. He said that the casting out of demonic entities was one of the signs that the Kingdom of God had come. A large portion of the ministry of Christ involved dealing with demons. It is the example of Christ and the authority of His name bestowed on those in Apostolic Succession that provides the legitimate basis for dealing with the demonic. Christ ministered to "all" who came with demonic afflictions. The Apostle Peter said of Christ:

... God anointed Jesus of Nazareth with the Holy Ghost and with power: who went about doing good, and healing all that were oppressed of the devil. -Acts 10:38

Demons are used by Satan to oppose God, His plan and purposes, and His Church. They also war against Christians to keep them from the truth of the Gospel and from participation in the Church Militant. Demons control specific physical localities (principalities) such as the prince of Persia mentioned in Daniel 10:12-13. Demons also work through people to accomplish Satanic objectives in the world. Opposition to God's will is Satan's main objective. The word "Satan" means "adversary." Satan is primarily God's adversary (Job 1:6; Matthew 13:39). He is secondarily, humanity's adversary (Zechariah 3:1; I Peter 5:8). As you have already learned, demons have different natures.

Remember that one demon identified himself in I Kings 22:23 as a "lying spirit." A "deaf and dumb" spirit is identified in Mark 9:25. Demons of various natures operate as spirits of infirmity, seducing spirits, and unclean spirits. Satan uses them to afflict humanity in body and spirit.

Demons of Infirmity- These are demonic entities that can afflict the bodies of Christians as well as unbelievers. Read Luke 13:10- 17. This woman was afflicted with a spirit of infirmity. She was present in the Sabbath services and Christ called her "a daughter of Abraham." Yet her body had been afflicted by Satan for eighteen years. For other examples of demonic powers afflicting the body see Matthew 12:22; 17:15-18; Acts 10:38; II Corinthians 12:7.

Seductive Demons- These spirits afflict the spirit of man, seducing him to believe doctrinal lies and be condemned to eternal punishment. They are the spirits of false doctrine, cults, false Christs, and false teachers:

Now the Spirit speaketh expressly, that in the latter times some shall depart from the faith, giving heed to seducing spirits, and doctrines of devils. -I Timothy 4:1

These seducing spirits are deceptive. They actually work miracles which lead some to believe they are of God: For they are the spirits of devils, working miracles, which go forth unto the kings of the earth and of the whole world, to gather them to the battle of that great day of God Almighty. -Revelation 16:14

Seducing spirits include the "spirit of divination" mentioned in Acts:

And it came to pass, as we went to prayer, a certain damsel possessed with a spirit of divination met us, which brought her masters much gain by soothsaying.

-Acts 16:16

Such spirits of divination or "familiar spirits" operate in psychics, channelers, sensitives, shamans and those who advocate spirit guides. Through pagan, New Age and even more blatantly Satanic methods the spirits of divination foretell the future or discover knowledge which is naturally unknown. Warnings against familiar spirits are given in Leviticus 19:31; 20:6; Deuteronomy 5:9; 18:10; Leviticus 20:27; and I Samuel 28:3. Seducing spirits sear the conscience, seduce, entice, tempt, allure, interest, fascinate, excite, arouse, attract, and deceive. Seducing spirits are active in causing "spiritual wickedness in high places." They are present in every cult and wherever false teaching is promoted. Seducing spirits entice men and women to worship idols and even Satan himself.

Unclean Demons- These demonic entities afflict the behavior of man. They are responsible for immoral acts, unclean thoughts, temptations and other strategies of Satan used to bind men and women. When Satan controls individuals with unclean spirits, he can also operate in homes, churches, and entire nations as these groups are composed of individuals. This is how Satan works in the various levels of structure in society. For examples of unclean spirits see Matthew 10:1; 12:43; and Mark 1:23-26. The priest should be prepared for all manner of sexually explicit language, talk, and even enticements when dealing with such demons. Intercessors and investigators are cautioned NOT to give heed to the things these and other demons say and/or do. The goal is to shock, stun, cause doubt, and ultimately entice the mind to ponder things of an immoral nature greatly reducing the effectiveness of the exorcism process.

OPPRESSION, OBSESSION, POSSESSION

Demonic entities can oppress people. To oppress means to bear down, come against, or bind from the outside. This oppression is accomplished by demons in various ways. They cause depression, create negative circumstances, and insert wrong thoughts into the mind such as thoughts of suicide, immorality, unbelief, fear, etc. Demons create Satanic circumstances and situations which tempt men to sin:

How God anointed Jesus of Nazareth with the Holy Ghost and with power: who went about doing good, and healing all that were OPPRESSED of the Devil; for God was with Him. -Acts 10:38

Demons can also possess the human body. Demon possession is a condition in which one or more demons inhabit the body of a human being and take complete control of their victim at will. "Possession" does not mean a person is not responsible for his or her own personal sin. The responsibility rests with the factors that led to his/her condition. Possession can happen willingly. A person may desire to be taken over by demonic entities in order to conduct seances, pronounce curses, become a witch, or secure some other supernatural power. Possession can also occur unwilling. An individual does not ask to be possessed, but through sinful thoughts, actions, or contact with the occult possession results. Demonic powers operating in parents and the sins of the parents can affect the next generation. (See Exodus 20:5; 34:7; and Deuteronomy 5:9.) This accounts for demon possession or oppression of children such as recorded in Mark 7:24-30 and 9:17-21.There is also such a thing as demon obsession. This is a condition where one becomes obsessed by an interest in or preoccupation with demons. It is an unusual interest in the occult, demons, and Satan which controls interests and pursuits in a dictating manner. Such obsession with demon powers can lead to possession.

CAN DEMONS ATTACK CHRISTIANS?

They can, but it is made much more difficult because the Holy Spirit cannot inhabit the same temple as a demonic entity:

What? Know ye not that your body is the temple of the Holy Ghost which is in you, which ye have of God, and ye are not your own? For ye are bought with a price:

Therefore glorify God in your body, and in your spirit, which are God's. -I Corinthians 6:19-20

When you become a Christian, are baptized and confirmed (filled with the Holy Spirit), you cannot belong to Satan and be filled with his spirits at the same time. The Holy Spirit will not abide in the same "temple" with Satan. But this does not mean Christians cannot be affected by demonic entities. It is these powers against which we wrestle. Satan uses demonic powers to attack believers from the outside through oppression, the symptoms of which were previously discussed. But he cannot possess the dedicated Christian, except with divine permission (these cases are very rare). To "possess" indicates internal occupation. To "oppress" or bind indicates control or severe influence from the outside. The activities of Christians can be demonically manipulated if they allow demonic entities to oppress them. Such oppression permits Satan to use the client for evil purposes. This is what happened when Peter, a disciple of Jesus, was used of Satan to try to divert Jesus from suffering for the sins of all mankind. When Jesus described the suffering He was to go through, Peter said:

...Be it far from thee, Lord: this shall not be unto thee. -Matthew 16:22

Jesus said to Peter:

...Get thee behind me, Satan: thou art an offense unto me: for thou savorest not the things that be of God, but those that be of men. -Matthew 16:23

Jesus did not mean Peter was actually Satan. He recognized that at that moment Peter had allowed Satan to operate through him. He was not demon possessed, but he was allowing Satanic spirits to influence him.

Believers, by their own actions, give place or make room for Satan to use them. -Ephesians 4:27

When a person is baptized and sealed in the Faith, his name is written in a special book in Heaven called the book of life. Only those whose names are in this book will be residents of Heaven for eternity.

And whosoever was not found written in the book of life was cast into the lake of fire. -Revelation 20:15

It is possible to have your name written in the book of life, but later blotted out because of turning back to sinful living:

He that overcometh, the same shall be clothed in white raiment; and I will not blot out his name out of the book of life, but I will confess his name before my Father, and before His angels. -Revelation 3:5

If a Christian continues in known, unconfessed sin, there is a point at which he can cease to be a Christian. The Apostle Paul expressed his own concern that he not be "cast away" after preaching to others:

But I keep under my body, and bring it into subjection: lest that by any means, when I have preached to others, I myself should be a castaway. -I Corinthians 9:27

Paul realized that sin, especially continued unconfessed willful sins of the flesh, could result in the loss of his own soul even though he had preached to others. By continuing to live in sin the client will eventually end up in a condition of serious mortal sin which after a prolonged period of time removes them from participation in the mystical Body of Christ. This means they are no longer a true follower of Jesus Christ. When this state occurs, the client has opened his or herself up to greater attacks of the Adversary, including the possibility of demonic possession. This is why it is important when you sin to immediately confess all sin to a priest and turn from unrighteousness:

If we confess our sins, He is faithful and just to forgive us our sins, and to cleanse us from all unrighteousness. If we say that we have not sinned, we make Him a liar, and His Word is not in us. - I John 1:9-10

In all cases the priest should strongly encourage nonbelievers to embrace the faith, be baptized and confirmed, and make a good confession. If the family are Christian they are encouraged to embrace the Faith, make a good confession individually, and then seek the solace of pastoral counseling which may or may not include exorcism of property or persons, depending on the need.

DEMONIC CONTROL

Demons gain control in several ways:

1. **Through generations-** Demons may oppress or possess a person or family because of previous possession or oppression of the parents. This accounts for demonic influence over children (Exodus 20:5; 34:7; Deuteronomy 5:9).

2. **Through the mind-** If Satan can control the clients thoughts, he will eventually control their actions. Lack of mental control eventually results in lack of use of the will. This leads to sinful actions. Continuing in sinful thoughts and actions can lead from oppression to possession and finally to a reprobate mind such as is described in Romans chapter one. This is a mind totally controlled by evil thoughts. Demons also gain access through mind-altering drugs which reduce the ability to resist demons and grant increasing access. "hypnosis" or "mind control" techniques also provides an entrance point.

3. **Through sinful actions-** Sinful thoughts are soon fulfilled by sinful actions. For example, the thought of adultery is fulfilled in the actual act of adultery. Sin is rebellion, and rebellious thoughts and actions provides an entry point for

demonic activity. When a Christian continues in sinful thoughts or actions they "give place" to the demonic (Ephesians 4:27). Sins of involvement with the occult, including objects, literature, seances, etc., are actions which are especially dangerous and attract demonic entities. A Christian who lives in sin is open not only to oppression of demonic entities, but also possession. As you have learned, there is no neutral ground in spiritual warfare. You are either on the side of good or evil. You belong either to God or Satan.

4. **Through desire-** Some people desire and request of Satan to be under the control of demons powers. They do this for purposes of having supernatural power or performing supernatural acts. Those with “spirit guides” or “psychic ability” should NEVER be used in an investigation nor consulted for any reason whatsoever.

5. **Through an empty "house"-** Demons consider the body of the person they inhabit as their house (Matthew 12:44). When a person who has been delivered from demonic possession does not fill his spiritual house with the Holy Spirit, reentry may occur.

6. **Through permission-** Sometimes God grants permission for activities of demonic entities to accomplish special purposes. This can be allowed as a trial of Christians as in the case of Job. It can also be judgment for sin as in the case of King Saul.

CHAPTER SEVENTEEN
THE SIGNS

Dealing with demonic entities is not something to be engaged in by paranormal investigators, ghost hunters or demonologists. Christ conveyed this authority only to the Apostles and their successors:

And these signs shall follow them that believe: In my name shall they cast out devils... -Mark 16:17

And when He had called unto Him His twelve disciples, He gave them power against unclean spirits, to cast them out, and to heal all manner of sickness and all manner of disease. -Matthew 10:1

And He called unto Him the twelve, and began to send them forth by two and two; and gave them power over unclean spirits. -Mark 6:7

And these signs shall follow them that believe: In my name shall they cast out devils... -Mark 16:17

Heal the sick, cleanse the lepers, raise the dead, cast out devils: freely ye have received, freely give. -Matthew 10:8

However, even priests should not rush into exorcism without proper preparation, as the sons of Sceva discovered (Acts 19). It is also important that priests in this area of ministry do not become overly demon conscious. We are not called to be "demon hunters". We are called to be priests of the Most High, to offer the Holy Eucharist, and to tend His flock. Those who are too fascinated with this area of ministry, or who seem to delight in its discussion are not suitable exorcists and should not be mentored.

DETECTING DEMONIC PRESENCE

The exorcist must be a person of keen discernment. To

overcome demonic powers it is important to be able to recognize their presence and tactics. The Holy Spirit has provided a special spiritual gift for this purpose. This gift is called "discerning of spirits" (I Corinthians 12:10). To discern means "to discover, evaluate, and make a distinction between." The gift of discerning of spirits enables an exorcist to discern the spirits operating in others. It permits him to discover, evaluate, and identify evil spirits. The gift of discerning of spirits is very important when dealing with preternatural investigation. It enables you to discern whether or not a person has a demonic entity operating through or against him. It prevents deception by recognizing when other more plausible answers are available. The well trained exorcist is also able to recognize the evil tactics and motives of demonic entities. There are six forms of diabolic influence.

Temptation- The ordinary way in which all of us are subject to as fallen humanity. After Adam and Eve fell they in effect conceded influence over certain aspects of our bodies. This is where the central focus of the battleground is- the body. All of the sins of the world appeal to the flesh and thus these are the things they use to appeal to us. Sin feels good, otherwise we would never engage in it. And as an extension they can influence your thoughts. Every sin begins as a thought, and every past sin remains in your memory and they already know about them because they've seen them. They will go back into your memory, no matter how long ago the sin, and pull it out as a temptation. Normally these temptations are in areas you need to work on and deal with. These areas lack virtue and therefore open us to demonic attack.

The next five are considered extraordinary forms of diabolic influence.

Demonic obsession- This is when the person's thoughts are bombarding them through the influence of the demonic. Their minds are fixated on any given thought. We see an extreme rise of this due to the ease of access to pornography. These tend to be very grave sins, or what are sometimes called mortal sins. What most people don't know is that the expected results of mortal sins is demonic possession. It is only kept from occurring because God in His grace keeps it from happening in the vast majority of cases. When one is in a state of grace, one is subject to God, but when one commits a serious sin one moves away from God and places oneself under the influence of Satan. Usually you're using your body in a way that greatly offends Our Lord which empowers demons. What many do not realize is that most of the victims of this are women. There are two reasons for this. The Church Fathers tell us that Satan has a particular hatred for women, because it was through a woman (Mary) that his head was crushed. The other reason is that women are often victimized. Now why does that make a difference? If something or someone is used badly, it too is subject to Satan. When someone is raped, molested, or abused they are being used in a disordered fashion, and it opens the door for the demonic to attack the woman herself. The vast majority of exorcism cases reported by priests around the world are women who have been raped, molested or abused. Likewise when you use your mind badly Satan can come in through that open door influencing those sinful thoughts to a greater degree. How does one tell if it is diabolic or psychological? If the priest prays over the person and they are able to think in a normative way for a period of time, and then slowly it comes back it is diabolic. If it is psychological the prayers won't change the situation at all. This is one of the primary diagnostic tools of an exorcist in this regard. This can sometimes be recognized by an uncontrollable and unusual preoccupation with demons, Satan, or the occult. Such a person may dabble in occult practices, constantly credit everything to Satan or demons, or be preoccupied with the study of demons and Satan.

Demonic oppression- This is primarily external to the individual. One's health with decline, relationships implode for no reason, your job is lost, finances collapse, etc. There is a form of oppression that is fast becoming more common, and this is a state wherein the demon doesn't possess the person, but rather speaks through them. It is the same thing that happens in seances or with spirit channelers. Psychics, channelers and the like are not contacting the spirit of some dead person, but merely opening the door to a demonic entity. Sometimes a demon may actually posses the person, but there is a higher demon in charge who doesn't possess the person, yet controls the situation from outside.

1. A physical binding: The "daughter of Abraham" who Jesus relieved of a spirit of infirmity was bound physically. See Luke 13:10-17. Chronic sickness may be demonic oppression. All illness is not caused by demonic powers. Some illness is caused by a violation of natural laws, such as not eating properly or drinking bad water. Some illness is also chastisement.

2. A mental oppression- Disturbances in the mind or thought life such as mental torment, confusion, doubt, loss of memory, missing time, etc. Restlessness, inability to reason or listen to others, abnormal talkativeness or reserve may be exhibited. All mental problems are not caused by Satan. Discouragement, depression, and disorientation can be caused by allergies to certain foods or a wrong chemical imbalance in the brain. Caution should be taken not to class illness or mental problems as being caused by demonic entities. Sometimes a simple change in diet or lifestyle will eliminate a problem if it is caused by physical causes. Always defer to medical and psychological professionals.

3. Emotional problems: Disturbances in the emotions which persist or recur, including resentment, hatred, anger, fear, rejection, self-pity, jealousy, depression, worry, insecurity, inferiority, etc.

4. Spiritual problems: Extreme difficulties in overcoming sin, including sinful habits. Rejection of spiritual solutions to

problems. Any type of doctrinal error or deception, including bondage to objects and literature of the cults.

5. Circumstances: Demons can create difficult circumstances which are oppressive. Such circumstances usually involve confusion and can immediately be identified as demonic because God is not the author of confusion (I Corinthians 14:33; James 3:16).

Demonic Possession- There are two types of possession. There is Full Possession wherein the person's entire body is subject to the control of the demonic entity. The person in this state has given their will completely over to the demon. As frightening as it may seem there are people who like being possessed. When someone comes to an exorcist with claims of demonic attack in their lives one of the first questions a seasoned exorcist will ask is *'Do you want to be liberated?'* What you have in operation here is the psychology of abuse. The demonic entities establish an abusive relationship with their victim. First they entice them, treat them nicely and once the person is under their influence they mercilessly abuse them, and blaming them for their tormented state. Sometimes however they will set up a relationship wherein the person does what the demon wants and the person is fine. If this person realizes the situation they're in and turn on the demon, that is when things get ugly. The entity begins to attack the victim and frighten or demoralize them so they continue to do the demonic entity's bidding. It should be noted that those who are perfectly possessed never seek an exorcist. There are certain things they get from the possession, some empowerment. In point of fact however, sin is weakness. Anytime the exorcist is dealing with a demon, as his goal is to subjugate the demon, to force him to tell you what must be done to make him leave.

1. Indwelling of an unclean spirit: This is demonstrated by a basic moral uncleanness and filthiness. It might

include the desire to go without clothing. For examples see Mark 5:2 and Luke 8:27.

2. Unusual physical strength: A person shows strength beyond normal capabilities. For examples see Mark 5:3 and Luke 8:29.
3. Fits of rage: These fits may be accompanied by foaming at the mouth. See Mark 9:14-29 and Luke 8:26-39.
4. Resistance to spiritual things: In the accounts in Mark 6:7 and 1:21-28, the demons knew Jesus immediately and asked Him to leave them alone. Fear of the name of Jesus, the saints, holy objects, holy places, prayer, and the Word of God and blasphemy of that which is spiritual are all symptoms of demon possession. Excessive blasphemy may be noted or contorted physical features and abrupt behavior changes when spiritual things are mentioned.
5. Changes in personality and/or voice: A person who is normally shy may become aggressive or violent. Actions as well as appearance may be affected. Moral character and intelligence may change. Voice may be altered. See Mark 5:9.
6. Accompanying physical afflictions: In cases of demon possession, these appear most commonly to be afflictions of the mental and nervous system. (See Matthew 9:33; 12:22; Mark 5:4-5). They can also include a general "pining" or wasting away physically. (See Mark 9:14-29).
7. Self-inflicted physical injury: In Matthew 17:14-21 there is the story of a man's son who would cast himself in the fire. In Luke 8:26-39 this demon possessed man cut himself with stones to inflict physical injury.
8. Terrible anguish: Luke 8:28 relates that this man went about crying because of the terrible inner torments caused by his possession.
9. Incapacity for normal living: This man could not live in society but lived in the tombs of the cemetery. See Luke 8:27.

10. Through non-scriptural methods, the ability to foretell the future or discover that which is unknown: The woman in Acts 16:16 is said to be "possessed" by a spirit of divination.
11. Speaking in a language unknown to the client, especially a dead language such as Latin. Sometimes languages such as Aramaic, Urdu, Sanskrit, etc. are encountered.

The following also may indicate demonic oppression or obsession:

1. Obsessive immorality such as involvement with extreme forms of pornography, adultery, fornication, masturbation, homosexuality, and other sex sins.
2. Strong compulsions toward eating disorders, suicide, self-mutilation, maiming, and murder.
3. Addiction to drugs or alcohol.
4. Trances, visions, and meditation which are not focused on or from the one true God.
5. Bondage to emotions such as fear, anxiety, depression, hatred, rage, jealousy, backbiting, envy, pride, bitterness, negativism, and criticism

SIMPLE PREPARATION FOR THE EXORCIST

- Make a good and complete confession.
- Fast at least three days before the exorcism.
- Offer the Holy Eucharist, pray the Breviary, and attend devotions.
- Discuss the experiences with your assistant after each session.

Disregard all the things the demonic entity will say, reveal, and entice you with, as well as manifest experiences you may see. Accept that the New Testament means exactly what it says. Accept it as true and act accordingly. You are the representative of Christ (II Corinthians 5:20).

INTERCESSOR PREPARATION

Whenever possible, a team of intercessors should be used when binding or casting out demons. Jesus sent out His disciples in pairs for this ministry:

And He called unto Him the twelve, and began to send them forth by two and two: and gave them power over unclean spirits. -Mark 6:7

This does not mean you cannot be effective alone, but there is strength in unity of prayer. Since strength comes from unity, those who are joining you in the exorcism should be similarly prepared with prayer and fasting. In cases of oppression and obsession, prepare the client. They need to have their faith built. (This may not be possible in the case of possession). Proper spiritual instruction must be given. Sometimes, God delivers without such instruction. But in exorcism ministry you want to properly use every channel prescribed by the Church to see the work done. Faith is one channel for God's delivering power and it comes by hearing God's Word, so instruction is important. Christ combined preaching and teaching with healing and deliverance and He instructed His followers to do so also.

THE PLACE OF EXORCISM

The ritual of exorcism is more properly performed in a Church, monastery, convent or rectory. Many have the misguided notion that this occurs in the bedroom of the victim only. As a priest you must understand that exorcism is a valid ministry of the Church. However, it is not necessary or even practical to do so in every case. Christ cast out the demons whenever and wherever he found them.

THE TIME OF EXORCISM

When you are ready to begin an exorcism session the following are basic guidelines of how best to proceed.

1. **Begin with a hymn-** We enter the presence of Christ the

King through worship and praise. Singing hymns or Gregorian chants establish an environment of holiness.

2. **Pray first-** Ask for wisdom and discernment before you begin the ritual.

3. **Decide whether to continue with the ritual-** Determine whether or not to repeat the ritual during a session or wait until another date. In most cases, you will pray the ritual, but in some, do not be surprised if the Lord directs you not to pray or to delay prayer. Jesus delayed healing in the case of the Syro- Phonecian woman's daughter and Lazarus. He did not do many works at all in Nazareth because of unbelief. The Lord may also direct you to delay until further instruction is given, i.e., they may need to deal with a sin problem, need more instruction, a curse or occult object is revealed, etc.

4. **Pray the ritual exactly as it is worded-**Stick to the text exactly. Deviation causes weakness in the process and disturbs the focus of the ritual itself. Do not spend time talking with the demon, should it manifest itself through spoken words outside what is required by the ritual. Jesus rebuked demons and told them to be quiet (Luke 4:34-35). Remember that any conversation with demons is dangerous because there are lying spirits. When forced to speak to the demon use he following as preparatory commands:

"In the name of Jesus Christ and on the basis of the authority of His power, His Word, His blood, and the Holy Spirit..."

...This establishes the power base for exorcism...

"...I bind you...."

...Christ taught to bind the demonic first before attempting to cast him out...

"...and I command you..."

...Exorcism is a prayer of priestly authority, not of entreaty. You can speak quietly, but you must take authority over the forces of evil in the name of Christ. Look directly into the eyes of the person as you speak.

"...the spirit of________" or "...you foul spirit of Satan..."

...if the spirit has been identified either through spiritual or natural discernment, then name it specifically; otherwise, generally.

"...to depart...."

...this is the casting out process...

"...without harming_______(name of person being exorcized), or anyone in this house, and without creating noise or disturbance"

...Sometimes the demon will try to harm the person or create disturbance.

"I forbid you to reenter this person..."

...Remember that Christ used this command...

SIGNS OF RELEASE

In cases of demonic possession, sometimes the demons come out with a struggle, such as crying out or throwing the person on the floor. When demons have departed (whether in possession or oppression), there will be a sense of release, joy, like the lifting of a weight. The victim will be able to receive holy objects, bless themselves with holy water, receive blessings, pray, etc.

ONGOING COUNSELING

After exorcism, those who have been possessed by demons should receive ongoing pastoral counseling and integration into the community life of the Church. When a demon is cast out, he will seek another body through which to operate. Christ taught that the departure of evil spirits leaves an empty place. There is danger of a demon returning to his former victim accompanied by worse spirits:

When the unclean spirit is gone out of a man, he walketh through dry places, seeking rest; and finding none, he saith, I will return unto my house whence I came out. And when he cometh he findeth it swept and garnished. Then goeth he, and taketh to him seven other spirits more wicked than himself; and they enter in, and dwell there; and the last state of that man is worse than the first.

-Luke 11:24-26

When a demon is cast out it is restless and discontent outside of a human body. It is only by indwelling and controlling a human life that a demon is able to fulfill Satan's evil purposes. This is why casting the demon out is not enough. Follow up counseling and ministry is necessary. The person should be immersed in the Word of God and prayer and become part of the Church, receiving the Sacraments as often as absolutely possible.

---

1. When you minister to a person experiencing demonic activity, you will almost always encounter a variety of elements that may be keys in keeping the person in spiritual turmoil. There are often unresolved hurts, spiritual issues, etc. that need to be addressed. Balanced pastoral counseling involves much more than simply praying the ritual of exorcism.
2. The first step in preternatural counseling is investigation of all claims. What we do in this process is determine whether the person is really in need of exorcism on either a personal or property level, or if there are other plausible reasons for the perceived phenomenon. This is a vital step that saves a lot of time and helps ensure that the clients physical, emotional, psychological, and spiritual needs are met. If you enter into a case with the preconceived notion that the person is in need of exorcism

you may add very dangerous imagery to potential psychological issues which may be the real cause. You also leave yourself open to litigation and can waste precious time and resources. Before a person is permitted to even undergo exorcism, they must meet the following requirements:

a. **They must be a Christian-** If they are not, then it is extremely difficult to exorcize a demonic entity. How can there be an effective exorcism without the confession forgiveness of sins, or without the baptism and confirmation of Christ's Church? It is vital that the person be baptized, confirmed, and make a confession before you can effectively pray the ritual of exorcism on their behalf. Exorcism is geared towards the Church Militant (Christians faithful to the historic Catholic faith).

b. **They must be willing to give up all areas of sin-** Example: If a client enjoys pornography and is unwilling to give it up, then it will be nearly impossible to cast out a demon that may be oppressing them with obsessive thoughts and diabolic temptation regarding sexual perversions without it coming right back. Please understand that it is possible to enjoy pornography or feel attracted to it, and yet be willing to let go of it at the same time. They must be willing to destroy these strongholds in order to receive and maintain their freedom the demonic. Furthermore, and this is very important; they must be willing to communicate about their past openly with you as their exorcist. It is important that you, as an exorcist, are aware of the areas of sin in their life, and the underlying roots of those sins. If they choose to hide something from you, it may very well keep you from being able to effectively exorcize the demonic entity.

3. They must be willing to convert to the Faith and enter the life of the Church Militant- This often involves taking catechism lessons, being baptized, confirmed, making confession, receiving the Sacraments, reading the writings of the Church Fathers, and daily Sacred Scripture reading and prayer. Doing this is vital to the tearing down of strongholds. They must be serious enough about their relationship with Christ, that they take His Church seriously. Counseling individuals who are not established in the Faith can be more time consuming and burdensome. It is much easier to counsel an individual who is strongly connected to the Church. However, in some cases, having this luxury is not possible, as by the time many desperate individuals come to us, there is little time to do everything we might like.

NOTES AND RESOURCES

INVESTIGATIVE QUESTIONNAIRE

The interview process and questionnaire are meant to be used by knowledgeable exorcists because the reasons for each of these questions is not explained in this questionnaire. A knowledgeable exorcist should know the reasons behind each of these questions. This insight is gained through proper mentorship to an experienced exorcist and through a proper seminary formation.

Part I

1. When did this start?
2. Was there any unusual things that took place (or you did) when this bondage started?
3. If this started when you were a child: Do you have ancestors who have suffered from a similar kind of experience?
4. What kind of experiences are you facing? (Fears, depression, voices in your mind, mental illness, physical illness, mental torment, spiritual torment, etc.. Please be as detailed as possible.)
5. What are all the things that have impacted your life? (Parent's death, trauma, a certain situation that changed your life, anything that 'changed' you.)

Part II

1. Do you have ancestors who have struggled with similar problems or mental illness?
2. Did your bondage start as a child and appear to have no reason to be there?
3. Do you have siblings who suffer from similar problems or oppression?

Part III

1. Have you been involved with extramarital sex? Are you attracted to an ex-lover? Is he or she a good/godly influence for you?
2. Have you been divorced?
3. Do you feel an unusual attraction to a past boyfriend,

girlfriend or lover (who is obviously not right for you)?
4. Do you let anybody dominate, control, or make your choices you?
5. Have you ever formed a blood covenant with another person? (Blood brothers, etc.)
6. Have you ever made vows or agreements with somebody in effort to strengthen the relationship or commit yourself to each other?
7. Do you see any ungodly relationships in your past where gifts were exchanged? (Are you holding onto something that was given to you from somebody you had an adulterous relationship with, etc.)
8. Have you ever had ungodly relations with an animal?
9. Do you have any pictures in your possession of somebody whom you may have an ungodly soul tie with? (A picture of you with somebody you had an adultery with, etc.)

Part IV
1. What do you think of your parents?
2. How would you explain your childhood?
3. Were you close to your parents while growing up? If not, why?
4. How would you explain your relationship with your parents? Was it good, bad or very cold?
5. Did you feel rejection from your parents?
6. Were either of your parents overly passive or controlling?
7. Have either of your parents been divorced? Remarried? Are your parents divorced?
8. How would you describe your relationship with your siblings growing up?

Part V
1. Were your parents married when you were conceived? Were you the right gender? Did your parents not want you, or want you to be different (gender, etc.) in any way? If so, explain.
2. Did you feel rejected as a child? As an adult? If so, by whom? Explain.

3. Did you face abuse? What kind (emotional, physical, sexual, etc.) and by whom?
4. Have you faced rejection from your peers, classmates, friends or those around you?
5. Have you ever been put down, belittled, or made fun of? If so, by whom? Explain.
6. If you have faced rejection or abuse, how did you respond? Do you feel you are still paying a price for it? If so, how?
7. How do you respond to rejection right now?
8. Do you reject yourself ? If so, why and in what ways?

Part VI

1. Is there anybody you feel edgy around? (Don't like them, feel anything in your heart against them, etc.)
2. Do you have anything against anybody? In other words, is there anybody that you have a hard time demonstrating the love of Christ to?
3. Has anybody wronged you that you haven't forgiven from your heart (thoughts, feelings, emotions, etc.)?
4. How do your view your siblings, parents, coworkers, etc.? Do you have any hard feelings against them?
5. Do you make a habit of blaming yourself for everything? Do you obsess over your mistakes and feel unusually guilty for them?
6. Do you deeply regret things that you've done in your past? Could you kick yourself over something you've done in your past? If so, explain.

Part VII

1. Are you a very positive or negative person?
2. Do you feel confident? If so, why?
3. Do you have a low self esteem? If so, why?
4. Are you domineering or controlling? If so, to whom, and in what ways? Why?
5. Are you an achiever? If so, in what ways?
6. Do you feel that you are always right and that if everybody did everything your way, this world would be a better place to live?

7. How do you treat your children? Husband? Are you controlling, passive, etc.?
8. Do you like people to 'look at you' (as in receive attention)?

Part VIII

1. Do you strive to feel accepted? If so, how does this affect your lifestyle? By whom do you want to feel accepted?
2. Are you always stressed out? If so, why?
3. Do you feel hurt? If so, by whom/what and why?
4. Do you feel good about yourself? If not, why?
5. Do you feel depressed? If so, why? When did it start? Did your parents or grandparents struggle with depression? If so, then do you know when it started and why? Do you have siblings who are also struggling? Do you feel your depression is rational or irrational?
6. Do you struggle with fears? If so, what is it that you fear? (Fear of heights, dying, being hopeless, failure, never marrying, etc.)
7. Do you worry about things? What things do you worry about? Why?
8. Do you struggle with anger? Do you have a short temper?
9. Do you have any insecurities? If so, explain.
10. Do you feel any self-pity or feel sorry for yourself? Have you ever felt this? If so, why?
11. Do you find it easy to hate people? If so, over what kinds of things would a person have to do to make you hate them?
12. Do you have any irrational feelings? If so, what are they?
13. Do you feel like something is wrong with you?
14. Do you feel excessively guilty over anything? Is this a continual problem?
15. Are you very confused and forgetful? (Beyond the normal)
16. Are you aware of any emotional wounds that have affected you?
17. Have you ever been deeply embarrassed over something? What was it?
18. Have you been in or are currently experiencing very difficult (depressing) circumstances which may cause you to feel hopeless or depressed?

Part IX

1. How do you explain your relationship with God?
2. Do you feel you aren't good enough to meet His standards?
3. Do you see Him as a loving father, or a dictator?
4. Do you believe that it's only by the Blood of Jesus that your sins are forgiven? Or do you feel you need to earn your forgiveness in any way?
5. Do you feel God's love in your life?
6. Do you feel like your sins are forgiven? Or do you feel guilty?
7. Do you feel excessively guilty in everyday life?
8. Do you feel that doing good things, you earn God's love and acceptance?
9. Do you feel that God is angry or upset with you?

Part X

1. Have you ever spoken something negative about yourself that has came to pass?
2. Have your parents, or those in authority over you spoken a curse over you?
3. Have you ever made a vow out of anger? If so, what?
4. Have you ever wished to die? Have you ever said it?
5. If you have made any vows or oaths, what are they?

Part XI

1. Do you have many friends? What kind of people are they?
2. Do you have a hard time trying to meet new people or make friends?
3. Are you socially outgoing or shy? If so, why?
4. How would you define your relationship with your spouse?

Part XII

1. Have you ever had immoral sexual relations? What kind? (Fornication, adultery, sodomy, bestiality, with a child, etc.)
2. Have you struggled with lust, fantasy or unholy sexual thoughts? If so, what kind?
3. Have you been attracted to pornography?

4. Do you have homosexual thoughts and desires? If so, have you acted upon those feelings?
5. How do you feel about your sexuality? (Do you feel dirty about it, or do you feel it's a wonderful blessing that God's given you?)
6. Do you withhold sex from your spouse or are you fidgety? Do you enjoy a healthy relationship with your spouse sexually? How does he or she react?
7. Have you ever been raped or sexually abused?
8. Have you ever woke up and felt a sexual presence with you?
9. Do you struggle or have you struggled with masturbation?
10. Do you struggle or have you struggled with any other sexual related thoughts, desires, or fetishes?
11. Is there anything sexually that you are ashamed of?

Part XIII

1. Do you have any addictions? If so, what kind?
(Drugs, alcohol, smoking, eating, sex, TV, etc.) When did they start?
2. Did anybody else in your family (siblings, ancestors, etc.) have a struggle with any addictions? If so, what? Who?
3. Have you ever had, or currently have any sort of obsession over anything? If so,what?

Part XIV

1. Have you ever been involved with any false religions? If so, why, when and how long? How do you feel about those beliefs now?
2. Have you ever been involved in any secret societies such as Freemasonry? If so, how deep were you involved?

Part XV

1. Have you ever shown interest in the occult? If so, in what ways? (Read up on it, dabbled in it, etc.)
2. Do you still feel drawn or attracted to the occult?
3. Have you had any interest in horror or thriller style movies or novels? Are you still attracted to these things?
4. Have you ever made a vow with the devil? If so, what?

5. Married Satan?
6. Worship a demon or Satan?
7. Have you ever put a curse or spell on somebody?
8. Are you aware of any curses or spells placed on you? If so, what? Who did it?
9. Dabbled with an Ouija board? If so, why?
10. Ever been a member of a coven? Explain.
11. Communicated with the dead? Explain.
12. Told somebody's fortune or went to see a psychic? Explain.
13. Ever read your horoscope?
14. Watched or been involved in a séance? Explain.
15. Been involved in New Age teachings? Explain.
16. Been initiated in a false religion? If so, what were you initiated into? When?
17. Have you ever had a spirit guide?
18. Have you ever been involved with meditation, yoga, reiki, or related activities?
19. Were you or anybody in your family superstitious? If so, who?
20. Ever been involved in astral travel? (Out of body)
21. If you have made any vows or oaths, what are they? Were there any sacrifices or rituals that was accompanied with them?
22. Have you ever made a blood pact before? If so, with whom (including persons, demons and Satan) and for what purpose?
23. Have you ever partaken in automatic writing, automatic drawing or automatic painting?
25. Any other involvement in the occult? Explain.

Part XVI

1. Are there any unconfessed sins? (Usually something you've done, that you know is wrong, but won't admit to it. An abortion, stealing, etc. are some examples.)
2. Is there anything you've been hiding inside that you haven't confessed?
3. Do you feel excessively guilty over some thing(s) you've done in the past? If so, what?

Part XVII

1. Do you have any idols, occult objects, or anything that could hold evil spiritual value in your home? If so, what? Any objects that hold evil spiritual value must be destroyed.
2. Do you have any gifts saved from sinful relationships? If so, explain. For example, if a man gives a woman a personal gift during an adultery, that needs to be sold or destroyed.

Part XVIII

1. Have you ever been exposed to extreme abuse or a traumatic experience? Did it have a drastic effect on your emotional or mental system? If so, what happen? How did it affect you?
2. Have you ever been diagnosed with Dissociative Identity Disorder (DID)?
3. Are you aware of any alters (other personalities) that you may have? (If so, tell me about them)
4. Do you have a memory gap where you cannot remember a certain time of your life?
5. Do you have false memories of things that really didn't take place?
6. Have you ever been in a car accident or other traumatic situation? Have you ever witnessed a tragedy in real life?
7. Do you feel you were abducted by "aliens"? Explain.

Part XIX

1. Do you struggle with any habitual sins? If so, what? Do you want to break those bad habits?
2. Do you struggle with any weaknesses such as lust, anger, hate, etc.? If so, what? Do you know where they came from or how they got started?

Part XX

1. Have you ever said something along the lines of, "I will never have children"?
2. Have you ever had an abortion or attempted one?
3. Have you ever had incest or ungodly sexual relations with somebody related to you? (See Leviticus 20:19-21,

as this can cause a curse to land upon you which needs to be broken)

Part XXI

1. Have you ever tried drugs? If so, how much, and how did it affect you? Why did you try drugs?
2. Have you ever thought about or attempted suicide?
3. Do you have any physical or mental disabilities, diseases or illnesses? Explain.
4. Do you want, and are willing to be delivered? Are you willing to make some lifestyle changes in order to be delivered?
5. Do you experience unusual confusion settle upon you as you try to pray, attend Mass, and read the Bible?
6. What kind of music do you like? (Please list all styles of music you currently enjoy, and give examples in each category you list, such as some names of artists and songs)
7. Have you previously enjoyed hard rock, metal, acid, alternative, rap, new age, or any other kind of worldly music? (Please provide some examples of artists and songs from each genre (type/style) of music you list)
8. Have you had any nightmares or weird experiences at night while supposedly sleeping?
9. Have you ever been in a trance or had an out of body experience?
10. Have you ever noticed time slipped right out from under you? For example, you look at your watch and it's 7:00pm, then you look again what seemed like 15 minutes later and it's 2:00am. This is a sign of a trance.
11. Have you ever touched or kissed a dead body? If so, explain whom and why and what happened afterward.
12. Do you feel that you somehow have to earn your forgiveness? Do you 'wonder' if your sins are truly forgiven -- all of them?
13. Do you have any physical infirmities, sickness or diseases? If so, please list them.
14. Are you on any medications? If so, please explain.
15. Have you ever had any other kind of weird encounter with

the spiritual realm?

Examination of Conscience

It may be helpful to go over a formal examination of conscience with the victim prior to or immediately after the series of questions. Often such an examination of conscience will help them recall things forgotten. An example of such an examination is as follows.

EXAMINATION OF CONSCIENCE WITH THE TEN COMMANDMENTS OF GOD

FIRST COMMANDMENT: I AM THE LORD THY GOD; THOU SHALT NOT HAVE STRANGE GODS BEFORE ME.

Sins contrary to the First Commandment are the following: neglect of prayer; ingratitude toward God; spiritual sloth; hatred of God or of the Church; tempting God (explicitly or implicitly, e.g. by exposing one's self to danger of soul, life, or health without grave cause); not behaving reverently when in church (e.g. not genuflecting to the Blessed Sacrament when entering or leaving the church, etc.); excessive attraction to things/creatures (e.g. over-affection to animals, sports fanatic, having movie star /music/TV idols, love for money, pleasure or power); idolatry (worshiping false gods such as giving honor to a creature in place of God (e.g. Satan, science, ancestors, country); superstition (ascribing powers to a created thing which it does not have); hypnotism (without sufficient cause); divination (communication with Satan, demons, the dead or other false practices in order to discover the unknown, consulting horoscopes, astrology, palm reading, fortune telling); attaching undue importance to dreams, omens or lots; all practices of magic or sorcery (e.g. witchcraft, voodoo); wearing charms; playing with Ouija boards or rotating tables; spiritism (talking with the spirits); sacrilege (profaning or treating unworthily the Sacraments, especially the Holy Eucharist, and other liturgical actions, as well as religious persons, blessed things such as sacred vessels or statues, or places consecrated to God); sacrilege by receiving a sacrament, especially the Holy Eucharist, in the state of mortal sin; simony (buying or selling of spiritual things); profane or superstitious use of blessed objects (sometimes done in order to remain in sin); practical materialism (one believes he needs and desires only material things); atheistic humanism (falsely considers man to be an end in himself, and the sole maker with supreme control of his own history); atheism in general (rejects, denies or doubts the existence of God, either in theory or practice, i.e. ignoring Him in the daily living of our lives); agnosticism (postulates the existence of a transcendent being which is incapable of revealing itself, and about which nothing can be said or makes no judgment about God's existence declaring it impossible to prove or even to affirm or deny).

Sins against Faith:

Willful doubt of any article of faith; deliberate ignorance of the truths of faith which ought to be known; neglect of instructing oneself in the faith according to one's state in life; rash credulity (e.g. giving credence to private revelation too easily or believing in a private revelations which has been condemned by the lawful Church authorities); apostasy; heresy; indifferentism (to believe that one religion is as good as another, and that all religions are equally true and pleasing to God, or that one is free to accept or reject any or all religions); reading or circulating books or writings against the Christian Faith or practice in such wise as to jeopardize one's faith; to remain silent when asked about one's faith; engaging is schismatic or heretical worship; joining or supporting masonic groups or other forbidden societies.

Sins against Hope:

Despair of God's mercy (to give up all hope of salvation, and the means necessary to be saved) or want of confidence in the power of His Grace to support us in trouble or temptation; no desire to possess eternal happiness in heaven or after this earthly life; presumption (to hope for salvation without help from God or to assume God's forgiveness without conversion, or to hope to obtain heavenly glory without merit); presuming on God's mercy or on the supposed efficacy of certain pious practices, in order to continue in sin; refusing any dependence on God.

Sins against Charity:
Not making an act of charity at regular intervals during life especially during times of necessity; egoism (one cares only about himself, praises himself, selfish, enjoys receiving praise) willfully rebellious thoughts against God; boasting of sin; violating God's law, or omitting good works through human respect.

SECOND COMMANDMENT: THOU SHALT NOT TAKE THE NAME OF THE LORD THY GOD IN VAIN

Sins contrary to the Second Commandment:
Dishonoring of God by profane or disrespectful use of the Name of God, or of the Holy Name of Jesus Christ; blasphemy (speech or gestures that have contempt for or insult to God, Jesus Christ, and the Church; perjury (to promise something under oath with no intention of keeping it, or breaking a promise made under oath); taking false or unnecessary oaths (to call on God to be witness to a lie); breaking vows or promises to God; talking during Liturgical worship and in a Church without sufficient reason or to the distraction of others.

THIRD COMMANDMENT: REMEMBER THAT THOU SHALT KEEP HOLY THE LORD'S DAY

Sins contrary to the Third Commandment:
Omission of prayer and divine worship, all unnecessary servile work, and whatever hinders the keeping of the Lord's

Day holy; engaging in unnecessary commerce, i.e. buying and selling on Sundays and Holy Days.

FOURTH COMMANDMENT
HONOR THY FATHER AND THY MOTHER

Sins contrary to the Fourth Commandment:
For Parents: Hating their children; cursing them; giving scandal to them by cursing, drinking, etc.; allowing them to grow up in ignorance, idleness or sin; showing habitual partiality without cause; deferring a child's baptism; neglecting to watch over their bodily health, their religious instruction, the company they keep, the books they read, etc.; failing to correct them when needful; being harsh or cruel in correction; sending children to non-Christian and other dangerous schools; neglect of directing them to attend Church on Sundays and Holy Days and to frequent reception of the Sacraments.

For Children: All manner of anger or hatred against parents and other lawful superiors; provoking them to anger; grieving them; insulting them; neglecting them in their necessity; contempt or disobedience to their lawful commands.

Husbands and wives: Ill-usage (i.e. using them without consideration for their own welfare and without regard to charity); putting obstacles to the fulfillment of religious duties; want of gentleness and consideration in regard to each other's faults; unreasonable jealousy; neglect of household duties; sulkiness; injurious words; neglect of attempting to secure means of supporting the family due to laziness or timidity.

For Employers: Not allowing one's employees reasonable time for religious duties and instruction; giving bad example to them or allowing others to do so; withholding their lawful wages; not caring for them in sickness; dismissing them arbitrarily and without cause; imposing unreasonable policies.

For Employees: Disrespect to employers; want of obedience in matters wherein one has bound oneself to obey (e.g. by fulfilling a contract); waste of time; neglect of work; waste of employer's property by dishonesty, carelessness or neglect; violating company policies without sufficient reason.

For Professionals and Civil Servants: Culpable lack of the knowledge relating to duties of office or profession; neglect in discharging those duties; injustice or partiality; exorbitant fees (this sin may also be included under the Seventh Commandment).

For Teachers: Neglecting the progress of those confided to their care; unjust, indiscreet or excessive punishment; partiality; bad example; loose or false maxims (i.e. teaching them things which are untrue as being true) giving in to idle distractions (e.g. partying and undue recreating)

For All: Contempt for the laws of State and country as well as of the Church; disobedience to lawful authority; breaking of civil laws.

FIFTH COMMANDMENT
THOU SHALT NOT KILL

Sins against the Fifth commandment include:
Murder; performing an abortion; having an abortion, aiding in someone procuring an abortion (the penitent should know that having, causing or aiding in an abortion causing one to be excommunicated); euthanasia; withholding ordinary means to a dying or terminally ill patient; suicide; attempts of suicide, serious thoughts about committing suicide; fighting; quarreling anger; hatred; desires of revenge; human torture; gluttony (excessive eating or drinking); drunkenness; abuse of alcohol, medicine or drugs; endangering other people's lives (e.g. by drinking and driving, by driving too fast, etc.); risking

one's own life or limb without a sufficient reason (e.g. daredevil stunts, Russian roulette, etc.); carelessness in leaving about poisons, dangerous drugs, weapons, etc.; mutilation of the body, such as castration, vasectomy, tubal ligation, hysterectomy (without sufficient medical cause); immoral scientific research and its applications; bad example or scandal; disrespect for the dying or the dead; not trying to avoid war; showing aversion or contempt for others; refusing to speak to them when addressed; ignoring offers of reconciliation especially between relatives; cherishing an unforgiving spirit; raillery and ridicule; insults; irritating words and actions; sadness at another's prosperity; rejoicing over another's misfortune; envy at attention shown to others; tyrannical behavior; inducing others to sin by word or example; injury to health by over-indulgence; giving drink to others knowing they will abuse it; taking contraceptive pills which may or may not be an abortifacient; use of prophylactic or barrier methods to avoid pregnancy; using licit means of avoiding conception while fostering a contraceptive mentality; direct sterilization; causing unnecessary suffering or death to animals.

SIXTH COMMANDMENT
THOU SHALT NOT COMMIT ADULTERY

Sins against the Sixth Commandment are the following:
Impurity and immodesty in words, looks, and actions, whether alone or with others, telling and listening to dirty jokes; wearing immodest clothing; buying, renting or watching indecent movies, television or books (pornography as well as books which contain impurity); masturbation; fornication (sometimes called premarital sex); prostitution; sodomy (homosexual practices); adultery; divorce; polygamy; incest; sexual abuse; rape; prolonged and sensual kissing; petting or foreplay outside the context of marriage and within the context of marriage not ordering foreplay to the consummation of the natural conjugal act; immodest dancing; dating without taking the necessary precautions to safeguard

purity or one's faith.

SEVENTH COMMANDMENT
THOU SHALT NOT STEAL

Sins against the Seventh Commandment are:
Stealing; petty thefts (e.g. taking things from one's place of employment to which one is not entitled or taking money from a family member without his permission); cheating; plagiarizing; breaking copyright regulations, (e.g. photocopying without permission); keeping borrowed or lost objects without making a reasonable attempt to restore the other's property; possession of ill-gotten goods; counseling or commanding someone to do injury to another person or to his goods; careless or malicious injury to the property of others; concealment of fraud, theft or damage when in duty bound to give the information; tax evasion by not paying just taxes; business fraud; dishonesty in politics, business, etc.; not paying just debts at scheduled time and neglecting to make reasonable efforts and sacrifices in this matter, e.g. by gradually laying up the amount required; not making reparation or compensation to someone suffering from unjust damages; forcing up prices by taking advantage of the ignorance or hardship of another; usury (lending money at high interest rates to someone in financial difficulty); speculation in which one contrives to manipulate the price of goods artificially in order to gain an advantage to the detriment of others; corruption in which one influence the judgment of those who must decide in legal matters; accepting bribes; appropriation and use for private purposes of the common goods of an enterprise; work poorly done; paying unjust wages or defrauding an employee of due benefits; forgery of checks and invoices; bouncing checks knowing that there is not enough funds to cover them; excessive expenses and waste; not keeping promises or contract agreements (if the commitments were morally just); gambling and betting (if they deprive someone of basic living needs for himself or others); excessive unnecessary waste of goods, resources, money or funds.

EIGHTH COMMANDMENT
THOU SHALT NOT BEAR FALSE WITNESS AGAINST THY NEIGHBOR

Sins contrary to the Eighth Commandment are:
Lying; boasting; bragging; flattery; hypocrisy; exaggerating; irony; sarcasm; unjust injury to another's good name either by revealing true and hidden faults (detraction); telling false defects (slander or calumny), talebearing, or spreading rumors; to criticize others, to listen with pleasure to others being criticized; gossiping; unjustly dishonoring another person in his presence (contumely); rash judgment (firmly believing, without sufficient reason, that someone has some moral defect); revealing secrets; publishing discreditable secrets about others, even if true; refusing or delaying to restore the good name one has blackened; baseless accusations; groundless suspicions; rash judgments of others in our own mind.

NINTH COMMANDMENT
THOU SHALT NOT COVET THY NEIGHBOR'S WIFE

The Ninth Commandment forbids all those impure thoughts and desires which we take deliberate pleasure in so thinking, or we willingly consent to it whenever these unchaste thoughts or passions come into our mind. The penitent should keep in mind that any sin listed under the sixth commandment in which one willing or deliberately entertains may have the same degree of gravity, i.e. either mortal or venial sin.

TENTH COMMANDMENT
THOU SHALT NOT COVET THY NEIGHBOR'S GOODS

The Tenth Commandment forbids the following:
Envy (desire another goods); jealousy (a zealous vigilance in keeping a good enjoyed by oneself from others); greed and the desire to have material goods without limit (avarice); the desire to become rich at all costs; businesses or professions who hope for unfavorable circumstances for others so that they may personally

profit from it; envious of someone else's success, talents, temporal or spiritual goods; the desire to commit injustice by harming someone in order to get his temporal goods.

FAQ

What are some of the signs of a possessed house?
There are many signs we can look for in a possessed home or building. Some of the things a person can look for are doors slamming when nobody is there, strange noises, reputation for calamities (people being pushed down stairs, finances always being drained, etc.), the air seems heavy (making it harder to breathe), animals acting fearful or weird (dogs barking like mad for no reason), and so forth. Often somebody with spiritual discernment will often pick up on a spiritual presence that doesn't feel right. It's not uncommon to visit a home and pick up on demonic presence before even finding out that there was demonic activity that's taken place there. I've picked up on something demonic before even entering a home before by just standing on the property discerning an unclean presence.

How do homes and land become demonically inhabited?
Sins of the inhabitants or previous inhabitants is the usual way, though not the only way. If things such as seances, voodoo, adultery, or incest have been practiced in a home, then demonic spirits may inhabit there. Sacred Scripture tells us that the deeds of its inhabitants can defile even the land on which it is practiced:

Leviticus 18:24-25,27, "Defile not ye yourselves in any of these things: for in all these the nations are defiled which I cast out before you: And the land is defiled: therefore I do visit the iniquity thereof upon it, and the land itself vomiteth out her inhabitants... (For all these abominations have the men of the land done, which [were] before you, and the land is defiled;)"

Jeremiah 3:9, "And it came to pass through the lightness of her whoredom, that she defiled the land, and committed adultery with stones and with stocks."

Ezekiel 36:17, "Son of man, when the house of Israel dwelt in their own land, they defiled it by their own way and by their doings: their way was before me as the uncleanness of a removed woman."

Jeremiah 2:7, "And I brought you into a plentiful country, to eat the fruit thereof and the goodness thereof; but when ye entered, ye defiled my land, and made mine heritage an abomination."

How do you exorcize a home or land?

The first step to exorcizing a home, building, or property, is to dispose of any occult items. If there are occult books, Ouija boards, crystal balls, new age items, dream catchers or other items on the premises they must be removed and burned. The next step is to go through each room, praying the ritual of exorcism and blessing each room, dedicating it to the Lord. Just remember that you, as an exorcist, have the authority needed to drive those spirits out. Also keeo in mind that while exorcism can be a one-time event, it can also be a process. Many times it takes multiple sessions before a person or place is completely freed of demonic influence. Sessions can last up to several hours, depending on the response of the demons.

AN EASTERN CATHOLIC RITUAL OF EXORCISM

INTRODUCTORY REMARKS

The exorcist should wear an alb and a purple stole during the prayers of the ritual of exorcism. After making the sign of the cross over the victim, place the ends of the stole on this person's neck. One may have two normal sized stoles sewn together in order to have a very long stole to extend from the priest to the victim's neck. It is truly amazing how the blessed stole calms and controls the possessed person. Certainly one initially may encounter violent reactions, but that is to be expected. The stole not only symbolizes, but demonstrates the power of the priesthood. Jesus binds the evil spirits with the use of this sacramental. The priest should also place his right hand on the head of the victim. Of course, the imposition of hands was used by Jesus to heal the sick. The church imitates this use in the Sacrament of the Sick and in other ways. Christ blessed children in this way. It has been noted by many individuals that hands of the priest's calm or burn them. If an assistant priest is present, they also may place hands on the person's head. A Bible containing both the Old and New Testaments should be on hand when questioning and commanding the demons to respond. After invoking the Holy Spirit, there is surprising response and confirmation, which are keys to opening up and freeing the person. The Rite of Exorcism uses passages from John 1:1-14; Mark 16:15-18; Luke 1:17-20; Luke 11:14-22; also use what ever passage the Holy Spirit inspires. This can hasten along deliverance and yield many crucial answers to the puzzle. Although the Blessed Sacrament is the Body and Blood of Jesus, True God and True Man, and not any mere sacramental, it is an excellent practice to use it to bless the sick and possessed. The Blessed Sacrament should not be placed on the head or any other part of the body of the possessed persons, due to the possibility of desecration. This rule or admonition need not apply in those cases where there is no danger or irreverence, that is cases in which the person's actions are nonviolent. It is truly astounding to observe how many days (when proper use of the Blessed Sacrament is applied to the body of the possessed), can be taken off the whole length of time needed to dislodge the demons. It shortens the process. It may be wise in other cases for the priest himself to carry around his neck the Blessed Sacrament in a Pyx. This may prove at times, necessary for protection. Then there is the crucifix, which should always be present. The victim will often stare at the cross and be forced to look away. The cross is symbolic of the defeat of Satan through the death of Christ. The long prayer for Solemn Blessing of the Crucifix, "Ut quóties triúmphum divínae humnilitátis, quae supérbiam nostri hostis dejecit" and (how often the divine humility has triumphed casting out the pride of our enemy). "Dignáre respícere, bene + dícere et Sancti + ficáre hanc creaturm incensi, ut omnes languores, omnesque imfirmitates, atque insidiar inimici, odorem ejus sentientes, efffugiant, et separatur a plasmate tuo; ut num quam lædatur amorsu antiqui serpentes" (Deign to care for bless and sanctify those being inflamed by passion and weakness, any sickness, deceits of the foe and suspicious resentments felt by them. Be cast out and driven away from your creature) and "Numquam lædatur a morsu antiqui derpentis" (Never to be hurt by the bite of the ancient serpent).

Basic Rules

The priest who with the particular and explicit permission of his Bishop is about to exorcise those tormented by a demonic entity, must have the necessary piety, prudence and personal integrity. He should perform this most heroic work humbly and courageously, not relying on his own strength, but on the power of God; and he must have no greed for material benefit. Besides, he should be of mature age and be respected as a virtuous person.

Let the exorcist note for himself the tricks and deceits which evil spirits use in order to lead him astray. For they are accustomed to answering falsely. They manifest themselves only under pressure--in the hope that the exorcist will get tired and desist from pressuring them. Or they make it appear that the subject of Exorcism is not possessed at all. Sometimes, a demon betrays its presence, and then goes into hiding. It appears to have left the body of the possessed free from all molestation, so that the possessed thinks he is completely rid of it. But the exorcist should not, for all that, desist until he sees the signs of liberation. The Exorcist must remember, therefore, that Our Lord said there is a species of Evil Spirit which cannot be expelled except by prayer and fasting. Let him make sure that he and others follow the example of the Holy Fathers and make use of these two principal means of obtaining divine help and of repelling Evil Spirit.

During Exorcism, the exorcist should use the words of the Bible rather than his own or somebody else's. Also, he should command Evil Spirit to state whether it is kept within the possessed because of some magical spell or sorcerer's symbol or some occult documents. For the exorcism to succeed, the possessed must surrender them. If he has swallowed something like that, he will vomit it up. If it is outside his body in some place or other, Evil Spirit must tell the exorcist where it is. When the exorcist finds it, he must burn it. In order for Satan to be driven out of the possessed, the exorcist must be humble. He must rely on God and only God for his answers and direction. Sometimes God forces the demon inside the possessed to reveal truths. However, the exorcist must be careful not to believe all that the demon possessing the victim might say. The demon will reveal exactly what the exorcist wants to hear even though it is not the truth, in order to side track him. The exorcist, out of his own curiosity, should not ask questions to the possessed regarding matters other than the exorcism at hand. Only through much prayer, fasting and humility of the exorcist along with the willingness of the victim, and of course, the grace and Will of God, can one be freed of this affliction.

THE RITUAL OF EXORCISM OF A PERSON
INVOCATION

The invocations are recited by the exorcist; the responses by all.

Exorcist: Lord, have mercy.
All: Lord, have mercy.
E: Christ, have mercy.
All: Christ, have mercy.
E: Lord, have mercy.
All: Lord, have mercy.
E: Christ, hear us.
All: Christ, graciously hear us.
E: God, the Father in heaven.
All: Have mercy on us.
E: God, the Son, Redeemer of the world.
All: Have mercy on us.
E: God, the Holy Spirit.
All: Have mercy on us.
E: Holy Trinity, one God.
All: Have mercy on us.
(After each invocation, "Intercede for us.")
E: We ask you Almighty Father to send the
Holy Angels to surround us, to bless us, protect us, and to assist us in battle against the Adversary.
All: Intercede for us.
E: We ask Almighty Father for strength,
resolve and annointing in this task of delivering your creation from the tortures of the Adversary.
All: Intercede for us.

**** After each invocation: "Deliver us, 0 Lord."***

Exorcist: From all sin,
From your wrath,
From sudden and unprovided death,
From the snares of the Devil,

From anger, hatred, and all ill will,
From all lewdness,
From lightning and tempest,
From the scourge of earthquakes,
From plague, famine, and war,
From everlasting death,
By the mystery of your holy incarnation,
By your coming,
By your birth,
By your baptism and holy fasting,
By your cross and passion,
By your death and burial,
By your holy resurrection,
By your wondrous ascension,
By the coming of the Holy Spirit, the Advocate,
On the day of judgment,
Exorcist: We sinners,
All: We beg you to hear us.

After each invocation: "We beg you to hear us."

That you spare us,
That you pardon us,
That you bring us to true penance,
That you govern and preserve your holy Church,
That you preserve our Holy Father and all ranks in the Church in holy religion,
That you humble the enemies of Your holy Church,
That you give peace and true concord to all Christian rulers.
That you give peace and unity to the whole Christian world,
That you restore to the unity of the Church all who have strayed from the truth, and lead all unbelievers to the light of the Gospel,
That you confirm and preserve us in your holy service,
That you lift up our minds to heavenly desires,
That you grant everlasting blessings to all our benefactors,
That you deliver our souls and the souls of our brethren, relatives, and benefactors from everlasting damnation,

That you give and preserve the fruits of the earth,
That you grant eternal rest to all the faithful departed,
That you graciously hear us, Son of God,

Antiphon
Exorcist: Do not keep in mind, 0 Lord, our offenses or those of our parents, nor take vengeance on our sins.

E: Our Father, who art in heaven, hallowed be thy name. Thy kingdom come, thy will be done, on earth as it is in heaven. Give us this day our daily bread, and forgive us our trespasses, as we forgive those who trespass againts us. And lead us not into temptation.
All: But deliver us from evil. Amen.

Psalm 53
Exorcist: God, by your name save me, and by your might defend my cause.
All: God, hear my prayer; hearken to the words of my mouth.
E: For haughty men have risen up against me, and fierce men seek my life; they set not God before their eyes.
All: See, God is my helper; the Lord sustains my life.
E: Turn back the evil upon my foes; in your faithfulness destroy them.
All: Freely will I offer you sacrifice; I will praise your name, Lord, for its goodness,
E: Because from all distress you have rescued me, and my eyes look down upon my enemies.
All: Glory be to the Father, to the Son, and to the Holy Spirit; as it was in the beginning, is now and ever shall be, world without end. Amen.
E: Save your servant.
All: Who trusts in you, my God.
E: Let him (her) find in you, Lord, a fortified tower.
All: In the face of the enemy.
E: Let the enemy have no power over him (her).
All: And the son of iniquity be powerless to harm him (her).
E: Lord, send him (her) aid from your holy place.

All: And watch over him (her) from Sion.
E: Lord, heed my prayer.
All: And let my cry be heard by you.
E: The Lord be with you.
All: May He also be with you.
E: Let us pray.
God, whose nature is ever merciful and forgiving, accept our prayer that this servant of yours, bound by the fetters of sin, may be pardoned by your loving kindness. Holy Lord, almighty Father, everlasting God and Father of our Lord Jesus Christ, who once and for all consigned that fallen and apostate tyrant to the flames of hell, who sent your only-begotten Son into the world to crush that roaring lion; hasten to our call for help and snatch from ruination and from the clutches of the noonday devil this human being made in your image and likeness. Strike terror, Lord, into the beast now laying waste your vineyard. Fill your servants with courage to fight manfully against that reprobate dragon, lest he despise those who put their trust in you, and say with Pharaoh of old: "I know not God, nor will I set Israel free." Let your mighty hand cast him out of your servant, **N.**, (SIGN OF THE CROSS) so he may no longer hold captive this person whom it pleased you to make in your image, and to redeem through your Son; who lives and reigns with you, in the unity of the Holy Spirit, God, forever and ever.
All: Amen.

The Exorcist commands the demon as follows:
I command you, unclean spirit, whoever you are, along with all your minions now attacking this servant of God, be they demons, Nephilim, Watchers, or unclean spirits, by the mysteries of the incarnation, passion, resurrection, and ascension of our Lord Jesus Christ, by the descent of the Holy Spirit, by the coming of our Lord for judgment, that you tell me by some sign your name, and the day and hour of your departure. I command you, moreover, to obey me to the letter, I who am a priest of God despite my unworthiness; nor shall you be emboldened to harm in any way this creature of God,

or the bystanders, or any of their possessions.

The exorcist lays his hand on the head of the sick person, saying:
They shall lay their hands upon the sick and all will be well with them. May Jesus, Son of Mary, Lord and Savior of the world, show you favor and mercy.
All: Amen.

Next he reads over the possessed person these selections from the Gospel.

E: The Lord be with you.
All: May He also be with you.
E: The beginning of the holy Gospel according to St. John.
All: Glory be to you, 0 Lord.

A Lesson from the holy Gospel according to St. John
John 1.1-14

As he says these opening words he signs himself and the possessed with the SIGN OF THE CROSS on the brow, lips, and breast.

When time began, the Word was there, and the Word was face to face with God, and the Word was God. This Word, when time began, was face to face with God. All things came into being through Him, and without Him there came to be not one thing that has come to be. In Him was life, and the life was the light of men. The light shines in the darkness, and the darkness did not lay hold of it. There came upon the scene a man, a messenger from God, whose name was John. This man came to give testimony to testify in behalf of the light that all might believe through him. He was not himself the light; he only was to testify in behalf of the light. Meanwhile the true light, which illumines every man, was making its entrance into the world. He was in the world, and the world came to be through Him, and the world did not acknowledge Him. He

came into His home, and His own people did not welcome Him. But to as many as welcomed Him He gave the power to become children of God those who believe in His name; who were born not of blood, or of carnal desire, or of man's will; no, they were born of God. (Genuflect here.) And the Word became man and lived among us; and we have looked upon His glory such a glory as befits the Father's only-begotten Son full of grace and truth!
All: Thanks be to God.

Lastly he blesses the afflicted person, saying:

May the blessing of almighty God, Father, Son, (SIGN OF THE CROSS) and Holy Spirit, come upon you and remain with you forever.
All: Amen.

Then he sprinkles the person with holy water.

A Lesson from the holy Gospel according to St. Mark

Mark 16.15-18
At that time Jesus said to His disciples: "Go into the whole world and preach the Gospel to all creation. He that believes and is baptized will be saved; he that does not believe will be condemned. And in the way of proofs of their claims, the following will accompany those who believe: in my name they will drive out demons; they will speak in new tongues; they will take up serpents in their hands, and if they drink something deadly, it will not hurt them; they will lay their hands on the sick, and these will recover."

A Lesson from the holy Gospel according to St. Luke

Luke 10.17-20
At that time the seventy-two returned in high spirits. "Master," they said, "even the demons are subject to us because we use your name!" "Yes," He said to them, "I was watching Satan fall

like lightning that flashes from heaven. But mind: it is I that have given you the power to tread upon serpents and scorpions, and break the dominion of the enemy everywhere; nothing at all can injure you. Just the same, do not rejoice in the fact that the spirits are subject to you, but rejoice in the fact that your names are engraved in heaven."

A Lesson from the holy Gospel according to St. Luke

Luke 11.14-22
At that time Jesus was driving out a demon, and this particular demon was dumb. The demon was driven out, the dumb man spoke, and the crowds were enraptured. But some among the people remarked: "He is a tool of Beelzebul, and that is how he drives out demons!" Another group, intending to test Him, demanded of Him a proof of His claims, to be shown in the sky. He knew their inmost thoughts. "Any kingdom torn by civil strife," He said to them, "is laid in ruins; and house tumbles upon house. So, too, if Satan is in revolt against himself, how can his kingdom last, since you say that I drive out demons as a tool of Beelzebul. And furthermore: if I drive out demons as a tool of Beelzebul, whose tools are your pupils when they do the driving out? Therefore, judged by them, you must stand condemned. But, if, on the contrary, I drive out demons by the finger of God, then, evidently the kingdom of God has by this time made its way to you. As long as a mighty lord in full armor guards his premises, he is in peaceful possession of his property; but should one mightier than he attack and overcome him, he will strip him of his armor, on which he had relied, and distribute the spoils taken from him."
E: Lord, heed my prayer.
All: And let my cry be heard by you.
E: The Lord be with you.
All: May He also be with you.
E: Let us pray.
Almighty Lord, Word of God the Father, Jesus Christ, God and Lord of all creation; who gave to your holy apostles the power to tramp underfoot serpents and scorpions; who along with

the other mandates to work miracles was pleased to grant them the authority to say: "Depart, you demons!" and by whose might Satan was made to fall from heaven like lightning; I humbly call on your holy name in fear and trembling, asking that you grant me, your unworthy servant, pardon for all my sins, steadfast faith, and the power — supported by your mighty arm — to confront with confidence and resolution this cruel demon. I ask this through you, Jesus Christ, our Lord and God, who are coming to judge both the living and the dead and the world by fire.
All: Amen.

Next he makes the sign of the cross over himself and the one possessed, places the end of the stole on the latter's neck, and, putting his right hand on the latter's head, he says the following filled with confidence and faith:

E: See the cross of the Lord; begone, you hostile powers!
All: The stem of David, the lion of Judah's tribe has conquered.
E: Lord, heed my prayer.
All: And let my cry be heard by you.
E: The Lord be with you.
All: May He also be with you.
E: Let us pray.
God and Father of our Lord Jesus Christ, I appeal to your holy name, humbly begging your kindness, that you graciously grant me help against this and every unclean spirit now tormenting this creature of yours; through Christ our Lord.
All: Amen.

Exorcism

E: I cast you out, unclean spirit, along with every Satanic power of the enemy, every spirit from hell, every demon, unclean spirit, Nephilim, Watcher, and all your fell companions; in the name of our Lord Jesus (SIGN OF THE CROSS) Christ. Begone and stay far from this creature of God. (SIGN OF THE CROSS) For it is He who commands you, He who flung you headlong from the heights of heaven into the depths of hell. It is He who commands you, He who once stilled the sea and the wind and the storm. Hearken, therefore, and tremble in fear, Satan, you enemy of the faith, you foe of the human race, you begetter of death, you robber of life,you corrupter of justice, you root of all evil and vice; seducer of men, betrayer of the nations, instigator of envy, font of avarice, fomenter of discord, author of pain and sorrow. Why, then, do you stand and resist, knowing as you must that Christ the Lord brings your plans to nothing? Fear Him, who in Isaac was offered in sacrifice, in Joseph sold into bondage, slain as the paschal lamb, crucified as man, yet triumphed over the powers of hell.

(The three signs of the cross which follow are traced on the brow of the possessed person).

Begone, then, in the name of the Father, (SIGN OF THE CROSS) and of the Son, (SIGN OF THE CROSS) and of the Holy (SIGN OF THE CROSS) Spirit. Give place to the Holy Spirit by this sign of the holy (SIGN OF THE CROSS) cross of our Lord Jesus Christ, who lives and reigns with the Father and the Holy Spirit, God, forever and ever.
All: Amen.
E: Lord, heed my prayer.
All: And let my cry be heard by you.
E: The Lord be with you.
All: May He also be with you.
E: Let us pray.
God, Creator and defender of the human race, who made man in your own image, look down in pity on this your servant, **N.**, now in the toils of the unclean spirit, now caught up in the fearsome threats of man's ancient enemy, sworn foe of our race, who befuddles and stupefies the human mind, throws it into terror, overwhelms it with fear and panic. Repel, 0 Lord, the Devil's power, break asunder his snares and traps, put the unholy tempter to flight. By the sign (SIGN OF THE CROSS ***on the brow)*** of your name, let your servant be protected in mind and body. ***(The three crosses which follow are traced on the***

breast of the possessed person).

Keep watch over the inmost recesses of his (her) (SIGN OF THE CROSS) heart; rule over his (her) (SIGN OF THE CROSS) emotions; strengthen his (her) (SIGN OF THE CROSS) will. Let vanish from his (her) soul the temptations of the mighty adversary. Graciously grant, 0 Lord, as we call on your holy name, that the evil spirit, who hitherto terrorized over us, may himself retreat in terror and defeat, so that this servant of yours may sincerely and steadfastly render you the service which is your due; through Christ our Lord.

All: Amen

E: I adjure you, ancient serpent, by the judge of the living and the dead, by your Creator, by the Creator of the whole universe, by Him who has the power to consign you to hell, to depart forthwith in fear, along with your savage minions, from this servant of God, **N.**, who seeks refuge in the fold of the Church. I adjure you again, (SIGN OF THE CROSS **on the brow)** not by my weakness but by the might of the Holy Spirit, to depart from this servant of God, **N.** , whom almighty God has made in His image. Yield, therefore, yield not to my own person but to the minister of Christ. For it is the power of Christ that compels you, who brought you low by His cross. Tremble before that mighty arm that broke asunder the dark prison walls and led souls forth to light. May the trembling that afflicts this human frame, (SIGN OF THE CROSS **on the breast)** the fear that afflicts this image (SIGN OF THE CROSS **on the brow)** of God, descend on you. Make no resistance nor delay in departing from this man, for it has pleased Christ to dwell in man. Do not think of despising my command because you know me to be a great sinner. It is God (SIGN OF THE CROSS) himself who commands you; the majestic Christ (SIGN OF THE CROSS) who commands you. God the Father (SIGN OF THE CROSS) commands you; God the Son (SIGN OF THE CROSS) commands you; God the Holy (SIGN OF THE CROSS) Spirit commands you. The mystery of the cross commands (SIGN OF THE CROSS) you. The faith of the holy apostles Peter and Paul and of all the saints commands (SIGN OF THE CROSS) you. The blood of the martyrs commands (SIGN OF

THE CROSS) you. The continence of the confessors commands (SIGN OF THE CROSS) you. The devout prayers of all holy men and women command (SIGN OF THE CROSS) you. The saving mysteries of our Christian faith command (SIGN OF THE CROSS) you. Depart, then, transgressor. Depart, seducer, full of lies and cunning, foe of virtue, persecutor of the innocent. Give place, abominable creature, give way, you monster, give way to Christ, in whom you found none of your works. For He has already stripped you of your powers and laid waste your kingdom, bound you prisoner and plundered your weapons. He has cast you forth into the outer darkness, where everlasting ruin awaits you and your abettors. To what purpose do you insolently resist? To what purpose do you brazenly refuse? For you are guilty before almighty God, whose laws you have transgressed. You are guilty before His Son, our Lord Jesus Christ, whom you presumed to tempt, whom you dared to nail to the cross. You are guilty before the whole human race, to whom you proferred by your enticements the poisoned cup of death. Therefore, I adjure you, profligate dragon, in the name of the spotless (SIGN OF THE CROSS) Lamb, who has trodden down the asp and the basilisk, and overcome the lion and the dragon, to depart from this man (woman) (SIGN OF THE CROSS **on the brow**), to depart from the Church of God (SIGN OF THE CROSS over the intercessors). Tremble and flee, as we call on the name of the Lord, before whom the denizens of hell cower, to whom the heavenly Virtues and Powers and Dominations are subject, whom the Cherubim and Seraphim praise with unending cries as they sing: Holy, holy, holy, Lord God Almighty. The Word made flesh (SIGN OF THE CROSS) commands you; the Virgin's Son (SIGN OF THE CROSS) commands you; Jesus (SIGN OF THE CROSS) of Nazareth commands you, who once, when you despised His disciples, forced you to flee in shameful defeat from a man; and when He had cast you out you did not even dare, except by His leave, to enter into a herd of swine. And now as I adjure you in His (SIGN OF THE CROSS) name, begone from this man (woman) who is His creature. It is futile to resist His (SOGN OF THE CROSS) will. It is hard for you to

kick against the (SIGN OF THE CROSS) goad. The longer you delay, the heavier your punishment shall be; for it is not men you are condemning, but rather Him who rules the living and the dead, who is coming to judge both the living and the dead and the world by fire.
All: Amen.
E: Lord, heed my prayer.
All: And let my cry be heard by you.
E: The Lord be with you.
All: May He also be with you.
E: Let us pray.
God of heaven and earth, God of the angels and archangels, God of the prophets and apostles, God of the martyrs and virgins, God who have power to bestow life after death and rest after toil; for there is no other God than you, nor can there be another true God beside you, the Creator of heaven and earth, who are truly a King, whose kingdom is without end; I humbly entreat your glorious majesty to deliver this servant of yours from the unclean spirits; through Christ our Lord.
All: Amen.
E: Therefore, I adjure you every unclean spirit, every spirit from hell, every satanic power, in the name of Jesus (SIGN OF THE CROSS) Christ of Nazareth, who was led into the desert after His baptism by John to vanquish you in your citadel, to cease your assaults against the creature whom He has, formed from the slime of the earth for His own honor and glory; to quail before wretched man, seeing in him the image of almighty God, rather than his state of human frailty. Yield then to God, (SIGN OF THE CROSS) who by His servant, Moses, cast you and your malice, in the person of Pharaoh and his army, into the depths of the sea. Yield to God, (SIGN OF THE CROSS) who, by the singing of holy canticles on the part of David, His faithful servant, banished you from the heart of King Saul. Yield to God, (SIGN OF THE CROSS) who condemned you in the person of Judas Iscariot, the traitor. For He now flails you with His divine scourges, (SIGN OF THE CROSS) He in whose sight you and your legions once cried out: "What have we to do with you, Jesus, Son of the Most High God?

Have you come to torture us before the time?" Now He is driving you back into the everlasting fire, He who at the end of time will say to the wicked: "Depart from me, you accursed, into the everlasting fire which has been prepared for the devil and his angels." For you, 0 evil one, and for your followers there will be worms that never die. An unquenchable fire stands ready for you and for your minions, you prince of accursed murderers, father of lechery, instigator of sacrileges, model of vileness, promoter of heresies, inventor of every obscenity. Depart, then, (SIGN OF THE CROSS) impious one, depart, (SIGN OF THE CROSS) accursed one, depart with all your deceits, for God has willed that man should be His temple. Why do you still linger here? Give honor to God the Father (SIGN OF THE CROSS) almighty, before whom every knee must bow. Give place to the Lord Jesus (SIGN OF THE CROSS) Christ, who shed His most precious blood for man. Give place to the Holy (SIGN OF THE CROSS) Spirit, who by His blessed apostle Peter openly struck you down in the person of Simon Magus; who cursed your lies in Annas and Saphira; who smote you in King Herod because he had not given honor to God; who by His apostle Paul afflicted you with the night of blindness in the magician Elyma, and by the mouth of the same apostle bade you to go out of Pythonissa, the soothsayer. Begone, (SIGN OF THE CROSS) now! Begone, (SIGN OF THE CROSS) seducer! Your place is in solitude; your abode is in the nest of serpents; get down and crawl with them. This matter brooks no delay; for see, the Lord, the ruler comes quickly, kindling fire before Him, and it will run on ahead of Him and encompass His enemies in flames. You might delude man, but God you cannot mock. It is He who casts you out, from whose sight nothing is hidden. It is He who repels you, to whose might all things are subject. It is He who expels you, He who has prepared everlasting hellfire for you and your angels, from whose mouth shall come a sharp sword, who is coming to judge both the living and the dead and the world by fire.
All: Amen.

Exorcism Prayers of St. John Chrysostom

E: O Eternal God, Who has redeemed the race of men from the captivity of the devil, deliver Thy servant/handmaid from all the workings of unclean spirits. Command the evil and impure spirits and demons to depart from the soul and body of your servant/handmaid and not to remain nor hide in him/her. Let them be banished from this the creation of Thy hands in Thine own holy name and that of Thine only begotten Son and of Thy life-creating Spirit, so that, after being cleansed from all demonic influence, he/she may live godly, justly and righteously and may be counted worthy to receive the Holy Mysteries of Thine only-begotten Son and our God with Whom Thou art blessed and glorified together with the all holy and good and life creating Spirit now and ever and unto the ages of ages. Amen.

All: O Thou Who hast rebuked all unclean spirits and by the power of Thy Word has banished the legion, come now, through Thine only begotten Son upon this creature, which Thou hast fashioned in Thine own image and deliver him/her from the adversary that holds him/her in bondage, so that, receiving Thy mercy and becoming purified, he/she might join the ranks of Thy holy flock and be preserved as a living temple of the Holy Spirit and might receive the divine and holy Mysteries through the grace and compassion and loving kindness of Thine only begotten Son with Whom Thou art blessed together with Thine all-holy and good and life-creating Spirit now and ever and unto the ages of ages. Amen.

E: We beseech Thee, O Lord, Almighty God, Most High, untempted, peaceful King. We beseech Thee Who has created the heaven and the earth, for out of Thee has issued the Alpha and the Omega, the beginning and the end, Thou Who has ordained that the four footed and irrational beasts be under subjection to man, for Thou hast subjected them. Lord, stretch out Thy mighty hand and Thy sublime and holy arm and in Thy watchful care look down upon this Thy creature and send down upon him/her a peaceful angel, a mighty angel, a guardian of soul and body, that will rebuke and drive away every evil and unclean demon from him/her, for Thou alone are Lord, Most High, almighty and blessed unto ages of ages. Amen.

All: We make this great, divine, holy and awesome invocation and plea, O devil, for thine expulsion, as well as this rebuke for your utter annihilation, O apostate! God Who is holy, beginningless, frightful, invisible in essence, infinite in power and incomprehensible in divinity, the King of glory and Lord Almighty, He shall rebuke thee, devil! -- He Who composed all things well by his Word from nothingness into being; He Who walks upon the wings of the air. The Lord rebukes thee, devil! --He Who calls forth the water of the sea and pours it upon the face of all the earth. Lord of Hosts is His name.

E: Devil: the Lord rebukes thee! He Who is ministered to and praised by numberless heavenly orders and adored and glorified in fear by multitudes of angelic and archangelic hosts. Satan: the Lord rebukes thee! He Who is honored by the encircling Powers, the awesome six-winged and many-eyed Cherubim and Seraphim that cover their faces with two wings because of His inscrutable and unseen divinity and with two wings cover their feet, lest they be seared by His unutterable glory and incomprehensible majesty, and with two wings do fly and fill the heavens with their shouts of "Holy, holy, holy, Lord Sabaoth, heaven and earth are full of Thy glory!" Devil: The Lord rebukes thee! He Who came down from the Father's bosom and, through the holy, inexpressible, immaculate and adorable Incarnation from the Virgin, appeared ineffably in the world to save it and cast thee down from heaven in His authoritative power and showed thee to be an outcast to every man. Satan: The Lord rebukes thee! He Who said to the sea, be silent, be still, and instantly it was calmed at His command. Devil: The Lord rebukes thee! He Who made clay with His immaculate spittle and refashioned the wanting member of the man blind from birth and gave him his sight.

Devil: The Lord rebukes thee! He Who by His word restored to life the daughter of the ruler of the synagogue and snatched the son of the widow out from the mouth of death and gave him whole and sound to his own mother. Devil: The Lord rebukes thee! The Lord Who raised Lazarus the four-days dead from the dead, undecayed, as if not having died, and unblemished to the astonishment of many. Satan: The Lord rebukes thee! He Who destroyed the curse by the blow on His face and by the lance in His immaculate side lifted the flaming sword that guarded Paradise. Devil: The Lord rebukes thee! He Who dried all tears from every face by the spitting upon His precious expressed image. Devil: The Lord rebukes thee! He Who set His Cross as a support, the salvation of the world, to thy fall and the fall of all the angels under thee. Devil: The Lord rebukes thee! He Who spoke from His Cross and the curtain of the temple was torn in two, and the rocks were split and the tombs were opened and those who were dead from the ages were raised up. Devil: The Lord rebukes thee! He Who by death put death to death and by His rising granted life to all men. May the Lord rebuke thee, Satan! – that is, He Who descended into Hades and opened its tombs and set free those held prisoner in it, calling them to Himself; before Whom the gatekeepers of Hades shuddered when they saw Him and, hiding themselves, vanished in the anguish of Hades. May the Lord rebuke thee, devil! -- That is, Christ our God Who arose from the dead and granted His Resurrection to all men. May the Lord rebuke thee, Satan! -- He Who in glory ascended into heaven to His Father, sitting on the right of majesty upon the throne of glory. Devil: May the Lord rebuke thee! He Who shall come again with glory upon the clouds of heaven with His holy angels to judge the living and the dead. Devil: May the Lord rebuke thee! He Who has prepared for thee unquenchable fire, the unsleeping worm and the outer darkness unto eternal punishment. Devil: May the Lord rebuke thee! For before Him all things shudder and tremble from the face of His power and the wrath of His warning upon thee is uncontainable. Satan: The Lord rebukes thee by His frightful name!

Shudder, tremble, be afraid, depart, be utterly destroyed, be banished! Thee who fell from heaven and together with thee all evil spirits: every evil spirit of lust, the spirit of evil, a day and nocturnal spirit, a noonday and evening spirit, a midnight spirit, an imaginative spirit, an encountering spirit, either of the dry land or of the water, or one in a forest, or among the reeds, or in trenches, or in a road or a crossroad, in lakes, or streams, in houses, or one sprinkling in the baths and chambers, or one altering the mind of man. Depart swiftly from this creature of the Creator Christ our God! And be gone from the servant/handmaid of God _________, from his/her mind, from his/her soul, from his/her heart, from his/her reins, from his/her senses, from all his/her members, that he/she might become whole and sound and free, knowing God, his/her own Master and Creator of all things, He Who gathers together those who have gone astray and Who gives them the seal of salvation through the rebirth and restoration of divine Baptism, so that he may be counted worthy of His immaculate, heavenly and awesome Mysteries and be united to His true fold, dwelling in a place of pasture and nourished on the waters of repose, guided pastorally and safely by the staff of the Cross unto the forgiveness of sins and life everlasting. For unto Him belong all glory, honor, adoration and majesty together with Thy beginningless Father and His all-holy, good and life-giving Spirit, now and ever, and unto ages of ages.
All: Amen.
E: Antiphon: Magi from the East came to Bethlehem to adore the Lord; and opening their treasure chests they presented Him with precious gifts: Gold for the great King, incense for the true God, and myrrh in symbol of His burial. Alleluia.

The Magnificat

Luke 1:46 55

E: "My soul extols the Lord;
All: And my spirit leaps for joy in God my Savior.

E: How graciously He looked upon His lowly maid! Oh, see, from this hour onward age after age will call me blessed!
All: How sublime is what He has done for me, the Mighty One, whose name is `Holy'!
E: From age to age He visits those who worship Him in reverence.
All: His arm achieves the mastery: He routs the haughty and proud of heart.
E: He puts down princes from their thrones, and exalts the lowly;
All: He fills the hungry with blessings, and sends away the rich with empty hands.
E: He has taken by the hand His servant Israel, and mercifully kept His faith,
All: As He had promised our fathers with Abraham and his posterity forever and evermore."
E: Glory be to the Father, etc.
All: As it was in the beginning, etc.

Antiphon
Magi from the East came to Bethlehem to adore the Lord; and opening their treasure chests they presented Him with precious gifts: Gold for the great King, incense for the true God, and myrrh in symbol of His burial. Alleluia.

Meanwhile the home is sprinkled with holy water and incensed. Then the exorcist says:

E: Our Father ***(the rest inaudibly until:)***
E: And lead us not into temptation.
All: But deliver us from evil.
E: Many shall come from Saba.
All: Bearing gold and incense.
E: Lord, heed my prayer.
All: And let my cry be heard by you.
E: The Lord be with you.
All: May he also be with you.
E: Let us pray.

God, who on this day revealed your only-begotten Son to all nations by the guidance of a star, grant that we who now know you by faith may finally behold you in your heavenly majesty; through Christ our Lord.
All: Amen.

Responsory
All: Be enlightened and shine forth, 0 Jerusalem, for your light is come; and upon you is risen the glory of the Lord Jesus Christ born of the Virgin Mary.

E: Nations shall walk in your light, and kings in the splendor of your birth.
All: And the glory of the Lord is risen upon you.
E: Let us pray.
Lord God almighty, bless (SIGN OF THE CROSS) this home, and under its shelter let there be health, chastity, self-conquest, humility, goodness, mildness, obedience to your commandments, and thanksgiving to God the Father, Son, and Holy Spirit. May your blessing remain always in this home and on those who live here; through Christ our Lord.
All: Amen.

Antiphon for Canticle of Zachary:

E: Today the Church is espoused to her heavenly bridegroom, for Christ washes her sins in the Jordan; the Magi hasten with gifts to the regal nuptials; and the guests are gladdened with water made wine, alleluia.

Canticle of Zachary
Luke 1:68 79

E: "Blessed be the Lord, the God of Israel! He has visited His people and brought about its redemption.
All: He has raised for us a stronghold of salvation in the house of David His servant, And redeemed the promise He had made through the mouth of His holy prophets of old.

All: To grant salvation from our foes and from the hand of all that hate us;
E: To deal in mercy with our fathers and be mindful of His holy covenant,
All: Of the oath he had sworn to our father Abraham, that He would enable us
E: Rescued from the clutches of our foes to worship Him without fear,
All: In holiness and observance of the Law, in His presence, all our days.
E: And you, my little one, will be hailed `Prophet of the Most High'; for the Lord's precursor you will be to prepare His ways;
All: You are to impart to His people knowledge of salvation through forgiveness of their sins.
E: Thanks be to the merciful heart of our God! A dawning Light from on high will visit us
All: To shine upon those who sit in darkness and in the shadowland of death, and guide our feet into the path of peace."
E: Glory be to the Father., etc.
All: As it was in the beginning, etc.

Antiphon
E: Today the Church is espoused to her heavenly bridegroom, for Christ washes her sins in the Jordan; the Magi hasten with gifts to the regal nuptials; and the guests are gladdened with water made wine, alleluia.
E: The Lord be with you.
All: May He also be with you.
E: Let us pray. God, who on this day revealed your only-begotten Son to all nations by the guidance of a star, grant that we who now know you by faith may finally behold you in your heavenly majesty; through Christ our Lord.
All: Amen.

Athanasian Creed
E: Whoever wills to be saved must before all else hold fast to

the catholic faith.

All: Unless one keeps this faith whole and untarnished, without doubt he will perish forever.

E: Now this is the catholic faith: that we worship one God in Trinity, and Trinity in unity;

All: Neither confusing the Persons one with the other, nor making a distinction in their nature.

E: For the Father is a distinct Person; and so is the Son; and so is the Holy Spirit.

All: Yet the Father, Son, and Holy Spirit possess one Godhead, co-equal glory, co-eternal majesty.

E: As the Father is, so is the Son, so also is the Holy Spirit.

All: The Father is uncreated, the Son is uncreated, the Holy Spirit is uncreated.

E: The Father is infinite, the Son is infinite, the Holy Spirit is infinite.

All: The Father is eternal, the Son is eternal, the Holy Spirit is eternal.

E: Yet they are not three eternals, but one eternal God.

All: Even as they are not three uncreated, or three infinites, but one uncreated and one infinite God.

E: So likewise the Father is almighty, the Son is almighty, the Holy Spirit is almighty.

All: Yet they are not three almighties, but they are the one Almighty.

E: Thus the Father is God, the Son is God, the Holy Spirit is God.

All: Yet they are not three gods, but one God.

E: Thus the Father is Lord, the Son is Lord, the Holy Spirit is Lord.

All: Yet there are not three lords, but one Lord.

E: For just as Christian truth compels us to profess that each Person is individually God and Lord, so does the catholic religion forbid us to hold that there are three gods or lords.

All: The Father was not made by any power; He was neither created nor begotten.

E: The Son is from the Father alone, neither created nor made, but begotten.

All: The Holy Spirit is from the Father and the Son, neither made nor created nor begotten, but He proceeds.
E: So there is one Father, not three; one Son, not three; one Holy Spirit, not three.
All: And in this Trinity one Person is not earlier or later, nor is one greater or less; but all three Persons are co-eternal and co-equal.
E: In every way, then, as already affirmed, unity in Trinity and Trinity in unity is to be worshiped.
All: Whoever, then, wills to be saved must assent to this doctrine of the Blessed Trinity.
E: But it is necessary for everlasting salvation that one also firmly believe in the incarnation of our Lord Jesus Christ.
All: True faith, then, requires us to believe and profess that our Lord Jesus Christ, the Son of God, is both God and man.
E: He is God, begotten of the substance of the Father from eternity; He is man, born in time of the substance of His Mother.
All: He is perfect God, and perfect man subsisting in a rational soul and a human body.
E: He is equal to the Father in His divine nature, but less than the Father in His human nature as such.
All: And though He is God and man, yet He is the one Christ, not two;
E: One, however, not by any change of divinity into flesh, but by the act of God assuming a human nature.
All: He is one only, not by a mixture of substance, but by the oneness of His Person.
E: For, somewhat as the rational soul and the body compose one man, so Christ is one Person who is both God and man;
All: Who suffered for our salvation, who descended into hell, who rose again the third day from the dead;
E: Who ascended into heaven, and sits at the right hand of God the Father almighty, from there He shall come to judge both the living and the dead.
All: At His coming all men shall rise again in their bodies, and shall give an account of their works.
E: And those who have done good shall enter into everlasting

life, but those who have done evil into everlasting fire.
All: All this is catholic faith, and unless one believes it truly and firmly one cannot be saved.
E: Glory be to the Father, etc.
All: As it was in the beginning, etc.

Here follow a large number of psalms which may be used at the exorcist's discretion but are not a necessary part of the rite. Some of them occur in other parts of the Ritual and are so indicated; the others may be taken from the Psalter. Psalm 90 ; Psalm 67; Psalm 69; Psalm 53; Psalm 117; Psalm 34; Psalm 30; Psalm 21; Psalm 3; Psalm 10; Psalm 12.

Prayer Following Deliverance

E: Almighty God, we beg you to keep the evil spirit from further molesting this servant of yours, and to keep him far away, never to return. At your command, 0 Lord, may the goodness and peace of our Lord Jesus Christ, our Redeemer, take possession of this man (woman). May we no longer fear any evil since the Lord is with us; who lives and reigns with you, in the unity of the Holy Spirit, God, forever and ever.
All: Amen.

EXORCISM OF A PLACE OR HOME

Ritual of exorcism to combat the power of the evil spirits over a community or locality.

E: In the name of the Father, and of the Son, and of the Holy Spirit. Amen. Heavenly Father, we beseech you to send to our aid the mighty angles of the heavenly army, to defend us in the battle against principalities and powers, against the rulers of the world of darkness and the spirit of wickedness in high places. To come to the rescue of mankind, whom You have made in Your own image and likeness, and purchased from Satan's tyranny at so great a price. Your Holy Church honors their presence here with us. You have entrusted to these angels the task of leading the souls of the redeemed to heavenly blessedness. Lord of peace, cast Satan down under our feet, so as to keep him from further holding man captive and doing harm to Your Church. May Your holy angels O Lord quickly come and lay hold of the beast, the serpent of old, Satan and his demons, casting him in chains into the abyss, so that he can no longer seduce the nations. All: Amen.

Exorcism

E: In the name of Jesus Christ, our Lord and God, and by the authority residing in our holy ministry, we steadfastly proceed to combat the onslaught of the Adversary.

Psalm 67

E: God arises; His enemies are scattered, and those who hate Him flee before Him.
All: As smoke is driven away, so are they driven; as wax melts before the fire, so the wicked perish before God.
E: See the cross of the Lord; begone, you hostile powers!
All: The stem of David, the lion of Judah's tribe has conquered.
E: May your mercy, Lord, remain with us always.
All: For we put our whole trust in you.
E: We cast you out, every unclean spirit, every satanic power, every onslaught of the infernal adversary, every legion, every

diabolical group and sect, in the name and by the power of our Lord Jesus (SIGN OF THE CROSS) Christ. We command you, begone and fly far from the Church of God, from the souls made by God in His image and redeemed by the precious blood of the divine Lamb. (SIGN OF THE CROSS) No longer dare, cunning serpent, to deceive the human race, to persecute God's Church, to strike God's elect and to sift them as wheat. (SIGN OF THE CROSS) For the Most High God commands you, (SIGN OF THE CROSS) He to whom you once proudly presumed yourself equal; He who wills all men to be saved and come to the knowledge of truth. God the Father (SIGN OF THE CROSS) commands you. God the Son (SIGN OF THE CROSS) commands you. God the Holy (SIGN OF THE CROSS) Spirit commands you. Christ, the eternal Word of God made flesh, commands (SIGN OF THE CROSS) you, who humbled Himself, becoming obedient even unto death, to save our race from the perdition wrought by your envy; who founded His Church upon a firm rock, declaring that the gates of hell should never prevail against her, and that He would remain with her all days, even to the end of the world. The sacred mystery of the cross (SIGN OF THE CROSS) commands you, along with the power of all mysteries of Christian faith. (SIGN OF THE CROSS) The blood of Christ, (SIGN OF THE CROSS) commands you. Therefore, accursed dragon and every diabolical legion, we adjure you by the living (SIGN OF THE CROSS) God, by the true (SIGN OF THE CROSS) God, by the holy (SIGN OF THE CROSS) God, by God, who so loved the world that He gave His only-begotten Son, that whoever believes in Him might not perish but have everlasting life; to cease deluding human creatures and filling them with the poison of everlasting damnation; to desist from harming the Church and hampering her freedom. Begone, Satan, father and master of lies, enemy of man's welfare. Give place to Christ, in whom you found none of your works. Give way to the one, holy, catholic, and apostolic Church, which Christ Himself purchased with His blood. Bow down before God's mighty hand, tremble and flee as we call on the holy and awesome name of Jesus, before whom the denizens of hell cower, to

whom the heavenly Virtues and Powers and Dominations are subject, whom the Cherubim and Seraphim praise with unending cries as they sing: Holy, holy, holy, Lord God Almighty.
E: Lord, heed my prayer.
All: And let my cry be heard by you
E: The Lord be with you.
All: May He also be with you.
E: Let us pray. God of heaven and earth, God of the angels and archangels, God of the patriarchs and prophets, God of the apostles and martyrs, God of the confessors and virgins, God who have power to bestow life after death and rest after toil; for there is no other God than you, nor can there be another true God beside you, the Creator of all things visible and invisible, whose kingdom is without end; we humbly entreat your glorious majesty to deliver us by your might from every influence of the accursed spirits, from their every evil snare and deception, and to keep us from all harm; through Christ our Lord.
All: Amen.
E: From the snares of the Devil.
All: Lord, deliver us.
E: That you help your Church to serve you in security and freedom.
All: We beg you to hear us.
E: That you humble the enemies of holy Church.
All: Amen.

The surroundings are sprinkled with holy water.

EXAMS

CHAPTER ONE

- Write out the text of Ephesians 6:12
- What two "bodies" do we possess?
- According to the Letter to Diognetus, where does the soul reside and what "guards" it?
- What are the two realms of existence?
- Lactantius states that God has given what to Satan?
- What are the two spiritual kingdoms?
- Explain in your own words the basic origin of the conflict between man and the demonic.
- Write out the text of Revelation 12:9.
- What are Watchers?
- What are Nephilim?
- What reason does Tertullian say Satan had for deceiving man?
- What is it that separates man from God?
- Tertullian states that the foe is the most savage when______?
- What is the definition of spiritual warfare?
- Fill in the blanks: *You must recognize that all battles of life, whether_________, ________, __________, ___________, or with human _____________ are only outward manifestations of a spiritual cause.*
- Write out the text of Romans 5:12.
- What is the Fallen Nature?

CHAPTER TWO

- What is repentance? Provide two scripture verses that discuss repentance.
- Why is repentance important?
- List four reasons why repentance is necessary.
- Write out the text of Matthew 4:17.
- What is conversion? (Four points)

- What is justification?
- Write out the text of Romans 6:16-18

CHAPTER THREE

- What does it mean when we say God has a triune nature?
- Is God one? Provide a scriptural support verse for this statement.
- Name the Three Persons of the Holy Trinity.
- Write out the text of II Corinthians 13:14
- What does it mean when we say the Trinity is eternal?
- What does it mean when we say the Trinity is Sovereign?
- What does it mean when we say the Trinity is omnipresent?
- Define omniscient.
- Define omnipotent.
- Define unchanging.
- Define infinite.
- It is through what that we are freed from the bondage of sin?
- Fill in the blank: The Holy Spirit reveals _______ things that cannot be known through our ____________ faculties.
- List the four types of spiritual gifts the Holy Spirit bestows on the Church.

CHAPTER FOUR

- What are angels?
- Write out the text of Hebrews 1:14.
- What are Cherubim?
- What are Seraphim?

- Who is Michael?
- Who is Gabriel?
- List 5 attributes of the angels.
- List two ways angels minister in heaven.
- List two ways angels minister on earth.
- Fill in the blanks: Angels ________ God's will, ________, provide ________, bring answers to ________ announce, warn, instruct, bring __________, encourage, sustain, deliver, and intercede on behalf of the faithful in battle.

CHAPTER FIVE

- Write out the text of I Peter 5:8
- Give the Old Testament reference that describes the original position of Satan.
- Define "Lucifer".
- List the five "I WILL's" of Satan.
- According to Lactantius Satan was infected with what?
- List the six results of Satan's rebellion.
- List the attributes of Satan. (There are seven sets listed)

CHAPTER SIX

- Write out the text of I Timothy 4:1
- Fill in the blank: Demons are ________ angels.
- Write out the text of Jude 6.
- List five attributes of demons.
- List the three "organizational levels" of demons given in scripture.
- Fill in the blanks: Demons have _______ degrees of wickedness and ________.
- Fill in the blanks: Demons can ________ their functions.
- Define an "evil or unclean spirit".
- Define a "spirit of infirmity".

- Define “seducing spirits”.

CHAPTER SEVEN

- Give three different meanings for “the world”.
- Write out the text of II Corinthians 4:4
- What scripture verse was given to prove that the world is already judged and under the condemnation of God?
- What are the “rudiments of the world”?
- What is the “course” of this world?
- Write out the text of Ephesians 2:2
- What scripture verse was give to prove the world hates God?
- “The flesh” is another way of saying what?
- Define “lust”.
- Define “lust of the flesh”.
- List the works of the flesh mentioned in Galatians 5:19-21
- List the four basic categories of sins.

CHAPTER EIGHT

- Fill in the blanks: Satan's attack on the first man and woman, Adam and Eve, was really an attack on the ________ and _________ of God
- Satan is called the “god of________ _________.
- Write out the text of I Peter 5:8-9

CHAPTER NINE

- Write out the text of I John 3:8
- Fill in the blanks: When you submit yourself to Christ the King to become "an instrument of righteousness unto God," it means you bring your ______ and ________ in _________ with His purpose and plans.
- What is the reason Christ came into the world?
- Fill in the blanks: Although Christ came to bring the

peace of God (John 14:27; Philippians 4:7), and peace with God (Romans 5:1), His coming also brought _______ ________.

- Finish this statement: It is not possible to be neutral. We either live in complete...
- Fill in the blanks: The _____ of ________ is our manual for warfare and reveals God's spiritual battle plan.
- What are the three keys of prayer?
- List the five types of prayer.
- List five hindrances to prayer.
- List the six purposes of fasting.

CHAPTER TEN

- NO EXAM- Rather this chapter is simply to get thinking on the topic of "wrestling".

CHAPTER ELEVEN

- Write out the text of Ephesians 6:11.
- Write out the text of James 4:7.
- Define "resist".
- What does it mean to "resist in the faith"?
- Define "abstain".
- Write out the text of I Peter 2:11.
- Write out the text of Romans 13:14.
- List the parts of spiritual armor and what they symbolize.

CHAPTER TWELVE

- Write out the text of Romans 12:2.
- Give the scripture reference for "pulling down" and "casting out".
- Fill in the blanks: Demonic entities hate all mention of the ________ of Christ and the ______ of the cross.

- Finish this statement: The Holy Name of Jesus is not some magical phrase with which we conclude our prayers. It is a symbol of.....

CHAPTER THIRTEEN

- Fill in the blanks: Satan's primary focus of attacks occur in our ___________ and ________/_________ life.
- Why does Satan battle so strongly for the mind?
- List the thirteen ways Satan attacks the mind.
- Fill in the blanks: Any therapeutic effort towards healing must take into consideration not only the ______ and the ________, but also this soul and it's absolute need for ____________ with God as part of the *wholistic* healing process.
- Define "meditation".
- What is "inherited depravity"?

CHAPTER FOURTEEN

- Give the scripture verse used to prove that the body of the Christian is the temple of the Holy Spirit.
- List four ways in which demonic entities attack the body.
- List the nine physical signs that a demon has physically abused a victim.
- Why is the family a primary target of demonic attack?

CHAPTER FIFTEEN

- List and describe the four types of cults.
- Describe in your own words "Wicca".

CHAPTER SIXTEEN

- Fill in the blanks: Demons control specific ______________ _____________ such as the prince of

Persia mentioned in Daniel 10:12-13.

- What is a demon of infirmity?
- What is a seductive demon?
- What is an Unclean demon?
- Define demon possession.
- List the six ways demons can gain control.

CHAPTER SEVENTEEN

- List the ordinary way we fall under diabolic influence.
- List the five extraordinary forms of diabolic influence.
- Define "demonic obsession".
- Define "demonic oppression".
- What are the two types of possession?

Bibliography

- Arpaia, Joseph, *Psychiatric Times*, June 2000
- Boorstein, Seymour, *Transpersonal Psychotherapy*, Am. Journal of Psychotherapy, Vol. 54, No. 3, Summer 2000.
- Brown, Allen, *Master Unit 4: Anthropology,* 2010
- Eckhart, Meister; *The Complete Mystical Works of Meister Eckhart*, transl. O'C Walshe, Muarice2010
- Law, William, *The Complete Works of William Law,* 2010
- Prabhupada, Bhaktivedanta, A.C. , *Bhagavad Gita As It Is,*1972
- Sivananda, Swami, *What Is Meditation?, 2013*
- T.N. Venkataraman, Tiruvannamalai, *Talks with Sri Ramana Maharshi,1972,*
- Whitall, Perry, *The Mescalin Hypothesis*, Challenges to a Secular Society, Foundation for Traditional Studies, 1996.
- Meier, Minirth, Wichern, Ratcliff, *Introduction to Psychology and Counseling, Second Edition,* 2010
- LeVey, Anton, *The Satanic Bible,* 1976

21234757R00143

Printed in Great Britain
by Amazon